From Bags to Riches

One Woman's Journey from the Streets to the Stars

From Bags to Riches

One Woman's Journey from the Streets to the Stars

Written by Suzanne "Bag Lady Sue" Austin

Fusion Publishing Group
www.amytravisunlimited.com

ISBN 978-1-7335626-4-5

Printed in the United States of America
Published by Fusion Publishing Group
Butler, Pennsylvania 16002

Please visit www.amytravisunlimited.com/fusion-publishing-group
or email atravisconsulting@gmail.com

DEDICATION

To the love of my life… my daughter, Cheyenne.

TABLE OF CONTENTS

SPECIAL THANKS

To Amy Travis, a.k.a. "Honey Badger" … Without your help and mad skills, this book would never have become a reality. Your fierce work ethic, persistence, guidance, support, encouragement and above all infinite patience, made this come to life perfectly!

I know YOU were the answer to years of prayers. God needed me to be right where I am for it all to take place. You made one of my biggest dreams come true.

Please visit Amy's website at **www.amytravisunlimited.com**.

INTRODUCTION

Thank you for picking up this book. I am honored that you want to know my story!

Initially, I began writing this book for my daughter Cheyenne. I wanted to leave her my life story, so when I am gone, she would know it and be able to pass it along to her kids. I also wanted her to really know me. After telling some friends I was going to do this, they suggested I should share some of my stories with the awesome people I have met along my way through life.

Personally, I think everyone should write their life story down, even if only for themselves. It has been an awakening for me. The stories in the book certainly aren't all funny because—like most people that become comedians—early life was intense, a tad odd and even sad. Still, it was a hell of a lot of fun. Sometimes insanity is a blast.

When Bag Lady Sue came to life in 1980, I never could have dreamed she would become what she has become. The old bitch has made every kind of person laugh and has been seen, shared, and adored by people all across the USA. And, thanks to our troops, even many folks all around the world have experienced her.

I could never have imagined that an old army duffle bag full of thrift store clothes would help me create a life few people ever get to live.

When I was a runaway kid working as a stripper in seedy east coast dive bars at the tender age of fifteen, I couldn't even dream that someday I'd see my name in the lights of Las Vegas. I also couldn't know that because of "her," I would get to see all the amazing places I have or how many incredible lives I would touch and be touched by. Everyone I have met through it all has become a part of me, whether for a moment, a month, or my lifetime. I am grateful.

It is also hard to believe that since her beginning, the Bag Lady has had millions of dollars slide through her hands. I may not be rich, but I have lived like a freakin' Rockstar! Like most, I sure wish I'd have had some financial skills, but I was always more concerned with making love, having fun, and creating memories than I was about properly investing all that dough. As a result, I don't own many material things. However, the experiences and the memories are priceless to me, and in those, I am filthy rich.

Best of all, I have had the opportunity to share so many of them with my incredible daughter. Giving her life has also been amazing. Being self-employed gave me the freedom to be with her as she grew up and not have to leave her to be raised by others. I'm sad for families that have to go thru that to make ends meet. I simply believe life is to be lived, kids are to be nurtured, animals deserve kindness, good men should be appreciated, and dreams are to be chased. Looking back, I have no regrets.

Everything in this book is true. I have not colored it up or stretched the truth at all. I never needed to; my life has been incredible in every way, from the painful lows to the glorious highs. It happened just the way it was supposed to. We all have a story, and God has a plan. I wouldn't change a thing. Ok, maybe just a thing... or three.

For one, I would have invested more money in real estate and learned the stock market sooner. Looking at the soaring prices of real estate where I now live in Colorado, I could just kick myself! Honestly, though, I never thought I wanted to stay in one place long enough to be strapped down to a house. Even feeling that way, I should have bought rental properties. But que sera sera!

Secondly, I wish I had ended two of my relationships just a tad earlier. When I felt those relationships begin to suck the life out of me, I should have run. Try to never waste time, especially when you know that is exactly what you are doing.

Ok, there is no 3.

I have left some stories out because they are too sad or awful to tell. Either way, I found the courage to forgive, or at least let go and move on. Nothing can get in your way of finding joy, living a passionate life, and realizing your dreams… except you. We allow what we allow, or we make up our mind to stop allowing people to fuck with us! I stopped allowing things and people in my life that weren't lifting me up. I may not have realized the person was a life-sucking, douchebag right away, but as soon as I saw it, I bailed.

When I was younger there was a standard question among my close friends, "Wonder why Bag's relationships never last more than two years?" The answer is that it took about that long for them to get lazy, complacent, and boring. I can't stand to be bored! If things start to suck, change them. Period, You can! My favorite saying in AA is:

"The definition of insanity is doing the same thing over and over again while expecting different results."

With me, what you see is what you get, and—like many folks—my public and private lives are very different. At home I am the Kool Aid mom, in public, well, you know…

So, here we go! I hope you enjoy my story.

Kidhood

Being a kid on Pittsburgh's Southside was almost idyllic. Houses were all in rows with barely a walkway between them. If your neighbor's house caught fire, you were screwed too. The houses had stone fronts and porches, and on summer nights everyone hung out on their stoops (steps). No one ever ran you off or made you feel like you weren't welcome. Everyone knew everyone, unlike today. Old folks liked little children back then because little children had manners. They had these because Mommy and Daddy beat their little asses when they smarted off. Kids behaved and respected their elders, whether the elder deserved it or not.

Back then you really could walk around the neighborhood alone or with one friend at the age of six or seven because everyone looked out for you. No one really worried about someone trying to molest their kids, I mean I know it happened…hell, it happened to me. But no one ran around all paranoid about it. We just lived and let live for the most part. Life was wonderful and if it wasn't, we didn't know any better. Those Kardashian bimbo's and all the other entitled little SOBs weren't even a tadpole in pop's nuts yet. Television was very new and, at least in our house, still in black and white. You even had to get off your ass to change the channel. It was also closely monitored by a bunch of really conservative and uptight religious folks, so you only saw that they "allowed" you to see.

Mostly, I think people just had more damn sense and more heart. I also believe they were kinder overall, and much less selfish than they are today. See, my dad and pap and those guys worked hard for a living. Most people did.

When I was young, I remember hearing so many different accents from all over the world, because many were immigrants from different parts of Europe, Poland, Ireland, Germany, Italy, and others. Best of all, everyone was very, very loyal to this great country. Even the people who barely spoke English truly loved America. They were only one generation away, if any, from those who came across the pond on some smelly ship in the steerage hold to find a better life here in America. They were ready to work hard to make this country what it was. I am glad I had grandparents who came here the right way and earned every damn thing they had. I will always be thankful to have been born an American.

I remember sitting at the bar on Pittsburgh's north side when I was around six years old, listening to the oldies like *Duke of Earl* and *Blue Moon* till I knew all the words. My mom had friends that were with one of the big motorcycle clubs. Tough as they were it seemed they always watched out for me, my little brother and her. I have never felt afraid of any biker club guys or gals though I think clubs were much rowdier back in the day. Laws and men were different in those days. I remember one guy who was prospecting, or "patching in" to the local MC wearing a freakin' used Kotex pad around his neck. Now that is tough! I was seeing this stuff at six and seven, mind you. It is no wonder my mind hangs out in the gutter much of the time.

I had some wild times on Pittsburgh's north side. It was a tight little neighborhood where the saying was and still is, "You're either from the Northside, or the *outside*." One night, this big-mouthed lady came into the bar where my mom was working. I heard her say something smart to my mom. I watched Mom walk calmly around the bar and grab this broad by the hair, which came loose in her hand (wigs were big in the '70s). Mom pulled her off the bar stool onto the floor, and proceeded to beat her ass, still holding the wig in her fist as she punched the chick out.

It was really kinda funny. A guy jumped up to pull my mom off the chick. The bartender, Mom's best friend Tony 'Alkie' Elsessor, grabbed him around the neck with a tire iron and said, "I don't think so, motherfucker!" And that was that. I thought it was just plain cool. I can tell you, these guys were real badasses, not like many guys today who sport man buns & skinny jeans. I felt awfully safe in that bar with those guys.

Back then if you had it coming, you'd get it. Best of all, you would *own* that you deserved it and move on trying not to get "bang checked" again. It made us better humans, and with all that self-governing, we didn't have to go to court and make the government richer off fines. Now, everyone runs like a baby to tell on you when you fart in public. Pussies!

Looking back now, I see it was a pretty dangerous world for a little kid to be in, but at six I thought it was cool.

Mom also had a lady friend who was a madam named Mary, or "Chooch" on the street. She had a laid-out conversion van that she used to run hookers out of on East Ohio Street. When I was fourteen, I was at a strip club with my mom, (yep, only 14) called The Greenwich Village, and we ran into her. I was leaning on the bar and she tried making a move on *me!* Talk about being scared. That was my introduction to lesbians, bi-chicks, and strippers.

Mom

My mom raised me while being a bartender on Pittsburgh's north side, which was a pretty rough place to hang. My mom was a tough chick. She was about 5'10" with big tits and dark auburn hair. She was a pro at snatching money from the drunks without them ever having a clue. Good or bad, she taught me how to survive.

Growing up in the 'burgh it was just me, mom, my brother Yogi, and a multitude of stepdads. Mom didn't take any shit... not from girls, guys and surely not from me and my brother. We had many an ass beating and, more than one instance, that literally scarred me for life.

When my brother and I were young we found our uncle's box of Playboy magazines. We thought how cool it was to see all the pretty naked ladies. Mom knew we looked at them and said she didn't care as long as we didn't take them out of the house. Well... being eight years old, I, of course, didn't listen and took one to elementary school to show my friends. Some little lip flappin' son of a bitch blabbed to the teacher, and I got busted! They called my mom, and she came to school and got me. I remember she dragged me home, made me sit down on the couch and proceeded to cut my hands with a razor blade (!). After that, she sent my little brother to the corner store for Band Aids. Now, I was pretty screwed up over this for many years. It would be until my thirties before I would let anyone touch my hands, even those closest to me. The scars never went away.

Mom was raised to be a spoiled brat. I found out later, as did she, that it was probably due to the amazing amount of guilt her parents carried around. My mother was born in the 40s. Back then America was still very religious (Catholic in our case), and people lived with enormous amounts of guilt. At that time when girls got pregnant out of wedlock, it was just horrible. Many families made their daughters give up the "bastard" children for adoption to a Catholic charity, or if she refused, they would kick her pregnant butt out in the street. So many young girls had to suffer this kind of hell. Many families didn't want to or didn't know how to deal with all the hush, hush and backstabbing talk around town. It could ruin businesses, entire families' images, have them shunned in their neighborhoods, their farms, church life, and whole way of living.

Many of these families did things that today we can barely imagine. Here's where it gets interesting… I was raised mostly by my "aunt", "uncle", and "grandma" because Mom still had around twenty years of wild oats to sow. What mom didn't know was her big sister (the woman I thought was my aunt), was actually her mother! The woman my mom *thought* was her mother, (and I though was *my* Grandma) was actually *her* grandmother! So, my aunt was really my grandma, and my grandma was really my great grandma. God only knows who my uncle really was. Follow me?

Suzanne, Mom, and Yogi

None of us found out the truth until around 1998. My mom's mom got pregnant with her when she was a young, single, career woman. So, rather than have her image tarnished and her dreams crushed, her mom (my mom's grandma that I grew up thinking was *my* grandma) stepped up and secretly took on the mother role. Back in the old days, many babies were born at home and hospitals and birth registries just took your word for it when you came in and told them this particular baby was yours. That is how it happened. So, my mother grew up never knowing the truth, even though she lived with these folks every day. Crazy stuff. Still, in my eyes they were the kindest, most amazing, loving people on Earth, and I know they meant well.

In 1968, my aunt/grandma tried to take me from my mother because she thought my Mom was unfit. She basically raised me during my formative years, and I knew she loved me very much. Mom, on the other hand, had been living the party life and was always hanging out in the north side bars, often with us kids in tow. Sometimes, she would bring guys home. Some were not so nice to me. My aunt and uncle thought this shit should cease, so they basically stole us from my mother. I remember mom bursting through the door screaming at my aunt and pushing me onto the floor as she dragged my brother out the door. My mom said my brother would be fine. I think in Mom's mind back then little girls were more vulnerable to sexual abuse than little boys. But, boy, was she wrong.

During the shelter hearing, I remember the courtroom and judge's chambers very, very, clearly. I also remember my mom threatening that if I didn't tell the judge that I wanted to live with her instead of my aunt, she was going to beat my ass. I don't remember ever being as terrified in my life of anything as I was of my mom. So out of fear, I lied to the judge. I remember my aunt crying as she left the courthouse, and my mother yelling obscenities at her as she walked away with my uncle's arm around her.

My mom wasn't always horrible; she was just a bit self-absorbed, young and not as ready to be a parent or as stable as my aunt and uncle were. She was also not as affectionate, gentle and kind as they were. I am not sure I ever felt the same about my mom after that. I know she wanted her kids, but there have been many times when I wondered why. I realized Mom was going through her own shit growing up entitled, then becoming a single parent with two kids and still young and wanting to be a party animal, but it still didn't justify how she treated us.

Eventually mom let us go visit my aunt and uncles' house, likely because she missed having a baby-sitter. But sadly, my aunt died four months later of a brain hemorrhage. I remember the day. My uncle came home looking like he'd just lost his mind saying, "Dolly's in the hospital. She had a stroke. I'm going to be with her." She died that night. He was never the same again after he lost her. Back then all my mom could say was, "Good for her."

I understand Mom never forgiving her for trying to take us, but my mom should have looked in the mirror rather than blaming everyone else for pissing her off. I know now that people who are raised by over-indulging parents rarely turn out to be fine, upstanding, and benevolent citizens. They seem to always go through life feeling like the rest of the world should kiss their asses like Mommy and Daddy did/still do. I have an ex that still has yet to get Mom's boob out of his forty-eight-year-old mouth.

After my aunt died, it was only a matter of time before my uncle went to join her. I know his heart was broken beyond repair. To make things worse, he chain-smoked Pall Malls, drank too much coffee, and lived on cottage cheese and peaches. He wasn't a drinker, though. Neither of them had been. He still tried to be there for my brother and me, but his soul was dying away without her. I always dreamed I would find a love like that. Time will tell.

My uncle was the greatest man I'd ever known, and although I wasn't his blood, he loved me and my brother like we were his own children. After my aunt died, I don't think he saw much reason to go on. He dated some. He was, after all, a very handsome, passionate Scorpio, but he never once brought any women to the house. I always admired him for that.

The day my uncle died he came home from work early. I ran to the back door to hug him as always and asked, "How was your cottage cheese and peaches, Uncle?" He kindly but hurriedly moved me out of the way, saying, "Not right now, Honey," then he told my grandma to call an ambulance. We didn't know it, but he was having a heart attack. The cops got there before the ambulance and just put him in the cop car to take him to the hospital. That may have been a huge mistake. Either way, he waved goodbye to me as I watched from the porch, and I never saw him again.

Uncle Authur and Aunt Doris "Dolly" Bodine

My grandma passed away a few years later. All I remember was one day she was just gone. Also, a heart attack. I never stopped missing any of them, even to this day.

Dad

I didn't meet my father until I was twenty-three. He and my mother split up when I was just six months old, so I didn't remember anything about him. All I knew was what I'd heard from my mom. She always said how damn good-looking and funny he was. The weird thing was that I knew my dad's dad, his brother, and stepmom all my life but never actually met *him*. Imagine how that might make you feel? There was some sneaky shit going on there, I'll tell ya!

My paternal grandfather, Bill, whom we called Pap Pap, was a real trip of a guy. He just loved Vegas, Coke (the cola), chocolate, and women. He was an auto mechanic for 60 years, before and after World War II. I always loved being in his old garage on Pittsburgh's

Southside when I was little. I loved hanging around there with my older handsome cousins who always looked out for me. To get to Pap's garage, you had to walk down the streetcar tracks on 21st St. in South Side and turn onto a narrow cobblestone alleyway. Pap's shingle hung out above the door, with the blue and yellow State of Pennsylvania inspection station logo on it. I can still remember the dark, damp, musty smell, the light with the wavy tin shade that hung over his workbench. I even remember the grease and oil on the floor. It was so thick from years of wrenching motors on it that I could carve my name in it with a screwdriver.

I can still see the ancient brick walls and wood-beamed roof that were most likely laid by Irish or German immigrants. I remember looking at all the calendars of beautiful pin-up girls hanging on the walls. I wished someday I would be *that* kind of girl. I noticed that the boys sure liked looking at them too! Mostly I thought their outfits were awesome, and their smiles were so big and bright. There was also a sign on the wall that said, "Send A Girl to Boy's Town" that I only understood years later.

Pap never drank alcohol, but he literally ate a pound of chocolates or more a week and drank a half case of Coke a day for most of his adult life. He still had all his own teeth and was as much of a smart ass and pervert at age eighty-three as he was at nineteen. A car fell on him when he was about seventy-nine, and he still worked after that. I remember him coming to my first "wedding" in a wheelchair and having him call me about a year later to come see him in a veteran's home. Unknown to me at the time, he had planned his escape and I was to be the driver. I took him back to his house on the Southside, but eventually the cousins or whomever made him go back to the VA. He died shortly after that. His spirit was too free to be cooped up in some facility, I guess. I am pretty sure I'd feel the same way.

In getting to know my granddad, I imagined that my own dad had his demons, too. I was told my Pap pushed my dad's mother down the steps when she was drunk and killed her so he could bring a beautiful Italian woman he met during World War II back to America. Not sure how true that is, but I heard my paternal grandma was quite a drinker, and I know my pap was a bit of a perv. Don't ask me how I know. Ok, I'll tell ya. He grabbed my boob when I was like fourteen. I figure many of us had grand paps, dads or uncles that were a little, or even a lot pervy whether we knew it or not. He was lucky that is all he tried, or he never would have made it to eighty-three!

Throughout my young life, I always wondered why my dad never wanted to see me or meet me. When I met him later, I still never really found out. I think it is because he was a true alcoholic, and possibly a narcissist, both of whom cannot honestly care about anyone but themselves. They think they can, but they just can't. Not really.

When my mom would be mean to me, I used to wonder about my dad. I wondered if he was nice. I heard he was funny. I always heard how much I looked like him, and how I reminded my mom of him when I would smile or do something. It used to drive me nuts because I only had one picture of him to go on, so I had no idea what she was talking about. I pictured him as some kind of hero who would come rescue me. I am sure my perception of and need for men in my life had much to do with the fact he was M.I.A. I had "stepdads" who were mostly—but not all—assholes, so it made sense to fantasize about my real dad the *hero*. I used to ask my grand pap where he was, and I would always get the same lie, "We don't know."

One night when I was about seven, I was sleeping over at my Pap's house. My cousin Mark told me my dad was going to come to pick him up to take him fishing. I remember lying in bed in the room above the front door listening to hear my dad's voice, but too terrified to come downstairs to see/catch him. I was always mad at myself for not having the guts, even at seven.

It took me sixteen more years to finally find him. I couldn't understand why my dad would come to get my cousin but not want to see me. It made me sad for years. That side of the family kept it a big secret all my life, I always resented them for that.

When I moved to Texas in 1983, I even went two hundred miles out of my way to try and find him. I called my Pap and went off on him. I said, "I know you know where he is, now give me his damn address!" So, the old man did. Pap said my dad was at 798 Harrison Street in Decatur, Indiana, which just so happened to be close and on the way. So, my then sweetheart C.J. and I loaded up the moving truck for Texas we headed south to surprise dear ole dad. We got there and found the right street, but the numbers didn't go up high enough, so I called and freaked out on my Pap. Turned out, he had it wrong. My dad was in Decatur, Illinois, not Decatur, Indiana. Oh well, shot down again. I went on with life and tried to forget about it all. Until around two years later…

I was twenty-three and was living alone in an apartment in Houston, TX when I had a terrible, but very real dream. I dreamt I was in prison and my dad was on the other side of the fence. (I knew what he looked like from old pictures mom had.) I cried to him, "Please, get me out of here!" He said he couldn't and walked away. I woke up hysterical; literally with tears still running down my face. I guess I had actually been crying in my sleep. I was still feeling pretty out of it when I jumped out of bed, so I grabbed the phone and called my dad's brother/my uncle Bill, whom I had also known all of my life. I said, "Listen up! I know you know where my father is. If you don't tell me right now, I'm going to come to Virginia and burn your fucking house down! I mean it!"

Needless to say, he was a bit shocked. And now that I have met my father, I am sure his brother Bill did not doubt I would, since we are of the same genetic make-up. My father is nuts. So, he gave me the address and begged me not to tell my dad how I found him. I never told dad his brother gave him up because I threatened to set fire to his house.

After hanging up the phone with Bill, I went next door to my then boyfriend's apartment and woke him up. I said, "I found my dad. Get dressed; we're going to Dallas." We jumped in his old 1978 Cutlass, and off we went. My heart raced the whole way there, and a hundred emotions ran around in it. *Fear* was the biggest, even past anger. But I'd had enough.

When I arrived in Granbury, Texas, I got a room and lay down to take a nap. Meanwhile, my sweet boyfriend Archer took a drive past the address to see where it was, and if my ol' man was outside. He wanted to grab a picture or two of him in case he rejected me when I went to his door. (Archer got the picture, by the way.) The old man was leaning on his fence talking with a neighbor; he had no idea of the surprise he was about to get. Granbury, Texas was a small, dusty, old, blue collar, trailer park type of town, complete with horses and tumbleweeds in every yard.

For reasons I am not sure of, I stopped on the way, bought a rose and proceeded to take all the thorns off it. We drove up, and I had Archer let me out down the street. I headed up the hill, rose in hand, to a small yellow double-wide mobile home. When I stepped on the porch and rang the doorbell, I was more terrified than I had ever been in my life.

My dad opened the door, looked down at me and said, "Can I help you?" I could have shit a brick! He looked just like me. I saw myself in his eyes. The rest looked like me too: nose, jaw, the whole deal. His voice even sounded like mine! (I have a deep voice for a girl.) All I could do was stand there trembling like a coke addict. I tried to say something, but not one word would come out of my mouth. For the first of only two times in my life, I was *literally* speechless.

Finally, he said "Are you ok?"

I finally got it out, "Are you Jerry?"

He said, "Yes, who are you?"

I said, "I'm your daughter, Suzanne."

For a few long seconds, we just looked at each other and there was silence. Then he said, "Oh, come in," and turned to go into the house, leaving me on the porch while, no doubt, figuratively shitting his pants. I walked in the door and a lady that was sitting on the couch (his wife Louise) yelled, "Oh my God, Jerry, she looks just like you!" So, expecting to have something thrown at me, I turned for the door to run away!

Then he said "No, wait, Kid. Come on in. How'd you find me?

I said, "It doesn't matter, I just wanted to see your face."

Just then a beautiful blond girl about three years younger than me came running out of the back room and said, "Wow! Are you my sister!?" I stood there and said, "Uh, yeah, I guess so," and she ran up and hugged me.

That broke the dam, and I started to cry. My dad then did something that still pisses me off to this day. He told the girl—my sister—to go to her room. And he said it quite firmly. I thought, *What the hell?* Had I the presence of mind I have now, I would have said, "No! Wait! I want to know her!" but I was truthfully still in shock and just didn't know what the hell to think, say or do.

Louise said, "Hey, did you come with someone?"

Oh shit... Archer! The whole time, poor Archer was driving around the block real slow. I had even forgotten about him! So we invited him in and we all sat down at the kitchen table, all of us except my sister. I still don't know what the hell the deal was with that. I don't know where she was or why he didn't want us to meet. I can only imagine he didn't want me to know what a real jagoff he was to her through the years. Maybe he was abusive to her? Perhaps he wanted my image of him to stay good because her's was so jaded. Who knows?

Sue and Dad

I remember desperately wanting to talk to her more. I had a thousand questions to ask her. Most of all, I want to tell her I am sorry I didn't say something to make him let her come out.

So, Dad and I talked and laughed the afternoon away. He even called my mom and they chatted it up. The day turned into night, and as I sat across from him, I saw more and more of myself. Our mannerisms and voices were almost identical. We agreed to go to lunch together the next day in Ft. Worth... just us. On the drive up, he kept saying over and over again how sorry he was and what an oyster (his word for asshole) he was for not finding me. I said I forgave him. We had a blast that day! I see where my drinking bone came from. I also finally got to see where my retarded sense of humor comes from, and why I turned out to be so colorful! Thanks, Dad, for that—and only that.

Over the next seven years we kept in touch and we saw each other two more times. Now and then he would call me late at night, drunk. He cracked me up. He was a funny man, for sure. Then, when I was having my daughter, I called him from the hospital and told him he was going be a grandpa. For whatever reason, he went off on me about how I shouldn't have a kid, and I should be married, and blah, blah, blah. So, I hung up on him.

Five years went by before he finally he called me—drunk, of course. He asked me to please forgive him. He said that he wanted to fly me and my daughter Cheyenne down to Florida so he could take us to Disney World. I was so happy, and the kiddo got all excited. I told her, "We're going to Disney World to meet your grandpa!" We got to the airport and found there were no tickets. I called him and said, "Hey, there are no tickets here for us Dad" and he said, "Oh, I'm sorry, I forgot." That was the last time I ever spoke to him. I'm not even sure he's still alive. You can mess with me, but *never* hurt my kid!

On a side note, I just want to tell any men out there who have made children: Don't worry about the mother. You be there for those kids. You thinking the mother is a twat—even if she is one— is no excuse for you to shirk your fatherly responsibility. They are part of you and you them and they *need* you. If you are being an absentee father, or simply a sperm donor, please get off your butt and man up. If you don't want to BE a dad, at least be man enough to snip your ballsack. (This goes for absentee mothers, too, though I will *never* understand that one!)

It took me decades to catch up with my sister again. When I did, I found out her mom Louise died. She was a sweet lady.

Even when I got older, I never understood how mean my mom could be, especially to her own children. I have *never* harmed or degraded my daughter Cheyenne. There were one or two well-de-served minor spankings when she was a little snot around age three, and the one time we had the teenager vs. mom blowup in the hallway. Still, I always held back and maintained my composure, whether she knew how much or not.

One time, my mother and I took Cheyenne for a boat ride on the Good Ship Lollipop, a little riverboat in Pittsburgh. It was a long day and Chey was cranky. So, when we were walking through the Station Square Mall, she was being a bit of a hag. Suddenly, my mom snapped and grabbed *my* kid by the arm, lifted her off the floor and slammed her back down. Before she could even say, "You stop it and behave!" I got in her face, slammed her and screamed at the top of my lungs, "Don't you ever fucking touch my kid in anger again, or I will kill you! Not ever! Do you understand?!" The whole mall stopped and got quiet. I was out of my mind. I knew at that moment I could easily destroy anyone that ever harmed my child. There would be no second guessing.

I often think my mom being pretty mean is why I am often overly nice, even to people that do not necessarily deserve it. My belief is… it is not up to me to decide who gets what or who deserves someone to be kind to them or, in reverse, to kick their asses. That is God's job. It's called Karma.

By the time I was twelve, I had lost all the people that looked out for me and my brother. My grandparents and aunt had left a house—a beautiful hundred-acre farm in Mercer, PA, complete with its own lake—and a huge chunk of money to me and my brother. My mom decided we should sell her house and move into the one they left to us. I had lived there most of the time with my gram, aunt, and uncle anyway, so we did. Honestly, I was glad. I always felt safe there—much safer than the house my mom raised us in where all the craziness and abuse happened.

After a couple of years, my teenage years came and the madness that was in Mom's old house snuck into this one. I ended up running away from it all, regrettably leaving my little brother there to hear the shit.

Thankfully, I learned to forgive her. I know many people would say "how horrible," but I know many kids who have been so abused mentally and physically by their parents and their parents' boyfriends/girlfriends that it made mine seem like nothing. Besides, years later she asked my forgiveness sincerely, so she got it.

None of us are without some bad character defects, for sure. Still, when it is your mom, I think that it makes it harder to swallow. Your mother is supposed to be the place you go for nurturing and comfort. Even many indigenous tribes believe the grandmother should discipline the children rather than the mother because that separation is important for kids. Makes sense to me.

Mom and I were great friends for many years at the end of her life. We have had hysterical fun together and my mom is an absolute genius when it comes to perspectives on people. Her "I don't give

a flying shit what people think of me" attitude has made me the ballsy, color-ful, fearless broad I am today. I got a lot of my material from her and from our bullshit sessions. I miss her dearly now that she is gone.

Suzanne, age 12

The Mean Streets

My town was full of funny, friendly folks and when I was a kid. There were thousands of colorful, unique personalities on those streets. We weren't afraid to have *big* personalities; it was how you stood out from the crowd. The only ones who sat around passing judgement were bored, frustrated housewives and a few crotchety old folks. The rest of us were too busy having fun and becoming even more outlandish… because back then it was cool. We mostly minded our own damn business and had a "live and let live" attitude. If we didn't like someone, we just didn't give them a second thought.

Our neighborhood also had its share of hardcore alcoholics, bums, and nuts. I always wished I could learn all of their backstories. One of my favorites was Sweet Pea. She was a thin, cheerful, little grey-haired, hunchbacked lady who talked at high speed. She would walk up to you and start chatting away while intermittently rubbing her hand between her legs and sniffing it, never missing one beat of her rant about whatever. In a disgusting way, she was adorable!

There was a tall, scary dude with wild eyes that would walk up to you and scream obscenities. He would open his trench coat to flash you and then walk away still hollering. The first time he got me, I damn near had a heart attack! After a while, though, you just got used to him.

The very best of them was Elmer. He reminded me of a little troll that lived under the bridge in some old fairytale. He chewed tobacco, which would run down his white beard, leaving little brown trails. Elmer wore ladies' wigs like they were hats. He would walk up and down the street day and night singing at the top of his lungs. Occasionally he would yell at some random person, often scaring the shit out of folks who didn't know about him. He mumbled when he talked, and he talked to himself all the time. Then, out of the blue, he would just lie down in the middle of the street and stop traffic. He'd lie there, singing out loud for 10 minutes or more till the cops came and moved him out of the way.

I was working at a little diner on the main drag back them, and there was a window behind me. Elmer used to come by and knock on it, making me jump. He got a kick out of it. We would wave to each other and he'd smile, stick his tongue out at me through his toothless, chewing tobacco beard and I would stick mine out back at him, smile and blow him a kiss. He did this pretty regularly, and it got to be our thing.

One day, for no apparent reason, he came into the diner and brought me a little statue of the Virgin Mary. Elmer handed it to me, smiled, winked, and left. I saw him on the street a few days after that and went up and gave him a hug. I could tell he was surprised, but he hugged me back. I looked him in the eyes, and said, "Ok, tell me the truth. You aren't crazy at all, are you?"

He looked at me with a twinkle in his eyes that would have made Santa Claus jealous, smiled and winked again. I had a feeling... I honestly felt just then that he was actually more of a genius than a nut. I asked around on the street and found out Elmer wasn't his real name. He was, in fact, a very, very wealthy man who owned a large construction company that his sister managed for him. Some years back, his wife and son had been killed in a car accident, and he lost it. I never told anyone about the connection I had with him that day or after. You could say we became friends. I'd see him often, and he always brought me little gifts from the thrift store. He never said a word, but I could see the knowing and appreciation in his eyes. That was enough.

In addition to rows of narrow streets and old narrow buildings, the city's North Side had bars—lots of them. There wasn't just a bar on every corner; often there were three bars to a block. And they were always full beginning at 7 a.m. until 2 a.m. because the H.J. Heinz plant was making that fabulous ketchup twenty-four hours a day, so the workers had happy hour after every shift. I'm pretty sure Pittsburgh invented the term "bar hopping." You'd just stumble from one to another and party into the night with everyone else. It seemed perfectly normal to me. It was blue collar to the core.

Growing up in a tough town surrounded by tough people, so it would only make sense that I would try to act as tough as I could. I got in a few good fights along the path to adulthood. Most of them were just plain funny, others were scary and even life-threatening. Regardless, I am still here, so I am either more of a badass than I think, or I have badass angels. I'm guessing the latter.

My friends back then were nuts too. There was a guy that rented the upstairs efficiency apartment in our house from my Mom. His name was Jule. He was a trip! The dude was around my age and worked for McDonald's at the time. He lived on frozen Mickey D burgers he stole from work, and he had a big headstone in his bedroom with his own epitaph on it. Jule lost his dad and brother when he was a kid. They fell through the ice at North Park Lake, I think, and he watched them go under. I can't imagine what he went through. He was an awesome guy and he had friends, lots of them. We all used to hang together.

One of Jule's friends was a 6'7" Prince Charming looking, blond Aries named Jim. My mom managed to set me up with him covertly, and I am glad she did. We had a blast together for a few months. Jim drove a Jeep CJ and wore down puffer vests and hiking boots. He looked like he belonged in the Rockies far more than in the 'burgh. (I later bought that Jeep, kicked the mice out of the engine hold, towed it home and restored it mostly by myself.)

While we dated, we managed to get in scuffles with various other dudes. One time we were driving down the road and some douchebag cut us off, so I proceeded to go Tasmanian Devil on

him and got him to pull over. We all jumped out of our cars, and I grabbed a tire iron out of the trunk. So, he grabbed an axe…a big one! Seeing that his tool was bigger, I had to talk my way out of that FAST before I got my got my head chopped off.

Jim Holihan

Not long after that, we were all sitting in the local McDonald's and some big dumb jocks made faces at me through the window, and I lost it! The Taz in me struck again. I ran out into the parking lot fully prepared to go down fighting (I was a bit reactionary back in the day). I was calling these fuckers on and the next thing I knew, all my friends were behind me. A melee ensued. I was swinging on one and my girlfriend jumped on the back of another. The guys in our group went after another. Suddenly, someone yelled, "Cops!" and we all took off. No harm, no foul. I love that back then you actually felt like you were *alive*.

There were also incidents that were not so fun. When I was fifteen and on-the-run, I was out on the streets most of the time and therefore had acquired a reasonable amount of street smarts. I knew how to act much older than I was. Since licenses had no photo back then, you could get a fake I.D. almost anywhere, and I had one. I loved to dance and dress up in fancy dresses and heels. Disco was still big so I would go to Oakland, the college town of Pittsburgh, and hit the Sanctuary Discotheque at night.

One night, I was waiting for a bus to take me back to the house I was staying at in Braddock, PA. A van pulled up with four black guys and one white guy in it. The side door slid open, and before I knew what the hell happened, one jumped out and grabbed me. I fought back, but he was big. He and another guy dragged me into the rust-colored van. The door closed, and they sped off. I don't think you can understand the feelings of something like that unless it has happened to you. For me, terror was mixed with calm. I knew I had to remain calm if I was to find a way out. I remembered my mother telling me, "If you ever get raped, just go along with it and stay calm. That is your best chance of survival. If you see an out, then run like hell."

So, they were pawing on me and passing me back and forth tearing off my clothes while the driver is driving. Then he turned down a dark back road. At that point I was thought I was going to die because I knew all of them intended to rape me. When the van stopped, I only had my thong panties left on, nothing else, not even shoes. They had even broken the crucifix necklace from my neck.

One of the douchebags tried to get me to put my mouth on him. I did *not* want that to happen, so I thought that if I acted like I was going to throw up, they might let me out of the van. Doing the best acting job I had ever done in my life, I started choking like I was going to throw up right there. The one that owned the van said, "Dude! Don't let her puke in my van!" and another one opened the door. They probably figured I was naked, so I wouldn't run. They were wrong.

I saw the cross from my necklace on the carpeted floor, and I managed to grab it on my way outside. The moment I got out that door, I ran as fast as I could down the road. I didn't look back; I just ran. It was so dark. I could barely see, and the gravel cut my feet, but I didn't feel it. I just kept running. Suddenly, I saw headlights coming from the other direction, so I flagged the car down with one hand while trying to cover my bare breasts with the other. It was a nice couple who were on their way home from dinner. I still remember her face and her yelling, "Oh my God, Honey!" And holding me in her arms, trying to calm me down and get me into the car. She gave me a coat to cover up with, and they drove me to the nearest police station. The officers gave me stuff to wear and took me to the hospital. I am not sure what was worse... the rape attempt or the terrible shit they put you through at the hospital. I know it is necessary, but it was honestly horrible.

I still have that crucifix necklace in my jewelry box today. Every time I look at it, I am reminded how lucky I was to get out of that alive and basically sexually unharmed. I described the perps to the cops but never heard anything. It made me sad that they were still out there and would likely hurt another girl sooner than later. Since they hadn't been caught, it had to have seemed like a damn game to them.

I was seeing someone in a local motorcycle organization at the time, and one of my girlfriends ran to them and told what had happened. Of course, it got back to him. Apparently, these scumbags and their van were notorious in the South Hills. All I will say is, it was handled. Whoever says vindication is bittersweet is full of shit. It felt great.

Family Dysfunction

No family is perfect, but at least mine didn't try to hide it. In fact, they did just the opposite, which made for some real fun.

Everyone in our town knew about the goings on at 36 Hempstead Ave., West View, PA. Our little yellow brick house sat on a hill. All the houses were close together, so all the neighbors could hear each other's personal stuff. When my folks took it outside, it was showtime for the peeps in the hood, and everyone came out to watch the dysFUNction. See, back then we didn't need reality television. We made our own insanity.

One of my stepdads was a riot. One time, a neighbor was screaming at us kids for running through her yard and tried hitting us with pears from her pear tree. So, the next day when she went to work, my stepdad had her spare car towed away from the front of her house! He called the towing company in town and told them to come tow his car to the shop, as it was broken down. Then. he gave them *her* address, and we all sat on our porch and watched. Along came the tow truck. They knocked on her door, but of course, no one answered. So, they left.

He called and said, "Geez, guys, I saw you leaving my house. I'd just got out of the shower. Now I am leaving for work. Please come back and get the damn car." So, they did. That night, the woman came knocking on doors asking if anyone saw anything. Of course, we said no. We laughed our asses off.

It took her four days to find it.

Another time, a different mean old lady that lived next door kept throwing dog crap over the hedges into our driveway because, of course, it had to be *our* dogs that were crapping in her yard. Well, my stepdad had enough. He decided to have a little fun at her expense. He started by calling the beer distributor and having them deliver a half barrel of beer and ten bags of pretzels to her house for a 'going away party.' Of course, when they got there, she said she hadn't ordered the beer. Then he called two different taxicab companies and sent them to her house to pick her up. She was getting a bit distraught. After that he had a cake delivered saying, "Bon Voyage" Mrs. Whatever-her-name-was.

Then, at just about the point where she was ready to flip, he called the cops and acted like he was her husband, sounding all sad and freaked out saying he'd found his wife dead when he came home! So, of course, they call the Pinkerton meat wagon (County Coroner) to pick up the dead body. Two guys got to the door all dressed in their suits, knocked and somberly said, "We are here to pick up the deceased (insert her name here)", to which she screams, "What? I'm not dead! I'm alive! I'm alive!"

Boy, we had a ball with that one.

When I was two, my mom re-married a guy named Paul Yogmas, and made my little brother Yogi. Paul was a hardcore alcoholic who was actually a great dad, but apparently not the best husband. I remember the day he left. They had a big fight. He came up to our room and said, "I have to go, I'll see you again soon," and jumped out the second-story window. Apparently, my mom was on her way upstairs after him, knife in hand! Mom chased after him and tried to stab his car tires as he was driving away.

Occasionally he came back to see us and take us on his boat. He was always cheerful. That probably had something to do with the baby food jar of whiskey that he almost always had in his hand. The sad thing was, he *forgot to come* or *had something come up* more times than he actually showed. I remember my little brother sitting on the front steps waiting and waiting and waiting and then crying. I didn't really care if he came or not, but it broke my little brother's heart too often. Again, I will say, dad's *please realize* how much your kids need you! Even if their mom is a hag, you need to man up. It is *never* the kids' fault; own your part in it. My brother's dad died of cirrhosis at the age of forty-something. I am always sad when I hear of a death that could have been prevented.

Mom dated a few other guys and had a few husbands, but I don't think she ever really loved someone until she was about fifty. She hit another guy with an iron, smashed a plate on another guy's head, and had the most colorful vocabulary of anyone I knew. I once stood outside the living room window with my best friend Rachel, and together we counted how many times my mom said 'fuck' or some variation of it in a single phone conversation. Eighty-seven times in five minutes. You wonder where I get it? Ha!

Through the years, like most single moms, my mom went looking for the right guy and, instead, found a bunch of wrong ones. I was molested at six years old by some douchebag boyfriend of hers. He put his hand down my pants when I rode with him to get icicles for our Christmas tree. I was terrified and when I got home. I ran to my mom's arms crying but afraid to tell her what happened, mostly because I figured she'd stab him and go to jail. Even then I knew mom could handle herself. I am still not sure to this day if I ever told her. I do know I never saw that guy again, and I also cannot, to this day, hang icicles on my Christmas tree. Maybe she had a feeling. I wish I could have stabbed him.

There are some sickos out there, folks. Funny thing is, unless you have been there, they are so hard to spot right off.

Another of my mom's boyfriends was Robin Albright. Robin and mom ran a small asphalt paving company out of our house. I learned to operate heavy equipment and drive dump trucks at age fourteen. I remember having callouses so bad on my hands from using a hand tamper all day that they bled. I thought it was cool that I was such a badass for a girl and showed off my bruised hands with pride! Kids today would curl up in a ball and whimper like little sissies. No wonder this country is dying a slow death…

I remember when mom and Robin had a fight about furniture. Mom was bitching that she hated the furniture and wanted new stuff. So, my stepdad (for lack of a better word), who was a stalky northern Italian guy from the tough part of town, picked up every single piece of living room furniture over his head—sofa included—and carried it out through the front door. He arranged it outside right in the middle of the street. He sprawled across the big white velour couch with the red trim, and started yelling, "Come on down, people. Yard sale right here! Fine furniture, great deals. Everything must go!" I stood in my front yard embarrassed as hell, debating whether to laugh or cry.

This same stepdad—Robin—was most of the reason I ended up getting taken away from my house. My mom had somehow met some guy from British Columbia through some singles ad in a paper called The Globe (before internet dating) and ran off to Canada to hang with him in the woods for two weeks. Needless to say, this pissed off the step-dick, so he took it out on my brother and me.

One morning me and a friend cut class, and when the school called home, he got mighty pissed. So much so, that he came to the school and dragged me out of class onto the street. He took off his belt and proceeded to beat me mercilessly. The entire school saw it. I know because I saw them all pressed up against the windows and doors. One teacher came out and tried to intervene, but then he dragged me home. When my little brother stood up for me, he hacked up his minibike with an axe (I wished he would have hit the gas tank and had it explode in his damn face).

I was cut and bruised all over and in some serious pain. The next morning when I went to school, the staff was waiting for me. They pulled me right into the office before I even had a chance to get to my class. Then they proceeded to ask me what the hell was up and when I told them, they called the authorities and had me taken to a child welfare shelter. I am not sure what was worse, home or the damn shelter. McIntyre Shelter was full of some pretty tough characters, most of whom were simply lost, sad, abused, scared, angry kids.

When I first walked into the shelter, one of the big, black chicks started saying stuff. I just kind of cowered down, hoping she wouldn't beat on my already sore body anymore. So, within minutes of being put in a dorm room, I was gone. When no one was looking I sped off out the door through the woods and down the hill to the highway. I wandered about for a while trying to find a safe place to hide from the cops, whom I was sure had been notified to look for me. Luckily, I came upon a cool lady in a grocery store who must have had a feeling I was in a mess. I stayed with her for about an hour, then had to move on.

I was walking along the road when a nice-looking older man with a big-ass Lincoln Continental stopped and offered me a ride. I told him a bit of my story, and he bought me lunch. He was nice looking, rich as hell and seemed very kind. Next thing I knew, he was offering to put me up in a Holiday Inn until he could find me a place of my own. I agreed, knowing even then that eventually this guy was gonna want something. But for the moment, I was tired and needed some real rest.

So, for about five days he was a perfect gent. He took me shopping and bought me some really nice clothes. We ate out at fine restaurants and went to his private clubs so he could show me off. No problem there, but one night he dropped me off at the hotel and wanted to come in. I invited him in but said I was really tired, hoping he wouldn't make any moves. He went to kiss me goodnight and went for my tit, so I kind of brushed him off and said, "I'll see you tomorrow, and we can have some real fun, ok?" I went to sleep, got up early, packed my stuff and took off. I never saw him again. Nothing against hookers, but I never wanted to be one.

I would try staying with friends when I could, but they were also young, and their parents were not all that keen on having a runaway in their house. Even a sweet, funny one like "yours truly." Times were hard. In fact, … I still believe fifteen was the hardest year of my life.

At this point, I had run away for like the umpteenth time and was living on the streets. (I explain more in the next chapter about those early years.) One afternoon I was walking around in downtown Pittsburgh when man came up and asked me if I was on the run. I just stared at him, then I said, "Who are you?"

He said, "I might be able to help you."

There was something about this man that made me unafraid. He had a kind voice, a fatherly gentle nature about him and sincerity in his eyes. So, I told him that I was. He told me his name was John Paytak and that he had a home for kids like me, and that he would be glad to help me if I would let him. He offered to buy me lunch so we could talk. I was starving, so I agreed. It turned out he ran a Christian group home called Circle C for abused and neglected kids like me. He told me I would be safe, and he could help me get back home to my parents. He said I should at least go there to see it and talk to the great folks that were the house parents. If I didn't like it, I was free to leave. Looking back, I believe God was present in this.

I told him thanks, but I wasn't quite ready to be confined, and I sure didn't want to go back to my home. But I took his card, thanked him for lunch and split. When he hugged me, I felt real caring, and that was huge to me. I walked away all tough, but when I rounded the corner, I lost it. I sat in an alley and cried really hard. I hadn't felt loved in so very long. He just had an amazing heart, and a warmth you could not miss.

Two weeks later, I was picked up by the cops. They said I was considered "incorrigible" for running away from home repeatedly, so that took me to a Juvenile Detention Center. Juvie hall was a tad scarier than the shelter. This place had little cells with tiny windows that you couldn't squeeze through, metal beds with shitty foam mattresses, no handles on the sink, and no toilet seat on a cold metal bowl (I had to hover). The building had a big-ass fence around it with guards. These people were much tougher than the gals I faced in the shelter.

Suzanne, age 15

Another big black girl tried to intimidate me, but this time I wasn't having it. I was watching TV in the main room of the pod and she just walked over and changed the channel. I looked in her eyes and told her if she didn't change that channel, I was going to strangle her with my bra. She turned it back.

I still had his card, so I called John and he came to my rescue. He had the judge release me into his custody, and off to the group home I went. It was a big cozy stone house on Pittsburgh's north side with four bedrooms; three beds to a room. There were about ten other girls there. I still remember some of their names today. Crystal, Robin, and Tara were my favorites. I would love to find them again. Crystal was a little missile twister with big eyes and curly hair like mine. Robin was a really tall, attractive, but tough blonde. Tara was a little skinny Latina or Italian gal; I don't remember which. We all became fast friends, even though Robin and I got into a big fight one night over I can't remember what. We duked it out in the bathroom, and I remember busting the towel rack off the side of the sink with some part of her. It was actually fun!

Shortly after I got into the group home, I received a call from mom whom I had not seen or talked to for months. She brashly said, "Here's the deal, you are either going to sign your half of Auntie's house over to me, or I am going to put your brother in a foster home and move to British Columbia. It's your choice." She didn't even say hello or ask how I was doing when she called. I was crushed.

But I signed over my part of the house to mom. The worst part was that after I finished the rest of my court-ordered six-month program, I had nowhere else to go. I went back home and had to deal with her bullshit again.

Even though I wasn't there long, I remember my time at the group home well. The house parents were seriously some of the finest humans I have ever met. I remember a few in particular. Veronica Bluey was the coolest. She was a born-again Christian who had been a former drug addict. I really loved her. Sue Anderson was a very cool older lady that we all just adored and then there was John, the man who found me. John was like a wonderful father to us all. Even years later—when I was back to running amuck—I thought about him often.

Stripped

I distinctly remember first time I was kicked out of my house at the age of fifteen and was living on the streets. I had no money and nowhere to go. I wandered around from friend's house to friend's house for a bit. Finally, I ended up running into this woman named Karen who lived four blocks from me in West View, Pennsylvania. When I told her my deal, she invited me to crash at her place till I got on my feet. I stayed with her for about two weeks—and boy—what an education I got while I was there! She was cool but was ten years older than me and a bit of a freak. She had worked as a model in New York back in the '70s. Karen was a gorgeous redhead with a very Euro, metrosexual attitude long before it was a thing. She had traveled around the world and had a lovely house in what was the well-to-do section called Wellington Heights.

We had some interesting parties at her place. I remember one evening I had a few friends over, and she came dancing down the stairs to David Bowie's *Fame* naked with only a silk scarf around her waist. Needless to say, she had lots of fans. All of my guy friends' balls were certainly clapping.

I didn't stay with her long, but we remained great friends. I do remember her being really depressed because she was aging and thought that her modeling career was over. She was still a knockout and had absolutely *no* inhibitions. She had married a very wealthy guy for his money, but just went through a nasty divorce. She came out of it with the house, though—and a kick-ass, full-length fox fur coat. I came to realize later that men often marry models and physically attractive women simply for their own egos. Often, they never actually *love* these beauties, and almost always seem to cheat on or mistreat them.

I realized—even at the age of fifteen—that I never wanted to marry for money. It seemed too dangerous for a gal to commit to someone who can hold so much over her head. No amount of money would be worth selling my own soul.

When that stint at Karen's was over, I was flat-broke again with nowhere to go. I remember looking through the paper one evening when I saw an ad for dancers. They were paying $200 to $400 a week! Well, I thought, *Shit, I can dance.* Back in the late '70s that was a hell of a lot of money, so I called. I scheduled an interview for the next day. I got on a bus with my last dollar and met the guy at his office. His name was Hugo, and he was pretty cool. He ran Talent Artist Enterprises in south Pittsburgh. We talked a while, and of course, I lied and said I was eighteen. Whether he saw through it or not didn't matter. I could tell he liked me, so he said, "I want you to audition." I was scared shitless, but hell, I was there, so I said, "Sure!" I was still thinking I was auditioning for some disco revue or something. My dream was always to be on TV and have my name in lights someday, so maybe this was my shot.

We got into his Cadillac and ended up down the road at some little old dive bar called The Thunderbird Lounge on Rt. 51. We walked in, and I saw this little 4ft x 8ft "stage" with lights all around it and mirrors on the wall and thought what a weird place for a disco audition. Then he handed me two Band Aids and a G-string and said, "In the back there's a little dressing room. Go put these on and pick a couple songs."

I could have shit! Fear took over my voice, and I could not say what I was thinking… *What the fuck are you talking about? Oh, hell no!*

I did manage to ask what I was to do with the Band Aids. He said, "You know, for your tits." Yeah, uh, no. I actually was not aware. Putting band aids on one's tits is not something nice teenagers from the North Hills typically need to do. WTF? But, with no other option and no money to get a bus back to West View, I put the shit on. I picked a song and hit the stage damn near naked except for the little G-string and Band Aids. I was never so terrified in my life.

I'm not sure what he saw in that performance because I was shaking like a leaf, …but either way, he liked me, and I got the job.

So, when we went back to his office, he called a club in Scranton, PA called The Thirsty Stone. After a quick conversation, he made a reservation for me for a flight. What? I have to get on an airplane? If I wasn't already horrified, I was at that moment. Hugo gave me two "costumes" consisting of tiny triangle tops and G-strings, bought me two packs of Marlboros, took me to the airport and I was off. I didn't even have any high heeled shoes.

I had never been on a plane before and was even more terrified than I was at back at The Thunderbird. Back then all you needed to get on board a plane was a ticket. I wasn't old enough to drive so I didn't even have a license. I remember sitting next to a priest, thinking, *my odds are better with him nearby.* I stayed really close and dug into his arm the whole time.

When we landed, this guy who was the classic perverted, groping grandpa was waiting for me. He picked me out of the crowd at the little airport. It must have been the hair. We left the airport and headed out to see the bar. It was in an old, old building that was probably built in the early 1900s and sat on a dark corner of the street in a city neighborhood. Boy, was it a dive! When we walked in, I suddenly remembered the stale bar smell from all the nasty little joints I'd hung out with my mom in when I was little. It was comforting in a way, I guess.

After that, we went to a big old hotel right in downtown and he checked me in. He advanced me ten bucks and left. I didn't have a toothbrush or even a suitcase. I was to start dancing the very next night. All this happened in one day. I remember lying there on the bed and how weird everything felt. It was strange being so far from home and alone… really alone.

The next evening, I was scared as hell to walk into the bar. My driver showed me to the dressing room, which was the back of an old grungy kitchen that hadn't been used for food—or even really cleaned—in years. In the room was an old padded stainless-steel chair and an old whitish Formica table, the kind with the little flecks of gold in it. I remember there was only a mirror and a small lamp on it and no door; just a thick gold curtain hanging between me and the bar. I was keenly aware that there wasn't any protection from the ravenous men who were swilling beer after beer, waiting for the stripper du jour to appear. The juke box was back there because it was just for the dancers to use. I was so afraid it wasn't funny. I had just turned fifteen three months prior to that day and I had been in bars with my mom since I was really little. But this was different. I was supposed to go out there and get up on the high, tiny stage and dance…with my top off. Good Lord!

For the first set I did, I couldn't muster the courage to take off my top. The guy who owned the bar came in the backroom and said, "Hey, Sweetie, you are gonna take your top off next set, right?" I remember crying through the three break songs before I had to go back up. I couldn't bail now; I had nowhere else to go.

I remember one of the songs was *I Go Crazy* by Paul Davis. I still cry a bit inside every time I hear that song to this day. I remember thinking I'm not gonna be able to stop crying in time to get back onstage. I felt so alone and lost and scared at that moment. I will never forget it.

Even all these years later as I'm writing this, I remember the room exactly: the old fridge, sink and stove, the little table, the smells and the sounds outside that curtain…

The break was over, and it was time to play my songs. I put the quarter in the jukebox, took a few deep breaths and went up on the stage. I took off my top after the first song, and that was it. Amazingly, all my inhibitions left the building in that moment. It was oddly freeing. The crowd went wild! Guys started throwing money at me onstage and whistling and yelling, "Beautiful!" Wow, I felt like a goddess. I couldn't get all of the money fast enough and still dance. When I finished that set and went backstage, I remember thinking, *if those dickheads from junior high could see me now.* That night changed my whole life in ways I could never have dreamed of at the time. When I left the bar and went to my hotel, the little girl was gone and a woman had taken her place. For the first time in my life, I felt like the world was an oyster and I was the pearl. I counted my $200+ dollars and laid back and dreamed.

The next day I decided to go shopping. I had a big, smelly wad of cash and it was all mine. I could finally buy myself nice things that I could never have growing up on welfare checks and public assistance. I walked down the street and found a Fredrick's of Hollywood. I felt like I was actually in Hollywood. I bought some really high heels (circa *That '70s Show*) and two pairs of expensive, tight-ass, bell bottom jeans. I still have one pair in my hope chest that has a zipper all the way from the front to the back. If you unzip them, they end up in two pieces. I have still never seen another pair like them.

That night, a bigger crowd came, and I made even more money. It was hard to imagine that just two days before this, I used my last dollar to take the bus to an interview. I was rolling in dough. To transition from a shy, insecure kid who got picked on relentlessly at home and school to a young, sexually appealing woman—basically overnight—who now had fifty guys a night throwing money at me and telling me I was beautiful, was pretty amazing.

We closed a little early on the second night, so after work I took a cab back to the city and decided to go out on the town. I asked the cabbie where there was a good disco, and he dropped me off at a club called the OZ Discotheque. I might have been only fifteen, but I walked in like I owned the joint. I bellied up to the bar, ordered a Black Velvet and Coke, and went out on the dance floor all by myself. No one even thought to card me. I must have looked like I did this shit all the time. I didn't have any fear at all. Back then, driver's licenses didn't even have pictures so anyone could get a fake I.D. I remember dancing all alone on the dancefloor under the swirling lights, looking up at the big sparkling disco ball feeling like I was in some romantic movie. It was surreal.

On night three, I met a guy while I was dancing. He was sitting at the bar quietly, just watching me with this sexy look on his face. His name was Les. He was absolutely gorgeous; tall, dark, and handsome like the prince in Snow White. He was also about thirty years old. His black hair was kinda tossled, and his smile was genuine. I remember his face to this day. He was charming and had these kind eyes. For some reason, I just trusted him. He gave me a big-ass tip, so we sat at the bar during my break and talked. I really liked him a lot. Eventually, he said he had to go, but told me he'd be back tomorrow evening to take me to breakfast after work if I wanted. Even with all of the money and attention I was seriously lonely, so of course I said ok.

As I was finishing work the next night, Les called the bar. He was on his way so I waited outside for him so the owner could lock up for the night. As I stood out front, two drunk douchebags approached me and started saying shit like, "Hey baby, why don't you come home with us and make us breakfast?" To which I replied in my most smart-ass tone, "I have an even better idea. Why don't you two go home and eat each other?"

One of them grabbed me by my arm, and the other came up from behind me and grabbed me around my waist. I hit the one in front of me in the face with my overloaded purse that had a big rock and a chain in it. Just then, I heard a horn blaring and saw headlights coming at a high rate of speed. The car jumped the curb and slammed on its brakes. It was Les. He jumped out of the BMW and grabbed the one guy off of me and punched him square in the jaw. He then yelled, "Get in the fucking car NOW!" So, I did. After a few more punches, one guy was on the ground and the other took off. Les jumped in the car and we took off. It was like something out of a Clint Eastwood movie. Even though I was terrified, I must admit that it was exciting.

We went to a little diner to calm down and have a bite. I will never forget that place because it had a beautiful mural of a tractor-trailer painted on the main wall and its headlights were real and they lit up. (I went back there again a few years ago and, damn, that painting was still there!) As we sat there and talked, I felt I needed to let him know that I was only fifteen. To his credit, he handled it well and was a perfect gentleman.

I was honestly afraid to stay at the hotel after being assaulted by the two dirtbags earlier that evening, so I stayed with Les the rest of the week at his beautiful house. It was like nothing I had ever seen before. It sat on a hill and had huge windows from which you could see the city lights below. It had one of those islands the rich people had and carpet so thick I couldn't walk on it in heels. I remember the crystal lights, plush leather furniture, a big wine rack, and a fridge full of amazing food. I never wanted to leave.

I finished the week out, and Les drove me to the bus station. I kissed him goodbye and went inside to get a bus back to Pittsburgh. As I sat there, I realized not only had I changed and grown up ten years in a week, but—once again—I really had no place and no one to go home to. I had a boot full of money, and I was free as a bird. Just then, a bus pulled in that said Philadelphia. I had an old boyfriend by the name of Mike McCann who lived there, so I decided to go surprise him. I changed my ticket and off to Philadelphia I went.

The thing is, I had no idea how big and scary Philly would be. My goodness, it was enormous! I thought Pittsburgh was a big city. Philadelphia is gigantic. The bus pulled into downtown at night and realized I had no damn idea where I was going or how I was going to get there. I was very concerned.

Suddenly, an older black man approached me and said, "Girl, you look like you need some help. Where are ya goin'?" For some reason, I trusted him. He had kind eyes. I told him I needed to find my boyfriend, but all I knew was he was working at a Steak and Ale in Devon or Berwyn. He said he'd take me for $30. I agreed. Actually, I ended up getting off cheap because he had to drive me around for over two hours looking for the place. Back then there was no Siri. We finally found the right restaurant, and Mike's lime green car was parked in the lot. I laid my suitcase under the car in case he managed to go out a back door and leave before I found him. I figured he'd hit something and at least get out to look, so it would buy me some time.

I walked into the restaurant, plopped down at the bar like I did this shit daily, and ordered a Black Velvet and Coke. I began chatting with the bartender and observed. Finally, once I realized she was cool, I told her I was here to surprise Mike the chef, as we used to date. I handed her a picture of me and him that I had kept in my wallet and asked her to take it back to him. She did. Seconds later, I heard a loud crash, and he ran out of the kitchen to see me!

I'll never forget that moment, his beautiful smile, and the lights reflecting off his shiny black hair. I knew I couldn't stay very long, but it was great to see him. The next morning, after breakfast, I asked him to drive me to the bus station. I hugged him goodbye and never saw him again.

On the bus back to Pittsburgh, I saw a man I swore I knew. I could not stop looking at him, so finally I said, "Excuse me, but do I know you?" He recognized me, too. As fate would have it, I was sitting right next to my great aunt's boyfriend. He was a very kind man and knew my family history and drama. We sat together and talked away on the ride back to Pittsburgh. Before we parted ways, he handed me a fifty-dollar bill and said, "Here, take

Suzie, age 16

this. You might need something, and I wish I could do more to help you." Even though money wasn't the issue at that moment, I knew that God had put him there for me.

I continued to work for years. I traveled around the region dancing in some pretty tough places. Pennsylvania, West Virginia, and New York were very blue collar, and the bars and buildings were very old. They had the Creaky floors, old glass doorknobs, and that musty smell. The hard-boiled eggs and kippered fish they served from behind the bar for your dining pleasure were a far cry from the high-end steaks you find in night clubs today.

Most of the clubs were bars in old hotel buildings. Sometimes we would be put up in one of the rooms upstairs of the bar. I had to be really careful out there on the road because there was always an asshole or two in the crowd. One night in Altoona, I had just finished dancing and the bar was closing, so a friend offered to walk me up to my room. Boy, I was glad he did. When I opened the door to my hotel room, a guy jumped out! He saw the dude with me and jumped out my window and off the roof. He had been waiting there for me. I am sure he wasn't planning to rub my feet, read me a bedtime story, kiss me on the cheek, and tuck me in.

The next time it happened; however, I wasn't so lucky.

This was a horribly lonely, scary time for me. I wrote this poem when I was barely sixteen and on the run. I didn't have anywhere to go. In fact, no one even knew where I was… or cared.

> *Off down the stairway and onto the stage*
> *goes a pretty, young girl, who looks old for her age.*
>
> *Her heart is sixteen, but she looks twenty-one.*
> *Dancing half-naked pretending it's fun.*
>
> *Surrounded by men, who are staring and swearing,*
> *But not at the smile she has to keep wearing.*
>
> *Does she ever want children, a husband, a home?*
> *Someone to save her from being alone?*
>
> *Will she survive the hell of the night,*
> *Or will she just end it, and give up the fight?*

It was one of the loneliest and lowest times of my life.

Let the Good Times Roll

Even with all the craziness, my childhood wasn't all bad. Since the first time I ran away, I'd return home throughout the years when there was nowhere else to turn. I would stay for a few months or longer, depending on the step-dick of the day. Then I would leave again. I didn't stay ANYWHERE for too long, and I still don't.

Growing up in the '60s and '70s was an amazing time. Everyone knew everyone else. Freedom was still real, and America was still powerful. People were kinder to each other, and dreams were right within reach for almost everyone. The cops were so friendly that would drive you and your half barrel of beer home when they caught you partying in the woods, or on the city steps. We just happened to do it almost every summer night. They would, however, take your weed.

The little suburb of Pittsburgh I grew up in was called West View. It had a main street and even its own amusement park. West View Park was built in 1909. It was absolutely like something from an old-fashioned storybook with wooden roller coasters, a beautiful hand-painted merry-go-round, and an aerial tram that went almost the length of the park. There were antique cars, and the best haunted house before Disney World. I swear, they had every kind of cool ride they made at the time.

West View Park also had a gigantic, beautiful dancehall called Dance Land where famous musicians of the time came and played. I spent every day all summer there with my pals smoking joints and checking out boys. There was an arcade with a little dance floor, where we all used to dance to the old jukebox. The water fountain smelled like rotten eggs. The place was wonderful. Best of all, it helped me escape the home drama, which was pretty frequent. I remember being eleven and dancing in front of all the people in the arcade like it was the most natural thing in the world. My friend, Dawn H., was just as fearless as I was and we would dance for hours, not giving a damn who was watching. Nobody had the ridiculous hang-ups we do today or really cared about being judged, at least not my friends in my hood.

Summers were free and fun, and we all played outside and knew just about everyone in our whole town. We were gone from sun-up till the streetlights came on. If your ass wasn't home when they came on, it would get a warming.

When the Moon Comes Up

Our favorite past-time, though, was mooning. I think that knowing how to properly present your moon to an unsuspecting human is a lost art… mostly because today you could get arrested and labeled a damn sex offender. Good lord. That's another fun thing about the old days: there were no cell phones and no way for wimpy assholes to call the cops from a street corner when you assaulted them with your ass crack, unless they ran to a pay phone and happened to have your plate number and a dime handy.

My friends and I used to go mooning all the time. We even took turns driving so we could each see the looks on the faces of the innocent victims we showed our butts to. It was grand summer fun. There's nothing like the feeling of the warm summer night breeze blowing across your butt cheeks. Ahhhh! Mooning is good fun in the wintertime too, but with the windows up it's called "pressed ham!"

Even mom liked to get in on the fun. We had a good time together when I was home. She sure could be a blast when she wanted to be. Once I understood that my mom and dad were the products of dysfunctional families too, dealing with them was a little easier. My mom was a spoiled-brat-wild-child with over-doting parents, who was mostly a lot of fun to be around when she wasn't kicking my ass.

One afternoon, my mom and I were sitting at the house bored, listening to the CB radio. We overheard some construction workers on an off channel who were working on the highway near our house. There was a big U-shaped bend in the road in West View, aptly called the Horseshoe Bend. From what we could tell from the transmissions, one of the guys was on the downhill side of it, the other was on the uphill side of it, and both were checking out the chicks in the cars that passed by. One would see some hotties driving by and radio the other one to look for them as they passed him up around the bend.

"Hey Bill, you got two blondes in a red car coming your way. One has a great set of tits!" Then the other guy replied, "Thanks Bob! You have one coming your way too. Cute brunette in a mini skirt" and so forth. So, I told my mom we should go down there and mess with them. While unbeknownst to them, listening on the mobile CB radio to what their responses would be.

She thought it was a grand idea! So, we fixed ourselves up, jumped in the car and turned on the CB radio.

We went past the one guy, waved at him, and smiled. Then, of course, he says, "Wow, Bob, ya got two hot ones coming. A blonde and a redhead. Holy crap!" So, when we passed Bob, he was waiting and smiled and waved. Then the fun began… I told my mom to go past him and turn around up the road a piece. I then proceeded to drop my drawers and got ready to moon him.

We waited for traffic to go ahead, then just as we pulled right up beside Bob, and BAM! Out the window went my bare ass. I gave him a good long look, jumped back in the seat, smiled, winked, and we took off. My mom was laughing uncontrollably while trying to drive the car. Just then Bob jumped on the radio and told Bill, "Dude… Ya know the blonde and redhead in the grey car? Well, the one just stuck her fine ass in my face. Like right in it! They're heading back down your way. Be ready!"

Mom, circa 1979

However, I told mom to turn off the side street before we got around the bend and park the car, which she did. Now, here was Bill waiting like a dumb ass for us to come back but we didn't show. So, of course, he started getting really pissed at Bob because now he thinks Bob is a damn liar. Hysterical! You should have heard the insanity. They went from best buddies to "Bob, you lying mother-fucker. I can't believe you would bullshit me, Bro. They never did that!"

To which Bob replied, "Bill! I swear they did! They did!" "Well then, where the hell are they, man?"

Finally, I could bear it no more. I grabbed the radio and said, "Hi, boys…this is the Moon Maiden. Bill, Bob wasn't lying. I just had to turn off before I got to you. Have a great day! Bye now." Then we heard Bill say, "Please! *Please* come back! Come moon me too! Pleeeease!" It was a hoot. Life was so much simpler back then.

Another time, I was cruising up I-79 in Pennsylvania and happened to flash this cutie, who was driving a box truck. He honked, smiled big and war whooped as men naturally do, and then I sped off. A short time later, he cruised up beside me beeping his horn, and when I looked over… there he was sliding the side driver's door wide open, naked from the waist down, pecker flapping in the breeze. Good times, good times.

NoNo

My grandparents and great grandparents, although they died when I was younger, were a big part of my life. My great grandma Corrine, or "NoNo" as we all called her, died when I was twelve, but continued to have a huge impact on me. I often see her in myself.

NoNo was a vivacious and voluptuous beauty with light red curly hair. She came here around 1920 from Russia on a boat with her sisters through Ellis Island. She was born in Hungary. She was breathtaking, intelligent and had a grand set of tits. (I know this because they are hereditary. I have them too.) She also had a killer accent, and even at seventy years old, she could still get men to do anything she wanted. She would fix herself up and look glamorous anytime she left the house. She wore furs in the winter, even if just to go down the street to the local bakery. I learned years later that she did a bit of prostitution in order to survive during The Great Depression. But, from all I gathered, she became something of a higher class one, and yes—there is a difference… sort of.

She told me this story when I was a young girl: She was walking through the park in what is now Allegheny Community College near Western Avenue on Pittsburgh's north side. However, back then it was Ridge Avenue, where all the millionaires lived. The mansions are still there today along with part of the college. Being the shrewd Scorpio that she was, Gram figured out how to look rich and classy in dime store clothes. She knew that if she strolled about where the rich men were looking like she was rich, they would feel comfortable approaching her. And she could then get their money.

One day, a wealthy man approached her. They talked, had lunch, and began seeing each other. I am not sure what exactly happened—or for how long—but in the end, she had a fabulous mink coat and hat.

I remember walking to the store with her in her later years. We lived on a hill, and though she enjoyed walking down to go shopping, climbing back up the steep grade was hard for her. So NoNo—being NoNo—figured a way to hustle rides from the local men. The first time I saw her do this she said to me, "Ok, now you pay attention." She walked up to a young man in the sweetest voice, which was NOT her normal tone and said, "Excuse me, darling. I have a heart condition and my ride is nowhere to be found. Could I pay you two dollars to ride us up the hill to my home? It's so hard for me with all these groceries."

The guy would say, of course, "Oh absolutely, ma'am. It would be my pleasure!" And up the hill we'd go with her praising him all the way. She would hand him money knowing full well he would not accept it.

After thanking him profusely, she would say, "What a fine gentleman you are!" He would even carry in our groceries. The moment he left, she would look at me, wink, and say, "Now, that's how you do it, honey."

NoNo had a sister who was the complete opposite of her. My great aunt Hattie was a devout Catholic who NEVER missed a Sunday service. She worked hard as a seamstress for the same rich folks NoNo hustled! Aunt Hattie married young, but after her husband and young child died, she never remarried. She gave me a one-dollar bill in a Christmas card one year. Even after she passed, I never spent it. No matter how bad things seem, I remember that I am never "completely broke," thanks to Aunt Hattie.

Looking back, I see how Great Gram NoNo taught my mom how to use her feminine wile. I learned it also. I just chose to use it differently. I am and have always been quite a flirt, though, and I know where I got it from.

Grandma had many dates come to pick her up at her house when I was younger, and every one of them would show up well dressed in a jacket and hat carrying a box of chocolate covered cherries. Great Gram loved chocolate cherries.

Grandma NoNo

One day when I was about eight years old, I remember a date came to the house to pick up grandma. He forgot the chocolates. She opened the door, said a charming hello, then looked down at his hands and said firmly, "Where are my chocolates?"

He said, "Oh, Sweetie, I'm so sorry. I forgot. I'll bring you two boxes next time," to which she replied, "Oh hell no, you won't! Please, go get them now," and slammed the door in his face. (Notice she said please.)

Twenty minutes later, he was back with the chocolates. She said, "Why thank you so much, darling," kissed him on the cheek, handed him her mink coat, and off to dinner they went. She didn't bitch, nag, or make him feel less manly. She knew better. Gram understood, as I do, that men are much simpler creatures with a shorter attention span than women. It is not a shortcoming; it is in their DNA.

There was another day when I came home from school crying because kids were picking on me. I am sure it was because I had kinky hair, no tits yet, was incredibly shy, (yes, really) and well… I was just different.

Great Gram NoNo sat me down and said, "I want you to imagine you're dead." She got my attention, then she said, "Imagine your body is lying in a casket, and your spirit is floating above the room looking down. Who's going to be there? Your mom, me, your brother, a few good friends. They are gonna be crying and really sad you're gone. But you know what all the other hundred people there are gonna say? 'Wow, bummer Suzi died, huh? So, what are you all doing after the funeral? Wanna grab a beer?

"And there you go. All that worrying about what they think of you, and in the end, they aren't going to give a damn about you or the people you left behind. So, why the hell should you care what they think of you while you're here?" That really hit me and made amazing sense.

After that, I decided to start doing life my way and let them all figure it out. I am glad I did. NoNo's advice served me well over the next decades of my life.

Love Me or Leave Me

There's one thing that always surprises me… when a person meets someone who is happy, alive, sexy and full of fire, he or she falls for them because of these qualities. Then, for some reason, they start trying to change them into someone else. I just don't understand that. I know they usually do it because they are insecure themselves and feel threatened by an outgoing or sexy partner. Other times, I think that—in the beginning—it is hard to see the real person you are falling for because your head is in the clouds… or your legs are over your head.

I remember a few times men tried to "settle me down," or change me. Obviously… they failed. They are not with me anymore, and I am still me. I even bought a fun shirt that says, "I'm not with stupid anymore."

The first time I encountered this, I was about eighteen and working as a stripper in Pittsburgh. I first started working as a stripper at the age of fifteen when I was on the streets and had to make some quick cash. At this point in time, I had been stripping for two years. My 'man of the year' played the *Honey, it bothers me that you show your body to other men. Can't you get a* real *job?* card. Since he asked instead of demanding, I figured I would give it a whirl because I thought I loved him very much at the time, and he was a good dude.

So, I got a job as a waitress at a restaurant that is Pittsburgh's equivalent to Denny's, but with far better food. It's called Eat-n-Park. I enjoyed working with the other employees and made a couple of good friends, but the money was crap compared to what I was doing before. I also had to put up with way more sexual harassment there than I ever did in the clubs. Seriously!

By the sixth day, the job was already wearing me down. The 'Counter Bums' (a.k.a. cheap old men that don't tip but suck up your seats all morning) were on my last nerve. They would grab my ass and condescendingly yell, "Hey, Doll face. How 'bout some more coffee?" These guys had done this so many times that, on the seventh day, I dumped a plate of spaghetti on the biggest asshole's lap, grabbed my purse and walked out the door before they could fire me.

When my boyfriend got home that night, I walked right up to him, hugged him and said, "When you can pay me $50,000 a year to sit home and suck your dick, I will gladly quit stripping. Until then, fuck you. I'm going back to the job I love. You are free to go if that still bothers you." He adapted.

Another time, I tried working a *real job*. When I was just nineteen, I took a break from dancing and got a job working in a nursing home in North Pittsburgh. I am so grateful for that experience. What an awakening. Looking back now, I see it also gave me a ton of material for what would become Bag Lady Sue's stand-up act, especially the physical comedy part of my character. Watching the old folks get around was fun. There were some very colorful people there, especially the patients.

I knew the job would teach me plenty. What I didn't know when I started there, however, was all the gross and sad stuff I would see and learn about. I was truly humbled as I realized that one day, I too could end up right there.

I remember my first day on the job. I got off the elevator in my crisp, new nurses' uniform. As I approached the nurse's station, I was horrified to see three nurses' aides running down the hallway, pulling an old woman backwards in her wheelchair, screaming, "Get out of the way!" The one aid said in a low voice, "Oh my goodness, I'm gonna puke!"

My first thought was, *My God! What kind of place is this?* When they rounded the corner to take her into a shower room, I saw her chewing on a mouth full of… well, *poo*. Yep, you betcha. Her very own *poo*. So—as I stood there in shock for a moment—my first reaction was to get back on the elevator and run like hell. But I decided this might just be a fun place to work, so what the heck… I'll give it a week.

The week turned into nine months, and it was, honestly, one of the greatest awakenings of my life. It not only humbled me, but it made me realize how valuable old people are to us young, dumb shits. We really take them for granted.

I used to watch for which patients had family come see them and which ones didn't. As I became more experienced, I was able to tell right away who had been a good person throughout their life—and who hadn't—often simply by how many people came to see them. The selfish, grouchy, entitled ones, were the loneliest and angriest. I couldn't tell if they were pissed at themselves or still blaming everyone else for their lot in life.

There were, however, others who were just *too* good to their kids. Whether intentionally or inadvertently, they had raised a bunch of entitled bitches and bastards whose only concern was how much money they were going to get when their old folks died. This was heartbreaking; it made me sick.

There was a woman there named Margaret. She couldn't see very well at this stage of life, but Margie must have been a wild one in her day. She was a bit 'out of it' for the most part, but when she was lucid, she would talk about getting laid in graphic detail! It made me laugh.

Sue working at Nursing Home

She would say things like, "My boyfriend will be here soon, and I intend to suck his dick," or "Get me to the john. I need to douche out my box in case he wants in." Other times she would say, "My goodness he has a big one! Yummy!" She also used to feed an imaginary dog at the same time I was feeding her. So, I would always leave her a bit of food on her tray for *him*.

I remember when I had to get her teeth out of her mouth after dinner. She would throw a fit. She'd clench her jaws together and tell me through her clenched teeth that there was no way I was getting her damn teeth. So, at first, I was puzzled. *Hmmm, how am I gonna get these teeth?* Then I thought about the dog. When I want to get my dog to take a pill, I disguise it in meat. Of course, the dog opens his Milk Bone hole and in goes the pill! So, I just told her here's a bit of food, open up, and when she did, I just snatched the damn teeth right out of her face. *HA! Gotcha.* She'd get pissed at me, but then she would laugh. It was fun.

I made a friend while there who I called Gram. She was the sweetest little, old, white-haired lady I ever met. She was as colorful as a rainbow. She had a couple of family members come by now and then. But for the most part, I was like her kid. We walked the halls and grounds, played cards and ate milk & cookies together, and—best of all—we talked about the old days. She had a way of making me feel like I lived back then too. I really grew to love her.

One day on our walk, she had a sudden, massive stroke. Out of nowhere, she just collapsed and died in my arms on the hallway floor. I was devastated. After that I had a hard time letting myself get too close to anyone there.

I really liked the white uniform and all. It made me feel important. Ironically, after I went back to stripping, I had kept that uniform and started doing a sexy nurse routine. I made a ton of dough with that one. The irony.

Try as I may to live a *normal* life, something always pulled me back into the strip clubs. It may sound odd, but it just felt like we were a real family. In addition, the money was awesome, the guys were flattering, and there were those people I had met along the way that really changed my life.

Ironically, a guy—who I actually met *in a strip club* and began dating—tried to suggest that I change the way I dressed. The nerve! I remember cruising down the road in my Jeep with top and doors off; the sun was shining, the wind blowing in our hair, and my skirt blowing up just slightly revealing only my outer thigh. I was eating an ice cream cone as we were driving down the road, when he suddenly said, "Tuck in your skirt! Why do you always have to dress so sexy?"

I responded by whipping the Jeep to the side of the road. I slammed on the brakes, hit him in the face with that ice cream and screamed, "Don't you ever try telling me how to dress, act, or feel. Ever! Are you my dad? Don't act like my dad, because I wouldn't fuck my dad! You got that?"

You see, ladies, sometimes you just gotta nip that shit in the bud right away. We made it over two years together, and he never once brought it up again. Things can be worked out.

We all like to think we are so damn different, but the truth is we all feel similar things. We dream similar dreams, want the best for our kids, want people to like us, want to have enough to be comfortable, have fun, feel love and passion, and get laid. And we hope to get enough of it done before we see that bright light. I think at the top of the list, though...we all want to love ourselves and to be loved for who we are.

Gram NoNo taught me that lesson, and I learned it well.

Suzanne, Mom, and Yogi (circa 1984)

Angels and Demons

In one form or another, I have always believed in God and the spiritual realm.

When I was fifteen, I had an experience which has stuck with me all these years. In those days, some of the parties I attended were pretty crazy. One particular night, I overdosed on a mix of uppers and downers while at a party down my street. I staggered home from the party and lay down in my bed, and then my heart stopped. (I wasn't lying when I said fifteen was the hardest year of my life.) My mom heard me talking to someone who seemed to be sitting with me, but when she saw no one there, she called the ambulance. I remember it so clearly. I could feel myself getting lighter and lighter and then—suddenly—my aunt, uncle, and grandma were there sitting on the bed and talking with me. They had died years ago! But to me, they were all as alive and well in that moment as I am sitting here right now. I distinctly remember what they were wearing.

The strange thing was that my friend Janet was there, too. The others were dead, but Janet was very much alive. Oddly enough, Janet—the only living person in the conversation—was the only one whose clothes I couldn't remember.

My grandma, aunt, uncle, and I talked about the party and the events leading up to this moment in time. We also discussed how bad things were at home. After a bit they said, "We have to go now." I pleaded for them to take me with them, but my aunt said, "It's not time for you to come with us yet. We love you, and we'll be back for you." Then they were gone. This was all I could remember when I woke up in the hospital.

The next day when I released and went home, I described their outfits to my mom in great detail. She confirmed these were the clothes each of them was wearing when they were buried. Interestingly, I didn't attend all of their funerals, just grandmas. How did I know what clothes they were buried in? I'm still not sure. I also couldn't understand why my friend Janet was also sitting on the bed with my deceased relatives. She just sat there looking at me, but never said a word.

Needless to say, all my friends were concerned when I got home the next day. My best friend Rachel came over to see me at my house, so I told her the story in detail. She knew my grandma and uncle before they died, but my aunt had died when I was five. I also told her about how weird it was that Janet was there, too. Why would she be there, we wondered? But like kids do, we blew it off and went about our lives.

Three months later, Rachel, a couple of our other friends, and I were hanging out in my backyard when Janet stopped over. As she walked up to us, we knew something was wrong. She said she had just been diagnosed with cancer. The doctors told her they wanted to take off her infected leg; otherwise, she was going to die. Rachel and I just looked at each other in shock. And at that moment, we both thought the same thing. We told Janet to let the doctors take the damn leg, but she said, "No fucking way! I'm not living like that!"

Janet died a few months later—she was only fifteen years old. She was one of the sweetest, coolest girls I ever knew. I will never know why I saw her the night my heart stopped. But from that day forward, I have no longer been afraid to die. Even when I feel lonely, I understand that I am never truly alone. There is *more* going on—I'm now convinced—than what we know here.

One night that same year, I ran away (again) after a big fight with my mom. It was a blizzardy night, but I didn't care. I'd had enough of getting pounded on and needed to just GO. So, I jumped out my window with little more than a jean jacket, a sweatshirt, and bell-bottom jeans on. It was snowing like a bitch, and the wind was ripping pretty good. I wasn't sure where to go, so I jumped on a bus and headed to the city to my then-boyfriend's house. When I got there, no one was home. I sat huddled in the doorway of his brownstone house and waited. No Joe. After a while I was nearly frozen, so I headed back to my neighborhood. The busses had quit running, however, so I had to hitchhike.

The snow fall reached eighteen inches deep at this point, and the wind was unreal. I was literally freezing to death. A guy stopped and picked me up, but on the way back to my neighborhood, he tried grabbing my breasts. I jumped out of his car at a stop sign and ran into the snow. I walked the rest of the way to a friend's house, shaken even more but afraid to knock on her door because I figured her mom would call mine, and I'd get another beating. I remembered there was an old, abandoned Volkswagen Beetle out back of her house, and I thought if I could get in it, I could get out of the wind and get warmer. I dug my way in through a snowdrift and laid on the backseat, shivering like I never had before. My pants were wet and so were my shoes. I simply could not get warm. I just lay there shaking all over for I don't know how long, and then—suddenly—I felt nice and warm and started to doze off.

Just then I heard someone call out, "Suzy!" real loud. It woke me up, and I started shivering again. I yelled, "Who's there? Hello?" but no one answered. I called out again, "Who's out there?" Nothing. At that moment, I thought of the Hans Christian Anderson story I loved as a child called *The Little Match Girl,* and realized it was the spirit of my grandma waking me before I froze to death. I must say, hyperthermia is a pretty decent way to go if you ever want to go. Hell, the Inuit people have been doing it that way for years. That way there's no pain, and their bodies feed the Polar Bears and wildlife, which in turn feeds and clothes their families. *However,* I was *not* ready to go. I know now, it wasn't my time. There was/is more I have to do. Maybe that is why I have been alright on my own all these years, because I never really feel alone.

Yet another time, my brother and I came home from school when we were living in the same house where my grandma had lived. My mom said, "Sit down kids, we need to talk." She then told us she had decided to sell the house. Instantly, the pole lamp in the corner of the dining room slammed to the floor all by itself and shattered, just like someone threw it down, HARD! My brother and I both looked at each other, looked at mom, and then yelled— at the same exact time, "See! Grandma doesn't want us to leave!" It was pretty crazy.

When my gram was alive, I used to hear her walking across the floor upstairs in the attic efficiency that was her home while we lived there with her. She would yell down for me and my brother to bring her stuff up. It was a cozy little apartment, and I used to love going up to sit with her. I remember her walking slowly up the steps to her place. Even after she passed, I heard the same noises.

A few years later, I had another freaky moment. I was sitting in my living room quietly on the couch reading a book. My beagle, Barney, was laying right in front of me (as always) on the floor. Our house was a ranch-style with the main living areas all on one floor so it was a straight shot from the sofa by the front window through the dining room into the kitchen. I always remembered my grandma sitting on the couch and watching her soaps when I was little. She would then slowly get up and walk across the house into the kitchen for her coffee, or whatever. She would do this many times a day. I remember it mostly because our kitten hid under the dining room table and would charge out from underneath when she passed by and attack her legs, which would make her jump and scream terrified… each and every time! To me at the age of nine and ten, it was a riot.

On this particular day, Barney suddenly looked up over the couch to his right, my left, and stared at something. Then his head followed it up from the couch and across the rooms into the kitchen. After that, he looked at me with a bit of concern on his face as if to say, *Did you see that too?* A few minutes later he did it again… looked from the kitchen across to the sofa and down. looking at me again as if to say, *Hey, asshole, did you see it this time?*

I did not think much of it at the time, figuring it might have been a bug or moth I could not see. However, after about ten minutes this happened again. This time the dog looked really scared as he watched it all the way to the kitchen again. Then he kept looking at the kitchen door, then me, then the door and so forth. I have to say, I started wondering what the hell was going on, but I still didn't make the real connection. Until "it" came back. This time it stopped right over my head. My beagle kept looking up and then at me, then he got up and ran off. Well, I did too! I jumped off the couch and bolted for the door, scared shitless. When I got outside in the front yard, it hit me. Maybe that *was* my Gram trying to tell me she was there.

After mom sold the house, life got even harder for me and my brother. We felt at home there even though all my grandparents had died and it was just us, Mom, and her boyfriends. After several years had passed, I no longer heard from or felt her anymore. I still talked to them when we would go by the cemetery and lie on their graves. I just wanted to be close to them and tell them about my life.

I always felt a certain level of comfort from those signs and feelings of gram's presence with me, but, honestly, I was still a little skeptical… until I *saw* her.

When I was about twenty-five, I moved back to Pittsburgh from Texas. I rented an apartment which, ironically, was laid out almost exactly like the old house we all lived in when I was younger. One fall day, I went out in my yard with my dog to feed the squirrels when I heard a bang on my screen door. I turned to see what it was, and Grandma was standing there behind the screen door glass, smiling at me. I saw her for about three seconds, smiled back and when I blinked, she was gone.

We saw her yet another time years later when I took my daughter back to the house where I grew up. As we walked through the yard, Cheyenne said, "Hey, Mom, there's a lady in that window up there looking at us." I didn't see her, but my daughter did. I know it was Gram.

Around this time, I had a really dear friend named John, a.k.a. "Tall Guy," who I lost to suicide. We met in a strip club I worked at and had become best friends. We hung out together all the time for many, many months. He was an amazing spirit and was so full of energy and life; he was electric. John helped me beat my fear of confinement in small spaces and heights by taking me caving and repelling one gorgeous weekend in West Virginia years before. He was gorgeous, intelligent, and an avid adventurer. Being with him was always a blast.

I will always be grateful to him for his patience at the cave entrance that day. He sat encouraging me gently as fear ripped through me as I tried to muster the courage to go into the small, dark hole and tunnel. He also showed me the power of conquering a giant rock wall (Seneca Rocks, also in West Virginia) with just a rope and my hands. I will never forget the self-confidence I felt on making it to the top. I just straddled the thin top ridge of rock and sat there, contemplating life. The view was incredible. I am so glad I did it!

John and I hung out like brother and sister until he hooked up with a psycho, drug-addicted bitch we will call "The Aries." Her name is not worth remembering. She managed to help get him hooked on dope, and when he tried to free himself of her, she would chase after him and stalk him in a way that should have landed her in jail.

About six months after he died, on New Year's Eve, I was alone in my house meditating, listening to Native American drum music and burning sage. (John and I had done it together, and though it freaked him out some, he really felt some intense stuff and had wanted to do it with me again. Sadly, he never got the chance.) Suddenly, my stereo started to cut out off-and-on. The lights didn't flicker, so I knew it wasn't a power shortage.

I don't really know why, but I called out, "Hello, John." As soon as I did, the stereo went back to playing normally. So, then I said, "Man, I don't know why you killed yourself, but I will always wish you would have called me first." I am not sure why that came out, but I just felt the need to say it. So, a few minutes later I went back to my meditations, but I simply could not get his mother out of my mind. I kept hearing inside my head, *call my mom.* (This meant his mom.) I tried to let it go, but I absolutely could not.

It was about 11:45 p.m. and I thought, *Man, I can't call his mom, she will think I'm nuts!* But finally, this feeling became so overwhelming that I grabbed the phone book to look for her number. I had only met her once, and I remembered her being a very kind soul. I looked and looked but could not find the number. His last name was a very common one and there were like ten thousand of them. And, for the life of me, I could not remember her first name. So being very frustrated, I called out, "John, if you want me to call your mom, you need to show me her damn number!" Immediately, I looked down at the phone book, and it jumped out at me... Regina!

I called her thinking, *she is gonna think I have lost it when I tell her this.* She answered and I said, "Hello, Mrs. M., Happy New Year and I am sorry to call so late. I don't know if you remember me, but this is Suzy, John's friend." She replied with a sweet, happy "Hello there! How have you been? My goodness, it is so good to hear from you."

John "Tall Guy" Murray

I said, "Well, I'm good, though you're probably gonna think I'm nuts when I say what I called to say. I was burning some sage, this thing I do now and then, and well... Your son's spirit was just here in my dining room. I think he wanted me to call you and tell you he is ok." There was silence, then she said, "Well, my God, thank you so much. He told me you used to burn that stuff together and how neat he felt it was. I have to tell you, Sue, last night I was praying by my bed and looking at his picture, and my candle just went out all by itself. I knew at that moment, he was here. I just knew it. Thank you for calling me; I needed to hear this. Happy New Year, Honey."

That is one of many experiences I have had with lost loved ones coming back. I absolutely believe there is more than just this life and that those you loved—who loved you—are there watching over you, waiting till you come to be with them. We are never alone. I have always firmly believed with all of my heart that this is not the end. Our soul never dies; it just goes somewhere else and changes form. Even though we can't *see* it, our energy is still around us in the universe. When a cell phone lights up for no good reason, or a stereo or lights flicker when the rest of the electric stays on, or when we hear an actual voice or feel a touch in the night, it is our loved ones who have passed telling us they are there. Trust your gut instincts always because that is where they are speaking to you.

I know that God was trying to get my attention through those I loved and trusted from the time I was very young. As I got older and actually started to read the Bible, I found many sections that made me think back to times in my life where God was indeed with me. Deuteronomy 31:8 says, "It is the Lord who goes before you. He will be with you; he will not leave you or forsake you. Do not fear or be dismayed" (ESV). Maybe He uses our angels to help guide and watch over us also.

Most everyone tries to find God, or something to believe in. When I started traveling to strip clubs at fifteen, I would always read the Gideon Bible when I was alone in those seedy motels. I didn't know much about the Bible—or God for that matter—but I would randomly open to a page and start reading. I don't remember everything I read, but I did this little exercise quite often. I would always get mad when I got to the part where women were supposed to "submit" to their husbands. *Why do WE have to submit to THEM?* The men in my life who wanted me to submit to them were the same ones who raped, molested, and abused me. It wasn't until much later in life that I read further and discovered that the "submission" thing was intended to go both ways.

Like most folks, I had all kinds of crazy theories about heaven, hell, and how we get there. I used to think if I did a bunch of good deeds, I was in with the Big Guy and all would be well. As I learned more however, I began to understand that It doesn't matter how "good" you are, because our level of good will never be enough to get us to heaven. Jesus prepared the way for us so that we don't have to live a perfect life—because we can't. I know I sure as hell have not! From what I gathered, all you have to do is ASK Him into your life, and He will do the rest. I did, and He has! So much in me is and has changed for the better. I pray my ass off… daily. I know without a doubt, I am heard.

Try it, what do you have to lose? As they say in A.A., "We are a work in progress."

I think God sees our hearts. Here are a quote I dig: Romans 3:23 says "for all have sinned and fall short of the glory of God." There is nothing we can do to *earn* our way into heaven. Salvation is a free gift for us; all we have to do is accept it, ask for it.

But this was a process for me. I didn't arrive there overnight. We all are on our own journey, and God is incredibly patient when it comes to allowing us to find our way.

Becoming Bags

I was now seventeen and had been stripping for a couple of years. My relationship with mom sputtered off-and-on throughout the years but was on at this moment in time. On this day Mom and I were shopping down in The Strip, the marketplace/warehouse district, in Pittsburgh. I spotted an old homeless lady and gave her a ten dollar bill. Having been homeless myself, I felt her.

Afterwards, my mom looked at me and said, "Ya know, you ought to get some old clothes and dress like [an old bag lady] and go onstage at the strip club." At the time, I was working at a place called the Night Gallery on Rt. 51. A guy we knew as Disco Darryl had turned an old mechanic's garage into a strip club.

I replied and said, "No way, that's lame." But Mom was so confident in the idea that she bet me fifty bucks that it would be a huge hit. Even though I still wasn't convinced that she knew what she was talking about, I thought *why not, at the very least it would be a riot*. So off to the thrift store we went. That day I bought one of those hideously printed polyester dresses that zipped up the front, an old slip, some lace up rubber boots, and a hug bra (which I stuffed with socks). I also got a few pairs of men's underwear and wrote some funny shit on them like "EAT ME", "KISS MY ASS", and "GO STEELERS". I blackened out a couple of teeth, found an old pair of black rimmed glasses, put on a hat and babushka, and went to work.

Mom came to the club that evening because—knowing me as she did—she figured I'd make this fun one way or another. Also, I was pretty sure she'd want to collect her fifty dollars and tell me, "I told you so!"

I asked one of the girls to play the *The Rodeo Song* on the jukebox and then walked in before the end of the other dancer's song so that I had time to mess with the crowd. On the way to the stage, I was talking to myself and acting like a nutjob. One guy—being a smartass—grabbed my behind so I started whacking him with my bag and continued to whack guys all the way to the stage. Unknowingly, I hit a couple members of the Pagan's Motorcycle Club with my purse, too! Luckily, they had a sense of humor.

I walked up on stage and began dancing like an old lady might. The place went wild. Everyone—including the other dancers—started throwing money on stage! I later discovered that most of the audience thought it was REAL, and I actually was an old bag lady.

The crowd roared as I left the stage and went to the dressing room. A couple minutes later there was a knock on the door. It was mom. She smiled and simply said, "I'll take that fifty bucks now, please." I hugged her and handed it over. After that mom came to many of my shows. Even with all of her flaws, I loved her deeply. She always encouraged me to chase my dreams.

And that was it. This is how "Bag Lady Sue" came into being. It was thrilling to find my life's calling (at least for twenty-three of the next thirty years).

Over the years, I developed the Bag Lady character by taking bits and pieces from my mom, great grandma and the *nuts* that hung out on the streets in my part of town. Sweet Pea, for example, was the old lady that used to rub her hands in her crotch and then sniff them, all while talking to you at one hundred miles per hour. I found her really adorable, so I worked that into the routine.

Being the Bag Lady has been the most consistently *fun* thing in my life. The crap I pulled off, and the situations I got myself into in-character have been a riot! One time, I even did the show on acid. That was a real trip (pun intended). I think it was the first time I truly realized how damn funny Bag Lady Sue really was… how funny *I* was. Performing as Bag Lady for a strip show was outstanding. It was very easy to remember and hard to forget. Most strippers—just like most comics—may stand out for one reason, or one joke or another. It is easy to forget names, but with Bag Lady Sue, no one ever forgets.

Early on, before Bag Lady Sue became a "thing," I was booked in downtown Pittsburgh at a real shithole called the Edison Hotel. The "Dirty Ed" as locals called it, was a turn-of-the century ten-story hotel that housed drug addicts, welfare recipients, and hookers. It even had an elevator operator complete with the old sliding metal gate on the doorway. I went upstairs to get dressed in one of the old rooms. But rather than entering from backstage, I wanted to make an entrance from the street. I knew it would be awesome because *this place was literally in Bag Lady Central.*

As I walked into the club to head to the stage the security guard, Coz, confronted me. He said, "You can't come in here, lady… sorry," and escorted me back out the door. So, I went around and came back in through the other door. Coz grabbed me again a bit more firmly and said, "I thought I told you not to come in here! Now off you go!"

I figured he was having fun with this, so I went along, never breaking character. I'm thinking *his boss hired me, right? He had to know it was me.* So as time was running out before my que to hit the stage, I tried again to get in. This time Coz was visibly pissed and grabbed my arm hard, so I tore my arm away and said, "Hey dickhead! it's me, Bag Lady Sue, how about you let me get onstage!"

If you could have seen his face… he looked like he shit a brick! He did NOT realize it was me and did, in fact, think I was actually a homeless lady. That was a real moment for me. Even though many folks had told me so, I knew then for sure that my disguise was damn good.

I have also had some neat experiences being Bags outside of the clubs. Once I was hired to do a promotional deal in Golden, Colorado, for a Ford dealership. I spent an hour in the sweltering heat in the back of a pickup truck parked in front of the dealership waving at and yelling at people passing by. The crowed loved it. While I was still in costume, my friend who I called the "Golden Bag Lady", and I went into town for a beer. She worked for the chamber of commerce in Golden and sent out welcome bags to new residents. I discovered that she also had a twisted sense of humor.

On our way, we stopped at an old western pharmacy called Voss Drugs to grab me some smokes. I like to stay in character when I'm dressed as the Bag Lady, so I thought I could have some fun with the locals. As I wandered through the store, the pharmacist suddenly came up to me and said, "Excuse me, Ma'am, but you need to put back whatever it is you stuck in your bag." I was thinking this guy knew who I was and wanted in on the fun, so I told him to piss off and told him that I didn't take no damn stuff.

Then he said, "Listen, you! Someone said they saw you stick something in your bag. Now give it back or I am calling the cops." I was trying hard not to lose it while continuing to blow him off. I was laughing my ass off as I walked into the back parking lot, trying to still stay in character, mind you. Not more than three minutes later, I was suddenly approached by two Golden city cops. I was thinking, *Uh oh, this can't be good.*

The officers said, "Excuse me, Ma'am, but someone said you took something from the store. Did you?" Staying in character, I yelled in my best gravelly Bag voice, "I didn't take nothin', Yinz!"

Then I singled out a real sweet one and said, "Boy, you sure are a cutie. How 'bout a little kiss?" as I leaned down slightly towards his crotch. He jumped back and the other officer busted out laughing. I mean… he was losing it.

Then one of the officers said, "Ma'am, where are you from? Are you from around here?" I was still hunched over in full Bag Lady Sue mode, talking to myself, while scratching my crotch, raising my hand up to my nose like I'm sniffing myself. They were trying hard not to laugh, but still trying to figure out what to do with this homeless nutjob, who apparently has lost her mind. Finally, another cop car pulled up. This guy was the chief. He had less of a sense of humor and got up in my grill and said, "Listen, Lady, if you don't tell us your name or where you are from, I am gonna arrest you." So rather than go on, I stopped, took off the hat, babushka, and glasses, wiped off my teeth, shook out my wild hair and said, "Seriously, Officers, I am just a comic doing a promo bit. Relax, would ya?"

You should have seen their faces! Their mouths dropped wide open and they were literally speechless. Afterwards, we chatted a bit. They realized I hadn't stolen anything, and that was that. I wished I had a camera phone at that time. I am certain this shit would have gone viral. As it turned out, my damn friend set me up and lied to the pharmacist. She's the one that told him I stole something. That BITCH!

Another time, I did a birthday strip-o-gram for a dude who owned a car garage on Warrington Ave. in Pittsburgh. It was a warm summer afternoon and some of his friends hired me to do a Bag Gram for his birthday. Everyone in the shop was in on the joke except the birthday boy. So, I came wandering down the street right in front of the shop where some nice motorcycles were parked. The garage doors were up so the owner of the shop could see me out there. I started staggering around, acting like I was going to fall over on the bikes, and he got nervous. Immediately he came outside and said, "Whoa, excuse me, Ma'am. Are you ok? Be careful now, please! Watch those bikes, ok? Can I help you?"

He was so damn sweet, so I said, "Oh, Honey, could I have a glass of water, huh? That'd be nice." So, he took me in gently and went to get me a glass of water. I wandered off again as if I was senile and headed back out the door. He came after me and got me back inside. His buddies, meanwhile, were losing it. He said, "Man, stop. You guys are dicks." He honestly had no idea what was going on. When I went for his pecker, he started getting scared and moved away. Then I really turned it on and started chasing after him. He was running around this van, trying to get away from me. His friends were just dying! It was so damn hard for me to stay in character. Finally—after I was sweating like a whore in church—I yelled at one of the dudes, "Hit the fucking music, ya dork!" Then I started stripping while *still* chasing the big guy around the shop.

I scared the living shit out of the big biker man. Once he realized I wasn't an old lady, he was even more scared that I was a dude! (That's happened more than once.) Afterwards, he was a little embarrassed, but he was also thrilled and gave me a big hug. I am sure he still talks about that to this day.

Once I did three birthday party grams in a row on a Saturday night while rocking a 104° fever. Two of the birthdays were for 80-year-old guys. At that point in time, I wasn't sure I would outlive them. It shows my work ethic. No matter what, the show *must* go on.

Original Bag Lady, circa 1982

Boys and Men

I've had my share of men in my life, for sure. I'm grateful for the experience to have known them and share different times in my life with them. I truly believe God brought these guys to me—particularly when I was younger—because I was pretty lost. Not having a father definitely influenced who I dated. Since the passing of my aunt, uncle, and grandma, there weren't a lot of people looking out for me... but there were a few guys who did.

David

Two months before I was released from the group home, I was permitted to take a job in my neighborhood in order to ease the transition. I began working at a little diner on the main street of Northside. That's where I met David; he was tall, blonde, and gorgeous. He served a few years in the Navy on a submarine and got out shortly before we met.

Dave's mom and dad were married for twenty-five years when we met and stayed together until they died. His father was a quiet, sweet, good man who retired from H.J. Heinz; a good old fashioned, hardworking, blue-collar, Pittsburgh-style, German man. His mom was Polish. This couple raised and deeply loved six kids, the last of which was born when his mom was around forty. They were the real thing. They lived in the Deutschtown part of

Pittsburgh's Northside, and their house always felt like home to me. My goodness, his mother could cook! They always seemed to be laughing and happy in that house. His mom taught me to cook, how to keep a good house.

David taught me to fish, drink, and drive. He also taught me how to fix cars! We rebuilt a '72 Chevy Nova damn near from the ground up and I participated in every bit of it. I've always loved getting dirty and learning how to fix stuff.

After my six-month sentence ended at Circle C, I returned to my mom's house. David used to like coming over late at night, half kicked in the ass, to surprise me. He almost always had a six pack with him. I was too young and naive to understand that he had a bit of a drinking problem. We just loved hanging out together. We also screwed like minks every chance we got.

One summer night, instead of coming in the front door like a normal person, David decided to climb in my bedroom window. Our house was a ranch style (all on one floor). We didn't have air conditioning, so all the windows were opened all summer long. The trouble was, he jumped into the wrong window… the bathroom window. He caught my mom on the crapper! All of a sudden, I heard a scream, then a thump, and then laughter. Immediately after that, I saw someone's head came through *my* window, so I threw a book at the intruder and lopped him right on the noggin. It wasn't until he fell out of the window, yet again, that I finally realized what the hell was going on. It was hysterical!

The problem with Dave was that he was a bit of a hothead, like many ex-military guys. I remember several altercations between him and others. One night we were driving down East Ohio Street partying (back then you could drink and drive. Ah, the good old days) when some dude cut us off and almost pushed us into a wall. Dave started calling out this guy through the car window. The guy pulled over and jumped out like a big badass, talking crap and puffing up like a peacock. David just walked right up and threw a roundhouse kick which landed on the side of the guy's head, knocking him down. Then Dave was beating his head off the bumper! I figured I'd better do something before someone got seriously hurt. Finally, I jumped in and grabbed David to break it up. We quickly jumped in the car and took off. We headed to the bar and partied till 2 a.m. Amazingly, I got served back then without any trouble everywhere I went. That was before photo I.D.s.

I used to love his stories about the Navy. I would sit for hours and listen to his tales and escapades from being on the submarine. He talked about all the ports he stopped in and the colorful people he met. David even introduced me to the amazing singer/ songwriter Harry Chapin when he took me to one of his concerts in the '80s. Harry was one of the great American folksingers and songwriters. You may know him from his song *Cat's in the Cradle.* David met Harry in Italy, and they even played basketball together once.

David

David had traveled all around the world and he was only twenty-two. Back then I had only been to Florida once and in a group home, so he fascinated me. But, man, he sure did like his beer. I didn't know many alcoholics back then except for the violent, mean ones like my brother's dad. David was mostly a happy drinker, and so was his mom. It was a family tradition to drink a lot. Thanks to David, I started partying back then a bit too much. It was fun at the time. He took me to bars that other kids my age would never even try. I already had a couple years of working at strip clubs at this point, so I'm sure that had much to do with it, too.

I was lucky to have met David and had him be my first real boyfriend. He sure knew how to be good to a woman. He made me feel safe in the world, at a time when no one really did. David was wonderful and fun. He loved me just for who I was. At the time, I really didn't understand what being a veteran really meant. Now I do. Thank you, Davy and all our brave and colorful veterans for your service to this great country.

Christopher James

A few years later I met C.J. when he rented the upstairs apartment in our house from my mom. C.J. was 6'4", about 220 pounds, and damn good-looking. He was from a small town in the Indiana and was a real all-American, earthy gentleman. He was funny, playful, sexy, adventurous, and full of life. He had recently graduated from college. At the time, I had moved out of mom's house and was living with David. Even so, I still spent a lot of time at my mom's. After living upstairs of her for a few months, C.J. asked me out. Although David and I were off and on at the time, I told him I couldn't because I was seeing someone.

Funny how things go. Even though I deeply loved David, his drinking had become more than I knew how to deal with. He and I had been dating for three years and, truthfully, I was about at the end of my rope. One night—drunk and delusional—David grabbed me by the throat and well …that was instantly the end of our cohabitation. I moved back in with Mom.

Ironically, David and C.J. ended up becoming friends, and we all hung out together occasionally. I must say… it didn't suck having two tall, hot guys to pal around with. One night the three of us were partying up in C.J.'s apartment and just having a grand old time hanging out at his kitchen table. (If you are from Pittsburgh, you'll understand that the kitchen table is usually the center of the universe when anyone is in your home.)

I went downstairs to grab something and when I went back up, they were gone. *What the hell?* So, I yell, "Hey, where the hell are you guys?" and they yell back, "We're down here!" I came to find out that they had snuck downstairs to the basement. Well, when I looked around the corner, there they were standing at the bottom of the cellar steps together… naked! I kinda wished I had a camera right then. Damn. Both of these well-endowed, gorgeous men standing there in all of their glory.

As beautiful as the sight was, I was honestly a bit shocked and didn't know what to say. I just stood there looking at them. My gosh, they were fantastic.

They said, "C'mon down here. Let's all take a shower!" So, I told myself, *Life is short, their dicks are long, why not?* I lept down those stairs like a gazelle that was being chased by a lion! Next thing I knew, we were all in the shower. We ran the hot water tank clean out, then the three of us went back upstairs and…we woke up together in the morning.

Sorry folks, but some things need to be left to the imagination.

So, after David and I officially split up, it was natural for me to be drawn to C.J. He taught me different things than I'd been used to learning and seeing. As a college graduate, He was able to raise me up a level from tough, blue-collar, street chick and made me a little classier and even a bit softer. Many of the men I knew before acted like spoiled children, so when I found C.J.—who actually cared for and supported me—it was easy to let my guard down and become more girly.

Once when we visited his hometown in Indiana, and it opened my eyes to what the heartland really is. He came from Crown Point, a lovely little midwestern town with a giant red stone courthouse in the center, surrounded by mom-and-pop shops and streets lined with huge oak trees. Everyone knows everyone and they all say hi to you. It seemed that every family had five plus kids, and things were incredibly normal.

After about six months in "Pleasantville," I had enough. The wanderlust finally got ahold of me, and I had to get out of there. I said, "Hell with this place! Let's get out of here and go to, ummm… Oregon!" So, we did.

Neither of us had much of anything. He'd lost everything in his separation from his ex-girlfriend before we met. When he moved into my mom's, the apartment was already furnished, and I stored most of my sentimental crap in Mom's basement. He sold his car to get out from under the payments, so we loaded up my new 1981 Datsun 310 hatchback and headed West. How exciting it was to

C.J.

be young, crazy, and free. We both believed that anything was possible. So, it was Oregon or bust.

On the way to Oregon we stopped in Mitchell, South Dakota, to see the Corn Palace. This is a big old building/museum that is covered in ears of dried corn that are laid out in beautiful designs: pictures of Indians on horseback, buffalos, cowboys and such. Then, of course, there is the world-famous Wall Drug. If you don't know about Wall Drug, it is actually just a pharmacy and store in the middle of nowhere. The owner had the brilliant idea to market their free coffee all over the world using simple road signs saying how many miles it was from wherever to Wall Drug. Genius! If you are in Oklahoma, for example, you will see a sign on the side of some back road saying,

"1000 miles to Wall Drug," or if you are in California, you will see one there saying how far it is to Wall Drug. Years later when I worked up north, there was even sign in Nome, Alaska, saying 2904 miles to Wall Drug.

We made it to Wyoming and camped in Yellowstone. It was July 2nd,1984. We set up camp by a beautiful stream and watched the sun go down. However, in the middle of the night, it started raining. The rain became snow. We were not prepared for this being "greenhorns" and all, so we nearly froze to death. I could never have imagined it being so cold in July. We crouched closer and closer to each other shivering like mad in the center of the tent until everything, including us, was soaked through with freezing rain. I was genuinely terrified. The Wyoming mountain wilderness was so dark that we couldn't begin to know what direction to get to the car! Neither of us could move because we literally had to share each other's body heat to keep hyperthermia from killing us.

Finally, after what seemed like an eternity, the sun began to rise, and we could see enough to get to the car. We packed up our sopping camp and headed into Jackson Hole, WY, about an hour south of Yellowstone. Jackson was a magical town. They filmed Clint Eastwood in *Every Which Way You Can* there in the '70s. I love the deer antler arches that surround the town square.

C.J. and I checked into a motel. After dinner we went to the town park to watch the fireworks. I was born on the 4th of July, so I love fire works! It was really cool watching them from on top of the mountain. They had a bunch of people running around putting the fires out when the sparks landed on the mountain side. This was as far west as I had ever been at that point in time, and I absolutely loved it.

After the fireworks had ended, we headed over to the Million Dollar Cowboy Bar. I wanted to turn twenty-one sitting in one of the saddles with my elbows on the bar watching the clock! Midnight came and with it a shot of Black Velvet. The first of a few. We laughed, played, and danced the night away to a real country band while we fell deeper and deeper in love. We were dating for eight months at this point, and—for the first time ever—I was excited for the future.

When we got back to our room, I looked at my calendar and realized my period was late. Ah oh. So, I told C.J., and we went and got one of those tests. The test was positive. We were gonna have a baby! I was thinking to myself… *now, there's a birthday present for ya.* Honestly, we were crazy in love and we were both excited. Scared, but excited. The trouble was, what to do now? Should we continue on to Oregon with no job and no place to live, or go back to Pennsylvania? The conversation started. It is one thing to be young and unemployed when it is just the two of you but add a baby in the mix and shit gets serious real fast. I was afraid to go through the whole thing without any family or friends beside C.J.; even though he was the kind of man that would take really good care of me and a baby.

I know we would have made many new friends in Oregon because we were both outgoing and gregarious, so that wasn't the problem. I guess it was just overwhelming, and we had very little money and knew no one in Oregon. After much debate, we were scared and decided to go back. Honestly, that is one of the few decisions I ever actually regretted in my whole life. I see now it all happened the way it was supposed to, but if I had it to do again, knowing what I know now, I would have kept going. Fear can be such a dream crusher.

C.J. had left a pretty decent job back East, but the position had been filled since he left. So, when we got back home to Pittsburgh, we got a small apartment. He started looking for work and I went back to dancing at the place where "Bag Lady Sue" got her start.

About a month later, we were in the shower and I doubled over in pain and started hemorrhaging. He rushed me to the hospital. After a few hours, it became clear that I lost the baby. That was rough to lose a child at twenty-one, but—as I've always believed—everything happens for a reason.

The entire reason we headed back to Pittsburgh had now vanished. He still hadn't found a job in the city, so he and I decided he should go back to Indiana and try to find work.

He did and found a great job with a tech company, but it kept him in Indiana. I had work in Pittsburgh, so we agreed to live separately. Since we were both now working and had money, we arranged for sexy, romantic weekends in various places around the country. Depending on the location, one of us would fly or drive out to see the other. That was a blast and I got to see so much of the USA during that moment in time.

One time, I flew to Boston to surprise him. I didn't tell him I was coming; I just jumped on a plane, got to his hotel, and slid my picture under his door. Then I waited at the bar till he got in from work and to his room. It was funny. I was sitting in a chair, hiding behind a newspaper just like in the movies. When I saw him come in through the lobby, I went up after him and waited outside his door until he found the photo. He yelled and opened the door. He was so glad to see me, and he showed me that by making love to me so perfectly that I still remember it.

Another time, we met in Florida and went to Disney World. The day we visited the park I thought it might be fun to drop a hit of micro-dot acid, so we did. I started to get off in the Hall of Presidents just as Lincoln stood up and walked to the podium to give the Gettysburg address! Wow. Talk about far out. I just sat there crapping my pants. Space mountain is a trip when you're trippin', too. I have honestly never laughed that hard since. We were losing it so badly that we actually lay on the ground right in the park and rolled around hysterically. There were about twenty Japanese tourists with cameras who thought we were photo worthy too. He and I had so damn much fun.

I had such great adventures trying to catch up with C.J. as we travelled around the country. I remember one time I was driving across Ohio on the Turnpike on my way to see him in Chicago. A trucker noticed my back wheel was tilted funny. So, he called me on the CB radio and told me I might want to pull over. I turned into the next rest area, and by then I had about eight truckers pull in with me to try to help. Those were the days when chivalry still thrived. One of the guys was also going to Chicago and offered to put my little Datsun on the back of his lowboy trailer; a flatbed used to haul heavy equipment. It's higher in the back and low in the middle, then high up front again. Well, I looked at this thing and said, "How in the hell am I supposed to get my car up there?"

He informed me that we could use a ramp to get the car up there. It was fun hearing the other truckers on CB trying to figure out why there was a little car on the back of this huge semi-trailer. What neither of us had thought about was how the hell we were going to get this damn thing down. We ended up standing in the rain on the side of the road near "Shytown" AKA Chicago, and I had to back this bitch down off the lowboy by myself while he lowered the ramp. Shit, I was a nervous wreck! If that damn car slipped off those wet rails, I was gonna be in trouble. But I just prayed and trusted my angels. God has always looked out for me, even long before I recognized it.

I was madly in love with C.J., but I was also young, alone, and unsure how it all was going to play out with us. He was still working in Indianapolis and I was in Pittsburgh. One night while I was stripping at The Night Gallery on Rt. 51, this guy came in. His name was Harry, and he was just adorable. When he asked me out,

I could see he was nervous as hell, so I said sure. He was shocked that I said yes. It was cute.

Over the next few months, we did a lot together and I learned so much fun stuff like how to shoot. He was a big-time man's man: fisherman, hunter, cowboy, and gentleman. I found out later he was also a virgin when we met, but he neglected to mention that. I was always a little bummed that he left that part out. I had a feeling… but I was a great teacher, and he was a damn quick learner. I was pretty honest with him about my long-distance situation, but he still wanted to see me. So, for a year I was seeing both of them. Yeah, I know in retrospect that was a trampy thing to do, but I was young, and everything seemed so uncertain when I looked at my future. I loved C.J. but I knew there was no way I was moving to Indiana.

Eventually, C.J. was offered a job in Houston, Texas. Even though I was dating Harry, too, I still met C.J. for romantic weekends. During one of our trips to Atlantic City, NJ, he asked me to move down to Houston with him. I was crazy about him, and… just plain crazy, so I did!

When I told Harry, he was pretty bummed. He had fallen hard for me, and honestly, I loved him too. He was very good to me, but another adventure was calling, and I had to go. There is an old Kenny Rogers song called *Scarlett Fever* about a guy who had eyes for a dancer he could never really have, and one day he came to see her, and she had moved on. That song always reminds me of him, and I know he thinks of me when he hears it too…because he told me.

At that time, 1983-86, Houston was still booming from the oil deal. The city had country bars, strip clubs, and restaurants by the thousands! It seemed everyone was young and wild, and each day brought something new and exciting to experience.

We found a great little apartment off Westheimer Ave., and I found a job at a Chili's-type of restaurant called J.J. Muggs. I really had fun working there. Half of the staff was gay. There was one black waiter, Darryl, who literally used to leap down the aisles, and his customers just loved him.

I made a couple of lesbian friends who also worked at the restaurant. They all thought I was just a hoot, so they started dragging me out to the gay bars with them and Darryl. One night, we were in this big club in town which had a balcony above the dance floor. My goodness, that place was wild! I remember standing on the balcony of this huge gay bar watching everyone dance around. Many were half-naked and on fire. Suddenly, in walks the most beautiful woman I had ever seen. She was perfect: her hair, dress, shoes, jewelry, body. She was absolutely stunning. The crowd parted like the Red Sea so she could walk down the stairs. I said to Darryl, "My goodness, look at that chick."

He replied, "Oh, honey, that's no chick, that's a man." I damn near fell over! This was my first experience with seeing a real live drag queen. Of course, I just had to run my ass down there and get a closer look, and I can tell you honestly there was no way of knowing. I was amazed.

When I got home, I said to C.J., "Look honey, you just have to go check out this gay bar thing! It's big fun!"

He wasn't the least bit intrigued. "I'm gonna feel so weird," he told me. Being a good ole boy from the Midwest, C.J. had never even seen a real gay person, let alone been in a gay bar. But I finally conned him into it because I knew he couldn't pass up an adventure. I loved that about him.

We went to a bar called Kindred Spirits on Richmond Ave. in Houston. I thought it would be safer for him because it was pretty much a lesbian bar. I decided we should go in separately, so we didn't look like a couple of perverts trying to pick up a third wheel for the kink wagon.

This is where it gets good… I go in, belly up to the bar, and order a drink. There was a big drag show going on. I had never seen a drag show before, so I was watching it when C.J. came in a few minutes later and stood beside me. I acted like I didn't know him. Just then two very gay queens—in full sequin gowns and '80s style wigs and, of course, mustaches—come strolling down along the bar saying goodnight to everyone and hugging their buddies as they were heading out the door. When they see C.J. they stop dead and one says to him, "My goodness honey, aren't you a tall drink of crème!"

He was so embarrassed that he started kicking me like I was supposed to rescue him, and of course, I turned the other way and continued to act like I didn't know him. Meanwhile, I was quietly laughing so hard I could barely breathe. Then the other queen says, "We have one phone number for both of us and a hot tub at our apartment. How'd you like to come home with us and jump in?" C.J. was stuttering and squirming like a fish in a net. I was nearly on my knees from laughing so hard. Finally, he spoke and said, "Oh, uh, thank you, but I am waiting for someone." They left bummed. He leaned over and whispered, "I'm gonna fucking kill you," in my ear. I finally cut him a break, and we saw some friends of mine at a table and went over to join them.

The girls from work were there and with them was one an extremely hot guy. We sat down, and the hottie came over and sat right next to C.J. After a few drinks and a lot of laughing, dancing, and great conversation, C.J. started kicking me again under the table, and I brushed him off because I was in the middle of telling a joke to my lesbian friend. What I didn't know was that hot-ass guy made a pass at MY hot-ass guy while my back was turned.

Dammit! I missed it. That would have been great to see. So, I asked C.J., "Well, you didn't kill him, so....?"

He was a bit freaked out but having fun. I think he actually kinda dug it a bit. Remember, we were young and childless, and Houston was just that kind of town. So, I said, "Well *hell*, try it. I want to watch." So, he did! I loved seeing my tough-ass man, letting his guy guard down for a minute. I think seeing two chicks getting it on is kinda gross, because I prefer men, but watching two straight guys kissing (or in this case one straight and one not) was hot as hell. Just my personal opinion. I will say this… C.J. was not gay. Not even kind of. It was simply one of those *what the hell*

experiences in life that just happened. Both he and I were very uninhibited, which turned out to be an awesome thing in the bedroom.

Around this time, I quit my job at the restaurant and "lied myself into" a great job doing construction with a huge company called Brown and Root, a division of Haliburton. I told them I had experience as heavy equipment operator. I wasn't entirely lying. I used to run a peanut roller and learned how to drive a dump truck at fourteen when I went on asphalt jobs with my piece-of-shit stepdad. At least he taught me something useful.

My boss at Brown and Root was a Texan named Blue. He was a trip. Blue had a ZZ Top beard and blue eyes. He was just a blast to work with. We mostly rode around in the pickup checking on all the Mexican's that did all the really hard work, but I also learned how to run various types of heavy equipment. The loader was my favorite. I used to roll down the new road we were laying on Interstate 10 and chase the Mexican's out of the way. They would swear at me in Spanish, so I got to learn a second language. Just the dirty words, of course.

I loved doing construction and hanging out with the guys all day. We all worked hard and got along… for the most part. One time, however, I had to kick the living shit out of one Mexican guy named Chiquile, partly because I never liked the jagoff, but mostly because he grabbed my tit.

He was sitting up on the backhoe on the side of the highway near the overpass with the service road below. Between the two of us was nothing but about twenty-five feet of concrete "rib wrap," the wavy concrete stuff that they pour to wrap the underpasses

Blue, Chiquile, and Crew

rather than just leave them dirt or rocks. When he grabbed me, I ripped his skinny little ass right off the backhoe and tossed him through the air. You can image his surprise! Out and down he went, hitting the concrete hard and rolling over and over all the way down to the feeder road… with me chasing after him. When we got to the bottom, I jumped on him and proceeded to pounding the daylights out of the little bastard.

Just in the nick of time, up pulled Mister Blue, who broke us apart. I was pissed, so Blue put me in the truck, reached in the ice chest in the back and grabbed a couple of California Coolers. So, I cooled off and went back to work.

Later that day, back in the yard, we were hanging out in the gravel lot when I heard someone running up behind me. I looked up into Blue's mirrored sunglasses and saw Chiquile coming at me!

He was seeking revenge. Just as he got in range, I swung back and elbowed him in the face. I knocked him out cold! He was down for the count. At that point I left, and Blue and the crew handled it.

Chiquile never messed with me again. Even with the drama, that was my favorite job while I was living in Texas.

C.J. and I were having some issues in the relationship. It wasn't his fault. To be honest, I was getting bored playing little Suzy Homemaker. We'd had so many fun adventures—and I loved him a lot—but I was young and wanted to experience everything I could in life. At the wonderfully fun age of twenty-three, I would watch him fall asleep on the couch every night, remote in hand. It just didn't do it for me. We went from wild romantic weekends to the rut of daily domestic life, and I could not adapt.

At this point I had been living with C.J. in Texas for about seven months. During this time, I kept in touch with Mom. She knew everything because we had more of a sister-*ish* relationship than one of a mother and daughter. We told each other everything. I had also kept in touch with both my exes, David and Harry, over the months since I moved down to Texas.

C.J. was going out of town for work soon for a weekend, and I happened to mention it to the other two. Harry never said anything, but David said, "Well, hell, I think I am gonna plan to come down there and visit you! I have a cousin in Houston, and I can see you both on the same trip."

What the hell, thought I, *why not? It would be great to see him again. We don't have to screw or anything, we will just be buddies. Ya know, have dinner, drinks, go country dancing and such.* The plan was set for him to come the day before C.J. left, and he would hang with his cousin until I dropped C.J. at the airport, then I would pick him up. No sweat. So, the day before C.J. left, I went to the airport and picked up David, dropped him at his cousin's house and went home.

That night me and C.J. were hanging out at the house in front of the idiot box (i.e. TV) around 7:30 p.m. when I get a phone call from my mom. "Whatcha doin'?" she asked.

"Oh, nothing," I said, "Just sitting here with C.J. watching TV. What are you doing?"

She proceeded to tell me, "I went to the flea market that day, bought some jewelry, took the dogs for a long walk, and… oh, by the way… Harry is in Houston at a hotel three blocks down the street from your house. He wanted to surprise you. SURPRISE!"

Whatttt?

She said, "Oh yes, and it gets better… He was on the same fucking plane with David, and he saw you pick him up at the airport!" Laughing like Satan she says, "Bwahaha! Let's see you pull this one off!" I damn near crapped my pants. Talk about a pickle. I was in a jar of them. You have no idea how hard it was to act that one out in front of C.J. while trying to remain cool.

"Oh really?" I responded to my mom, "Well, isn't that something?" I knew that Harry knew what David looked like from pictures I had shown him, but David had never met Harry.

I had to come up with a plan, and fast. I found out from her where Harry was staying. I told C.J. I had to run to the store for a pack a smokes and rushed out the door. I got to Harry's hotel, and when he answered the door, I hugged him and said how glad I was to see him! He was apologetic and he told me he missed me a lot and he wanted to surprise me, but he didn't know David was coming, too. I was so flattered. I wasn't mad at all. In truth, I was delighted. Still, I was in a bit of a situation.

Harry, embarrassed that his plan to surprise me didn't work out as planned, offered to leave in the morning since he knew David was there to see me, too. But I told him, "No! I got this!" I had a plan. So, I kissed him goodnight and headed back home.

I went to bed with C.J. that night. We woke up, slugged down some coffee and I took him to the airport. I dropped him off, ran to a pay phone, called David, and lied. I told him C.J. wasn't leaving till later, and that I'd pick him up at his cousin's house after C.J. left. I ran out to Harry's hotel, picked him up, and off we went to Galveston for the day. We had a lovely dinner, strolled along the beach, sucked some face, and came back to town. I dropped Harry off at his hotel, grabbed David at his cousin's, and spent that night and the next day and night with him.

Then, I took David to the airport, walked him to his gate, kissed him goodbye, grabbed a seat at the bar and waited. About four drinks later C.J.'s plane landed. The only one who knew anything in the end was poor Harry, who thankfully is still my good friend to this day. What a weekend!

Just around this time, C.J. and I met a girl who lived in our apartment complex named "Weezy". Weezy was a hot little blonde Libra with a punky shag haircut. She had gotten herself into a marriage-for-profit thing with some Arab, who paid her a bundle to get his green card. Had I known then what I know now, I would have seen the big red flag flapping in the breeze. But at twenty-two, fun was the order of the day and who or what she was screwing made no difference to me. I wasn't sleeping with her… yet.

She was in a bad situation. So, after she lost her apartment, C.J. and I ended up letting her stay with us. Before Weezy came around, things had started to get really boring between C.J. and me. Somehow without my even seeing it happen, we had settled into a routine. The house was furnished well, complete with fancy

T.V. and reclining chair. Trouble was, I was young, outgoing and in an exciting new city full of millionaires, cowboys, and adventures. I found myself going out more and more often alone.

Over time, C.J., Weezy, and I were hanging out all the time. Before I knew it, we ended up in the sack together. We were *very* close. Me and Weezy even flew to New Orleans to meet C.J., dressed in matching, sexy, outfits for a wild weekend of booze and debauchery. New Orleans is that kind of place, you know. I remember the three of us driving down I-10 back to Houston in the company minivan. Weezy drove while I rode…on C.J., and then I drove while…well, you get the picture. You could pull stunts like that before everyone had cell phones and recorded you.

For about a month it was all good. We all had a ball together, and then Weezy started wearing my clothes and borrowing my stuff without asking and other shit that annoyed me. After a huge blow out over God-knows-what, I just up and left. I figured they would have each other, and it would be cool. I just wanted out; it was time for another chapter in my life's story. The guys I worked with from Brown and Root Construction came over after work with trucks, and I was in my new apartment in three hours. By the time they came home from work, I was gone.

C.J. and Weezy ended up marrying each other a couple of years later, moving to Dallas and having a beautiful daughter.

I honestly kind of wish he and I could have stayed together, but again, it wasn't meant to be. Life just happens. C.J. was a stellar man and I am glad he was part of my story. He was really rather innocent before he met the old Bags. Houston in the early 80's was in the midst of the oil boom, so free love and Ecstasy were the "in" things. But I have to take credit, too, for corrupting the guy. But, boy, it sure was a blast!

Home on the Range

After I left C.J., I moved farther out on the west side of Houston, to a place called Rose Land Apartments, near Dairy Ashford and Westheimer. (Later, I found out it was nicknamed "Drugland Apartments".)

I was now single, free, over twenty-one, and in the cowboy capital of America. That was the coolest feeling ever. The world was open, and my dreams seemed like they were finally able to come true. Trouble was… I was not quite sure back then what I wanted. I knew I wanted to be famous and to have horses. That had been my dream all of my life. But, of course, now I needed to locate a sexy cowboy to go with them.

Being the go-getter I am, I set about trying to figure out where I might find said cowboy. Ironically, there was a little horse ranch down the street from my apartments called Abis Rent-A-Horse. (The owners last name was Avis, but they couldn't call it Avis because some corporate assholes at the rent-a-car place threatened to sue.) So, I went over to take a horse ride and meet the folks. This place was something right out of a John Ford western. A huge corral; a stable made out of 1800s barnwood from old, twisted up oak trees greeted you as you entered. There was also an outdoor office under a wooden canopy, complete with a fridge full of Miller beer, homemade lemonade, and whiskey.

The husband and wife who owned it grew up through the dust bowl days and lived there all their lives. They were real, live, Texas badasses. Miss Avis was a feisty seventy-something redhead who was just full of fire. Her face was very weathered from all the years in the Texas sun, but she was still quite lovely. She reminded me of Katharine Hepburn because she could ride a cutting horse and rope a steer better than most men, even at her age. Her husband was about ten years younger than she; he was the toughest, most John

Wayne-type, handsome cowboy I ever met in person. He rocked the bowlegs, Wrangler jeans, chewing tobacco and all. Together they ran this place and another big ranch on the other side of town. Neither one had an ounce of fat on them, nor did they take any shit from anyone. The most beautiful thing about them was how they were crazy about each other.

They took to me like flies on a horse, and we became fast friends. I made them laugh and helped them at the ranch. I happily took the horses out for trail rides, and they taught me how to be a real cowgirl. I learned the old ways of running a real, western ranch. For example, they taught me how to rope a steer and not to take too much crap from horses or men. I also learned that donkeys really are stubborn but have as much personality as a dog. My *least* favorite lessons were how to help untwist the inners of a colicky horse. I needed to walk beside him, so I didn't get kicked when I would slide my entire arm up his butt. I watched Miss Avis geld a colt once; she literally grabbed him by the balls and cut them off real quick with a sterilized knife. There is a certain whinny noise they make at that moment that is well… different from the others. (Men always hold on to their nuts when I tell that story.) Yeah, boy, how many times I have had flashbacks of that moment when one of my exes pissed me off.

What an amazing experience for a city gal from Pittsburgh! I rightly earned the nickname "Crazy Yankee" from them. They told me that no one else they knew could talk as fast as I could and still be understood. I remember how hard it was for me to *wait* for *them* to tell a story or complete a sentence. Words would fly out of my face at lightning speed, while they talked slower than molasses and paused between every three words for *literally* 5 seconds. As impatient as I could be, it was still awesome to watch. I remember leaning forward on the edge of my hardwood bench, waiting to hear the next thing coming. I was also waiting for my chance to jump in and again start flappin' my jaws. We would spend hours at the end of every day sitting under that old wooden canopy at the picnic table drinking beers, and "spinning yarns" (that's Texas-speak for telling stories).

In the year I hung out there, I learned to ride like Dale Evans, rope like Will Rogers, shoot like Annie Oakley, and drink like The Duke. I was only thrown three times… twice by the same damn horse, who, I swear laughed at me as I lay on the ground in front of him. I got kicked once, and stepped on at least 5 times, and bitten on the ass twice (not by a horse, but by a cowboy).

My favorite horse was a twenty-three-year-old black, retired police mount named Smokey. Smokey was a Tennessee Walking Horse and had a wonderfully smooth gate. Riding him was like sliding naked across a piece of silk. He was beyond sweet and cool as hell. If you pointed your finger at him like a gun and yelled "BANG," he would fall over… like a dog! There is not much, in my opinion, that compares with sitting on top of a big, beautiful horse feeling the wind in your hair.

I really enjoyed getting to meet all the different folks that would come out to ride the horses. Some knew how to ride when they came, and some did not. I especially liked the kids. They weren't afraid of anything. Their parents, however, were often big, fat, sissies. Working on that ranch made me stronger and gave me a confidence I certainly did not have before. Once I started working construction again, I couldn't wait to get off work so I could head over to the ranch and sit under that old wooden shanty, drinking a cold Miller High Life. I would then jump up on my horse and ride off and watch the sunset for a spell… slow and easy. That was Texas in 1983.

The most amazing discovery I made during this time, however, was that real cowboys are just plain sexy! How could I not love

Texas? The people were so real, strong, and colorful. The men were *men*! Every single one of them I met was a complete gentleman. They didn't appear to ever mind that I was a strong woman, nor did they use that as an excuse to become lazy or not do the things for me that men are just supposed to do. These guys were true gentlemen; they paid for dinner, opened doors, and waited until I was ready to receive their advances before they tried advancing. Most importantly, they all knew how to dance! My goodness, it was refreshing. I met a lot of wonderful fellas there and was never short on dates. Mostly, I was asked to go country dancing. Guys who are good dancers are always also good lovers. If he can kiss, dance, and cook, I guarantee he will be good in the sack.

There was a real live rodeo that went on every weekend about twenty miles west of Houston in a town called Simonton. It had been there forever, and in the '80s, it was alive and well. I found it by accident one evening when I took a drive to the country for some country fried steak. There was a lovely new roadhouse restaurant and bar that had a wraparound porch. After dinner, you could sit outside on the porch, watch the sun go down, and listen to the coyotes howling away. On my way to the restaurant one day, I noticed this giant red building. I still have never seen anything like it in all my travels. This place had an indoor dirt floor rodeo arena, complete with stalls and shoots. There was an amazing BBQ restaurant, and a country dance hall… all under one roof.

My mom came to visit me while I was still in Houston, and I took her to the ranch to ride and meet my new friends. We went to the rodeo place. I remember me and mom sitting there eating and being checked out ever so discreetly by all the hot-ass cowboys. When we finished dinner, one of them who was about thirty came up to us; he had a handsome face, tight Wrangler jeans, crisp button-down shirt, white cowboy hat, and a smile that could stop time. In the most gentlemanly Texas fashion, he put one hand behind his back, the other across his front, bent over slightly at the waist and said, "Excuse me, ma'am, could I please have this dance?" I swear both our mouths dropped open, and we must have looked retarded because we just sat there in shock. I could not believe how stunningly handsome and classy this guy was. Being the amazing daughter I was, I said. "Go ahead, Mom, have a dance!" So, she did. Then another equally gorgeous and gentlemanly cowboy came and asked me, and then another and another and… well you get the picture. We danced until 2 a.m. with just about every cowboy there. That was the night I first learned how to do the Two Step, and the Cotton Eyed Joe; both Texas type dances.

Mom and I had a great visit. I remember buying her a lovely Amethyst ring, which I gave to her while we were out in the backcountry riding. A year later, she told me she had sold it at a flea market. But hey, that was mom. She did say, however, that she now understood my attraction for Texas. Even though she missed me, it was good that I took the chance and went after something more.

Archer

Shortly after I moved into my new apartment at Drug Land, I was carrying laundry up to my apartment when I heard, "Hello." I looked up to see a very handsome guy; lean, tall, with wild dirty blond hair sitting on the steps the next apartment over from mine. I smiled, he smiled, and into my house I went. A few minutes later, I came outside to get something from my car just as he was walking up my steps. He was caught off guard when I came out and stopped. We just looked at each other awkwardly, and then he said, "Uh, hi, I'm Archer from next door. I was wondering if you might like to come over to my place for tuna casserole." Wow, how romantic? Ok, not really, but I had to admit it was a unique opening line. How could I say no?

I answered, "Sure!" He said to stop over in thirty minutes. This began my next relationship. The tuna was stellar, by the way.

Archer was one of the most fun guys I had ever met. He had a lighthearted way of living life. He grew up with a single mom and two brothers in a big house in Northern Illinois beside a lake. The winters were unbelievably windy and damn cold, so I guess that made him a bit tougher than some. His mom was a really unique woman of Polish descent, who taught school in the Polish part of South Chicago. His older brother was a Chicago City cop, and he and his younger brother were both locksmiths. I never lost my keys once until I started dating him.

Throughout our relationship, we made a few trips up to see his family in Illinois. I really adored them. I also got to experience many things I never had before like going to a Chicago Bear's game! It was so great getting to know many amazing people from that part of the country.

I remember him taking me to eat my first chocolate covered strawberry at a place called The Long Grove Confectionery, in Long Grove, Illinois. The candy shop was a darling little gingerbread-style cottage. I will never forget the way that juicy thing popped in my mouth and how incredible it tasted. (I meant the strawberry, not the man, though he was also delicious, too.) I don't think I have ever had one that perfect since.

There was another incredible place in the northern part of the state called Café Sarkis. The café was set up in an old train car and the food was incredible. For five dollars, you got a huge omelet, a piece of homemade sausage made by Sarkis himself with fresh Wisconsin brick cheese on it, home fries, toast, and coffee. If you were still hungry after that he'd give you more! Mr. Sarkis was a unique, colorful, very hardworking Armenian guy who always had a happy disposition. Everyone that walked in got a hardy hello, a kiss on the cheek, and a big hug. Yep, everyone got a hug over the counter… young, old, girls, guys, everyone. That was part of what made the place so amazing. The counter was lined with pastries, which you could help yourself to if you did not want a full breakfast. On occasion, Sarkis would slip Baileys Irish Cream in my coffee when I wasn't looking.

Honestly, I was really lucky to meet Archer when I did. Even though I loved Texas, I was at a pretty lonely place in my life, living by myself. He was just a blast to be around. He also had a bunch of friends who became mine, as well. For example, I met people like Ma Burns, who was a sexy, yet conservative white collar, brunette woman married to a blue-collar friend of Archer's. Jim was a laid-back, silly-ass, country boy, and Anne "Ma" was an educated, class act. They were a classic case of opposites attracting, but somehow it worked. She became a very dear, lifelong friend to me. I missed her terribly when we moved north. I loved having an intelligent friend to banter with.

Archer had another friend I grew to love also named Rob. Rob was a tall, very handsome, dark-haired, late twenty-something guy with an incredibly handsome face and dark piercing eyes. He was a sweet, kind, down-to-earth guy, who also just happened to be a master in the art of Ninjutsu. Before I met Rob, I knew nothing about this form of martial art other than what I had seen in old movies. I can now tell you from personal experience this is some special stuff. It is deeply intense, potentially lethal, and the master moves so quickly that it's very difficult to see him.

One night, I was sitting in my living room, and Rob was in my kitchen talking to me. In one second, he had moved to the complete other side of the apartment, and I never heard or felt him pass behind me. His movements were incredibly quiet. It was almost creepy and seemed unreal. I once saw him stop a fight once between two assholes at our pool, taking them both down so fast

I could not believe my eyes. There wasn't even a sound except the guys grunting as he held them to the ground and calmly asked them to knock it off. How I loved hanging out with him and Archer. It didn't suck being the envy of all my friends, hanging out with two incredibly sexy guys. Rob was single at the time, and I loved him like a brother. Until one night…

Rob, Archer, and I were hanging out at our apartment one evening talking, laughing, and wrestling around, and the next thing I knew, the three of us are in bed together. Suddenly, things were not funny… they were incredibly hot, intense as hell and deadly serious. Rob was, as you would imagine, a very intense guy. I remember at one point, Archer was behind me as I lay on Rob and as they both went inside me, Rob said, "Look in my eyes." I swear he had hypnotized me, and I felt as if I literally became a part of him; a part of them both. All three of us became one person at that moment. As long as I live, I will never ever forget that experience.

Archer & Rob

I am so thankful I got to experience these kinds of erotic moments in my life. But only because I experienced them with the beautiful-spirited men that I did. These two guys weren't even kinda gay, they were just about pleasing me, and… my goodness, they did.

New Beginnings... and Endings

I had a blast living in Texas, but I was still incredibly lonely. The man who was the reason I moved to Houston was no longer in my life, and there was no legitimate purpose for me to stay. I had a lot of fun with Archer, but I didn't see any great future for us. Besides, I missed my mom.

Being the spontaneous nut I am, I decided on a whim that I wanted to go home. After unloading most of my possessions over the next week, I packed my Datsun 310 and headed north. Archer was still working as a locksmith, so he wasn't ready to go with me… just yet.

Archer and I did the long-distance-dating thing for a while. He came to Pittsburgh a few times to visit in the summer of 1986, and even made a few friends there. Pittsburghers are so friendly. So after about six months of living apart, Archer made the decision to move north. He rented a small apartment about two miles from where I was living.

I realized during our time apart, though, that Archer and I were really better friends than lovers. It was a difficult decision—at first—for us to split but it proved to be the right call in the end. We just grew apart but remained good friends. I had no reason to dislike or be angry with him. As I always say, things happen for a reason. Archer ending up meeting a great gal named Holly, whom he married a couple years later. Not only was I invited to their wedding, but my boyfriend of the time also gave Holly away to Archer at their wedding! I remember being very happy for them.

After returning to the 'Burg, I found an awesome little house off the beaten path in the North Hills of Pittsburgh. I took my old job back stripping at local clubs. I was single and ready to party again. Every night during the summer, the guys and I would hang out in my garage, drink beer, and work on rebuilding my Jeep CJ-5.

Around that same time, I bought my first motorcycle: a brand new 1986 Honda Rebel. I taught myself to ride by drifting the bike down the slight grade in front of my house, then pushing it back up and doing it over again. I eventually learned to catch it in gear as it was drifting down the hill. For the next few weeks, I rode up and down my street a bazillion times.

The main problem with the Rebel was that it was so damn light. One time at a club, a group of guys picked it up and carried it off as a joke. They put it in the middle of the highway on the median strip! While I was working that night, they came running in the strip club yelling, "Bags, someone took your bike!" I jumped off the stage half-naked and ran outside to see what was going on. These assholes were standing there—pointing to my bike in the middle of the road—laughing their asses off. I did not laugh.

And then there was another time when someone taped a blow-up doll to the back seat on the bike. I actually liked that, though. I taped a fake join in her mouth and rode around with her riding shotgun for a while.

I would always ride around the lake at North Park, PA. I rode through the park one sunny spring day wearing my full-face helmet and leathers. When I pulled into the boathouse to use the head, I parked right next to three guys who were also on their bikes.

When I took off my helmet, shook out my hair, smiled and said, "Hi, Boys!" You should have seen their faces! See, back then there were not many girls on bikes, and I was, of course, rocking the Robert Plant hair, great tits, and size seven ass. Naturally, we all started chatting and next thing I knew, I had three amazing new friends: Shark, Dudley, and Woody.

Starting that day, we drank and rode together often. We all became really close, and I almost married one of them. Dudley stood about 6'4" and topped out at 170 lbs. soaking wet, and with his shoes on. Yep, he was really tall and skinny. Dudley and I dated for a while. He was a sweet guy but had a nasty tempter when he drank. Fortunately for me, I got to see this in fully display about one month before the supposed wedding. We got in a fight over something dumb, and he started screaming at me while we were driving in my car on our way to our favorite local bar, Bellasario's Lounge in North Hills. He annoyed me so badly that I pulled up to the bar and told him to get the hell out. This really pissed him off.

Dudley ripped my keys out of the ignition, jumped out of the car, and threw them at me over the roof! He then came running around towards me like he was gonna hit me. So, I pulled the door back and when he got close enough, I hit him with it. He came at me again, so I punched him right square in the face so damn hard he slid over the hood of my car onto the street. I must have knocked some sense into him because he got up and went into the bar. I went home and packed his shit, put it outside, and I was done. The end.

Shark and I remained good friends, even after the Dudley incident. He was a really nice-looking guy who worked as a guard at the county jail. I remember calling him the night I wrecked my Honda. While taking a sharp bend on a windy road in the north part of town, a car came at me in my lane. I swerved off into someone's yard, locked up the front brake, and jackknifed the bike. The bike threw me headfirst into the grass and I was out cold.

A bystander called the ambulance, and they took me to the hospital. I had no one else to call to come get me… except Shark. He was there in minutes, and he took me back to my house. I had a helmet and goggles on but no gloves, so my hands were really messed up. I also had a killer black eye, but my brains were reasonably intact, thankfully. The bike suffered some scratches too, but it also survived.

When we walked in the door to my house, I had to pee like crazy. I went to the bathroom and realized I could not get my pants down thanks to the swelling, cuts and bruises on my hands. What to do now?

"Oh, Shaaaaarrrk, I need your help, pleeeeeease."

I hear him from the other room say, "What do you need?"

I replied, "Well, I have a problem, I can't get my pants off." I hear a sigh, and in comes Shark. Just as he went to help unsnap my jeans, I stopped him and said, "Uh, by the way, I don't have any panties on."

"Oh geez, Bags, how in the hell do you expect Maurice to not act up?" (Yes, he named *it*.) I suggested that he should close his eyes, and he actually did! What a gentleman.

A year or so later I upgraded my bike. The thing with riding is… you *always* want a bigger bike. Besides, I got tired of coming out of the strip clubs at night to get on my bike only to find piles of rice under my pipes, fortune cookies stuffed in them, and chow mien noodles on my seat (this was done as a slam for owning a

Japanese-made bike). When I started looking to buy a Harley, a friend was selling a cool older Sportster, so I went to look at it. It was red, really tall, had mini-Buckhorn bars, and stock wheels.

I fell for it immediately and wanted to take it for a ride. I have to admit I was a bit nervous. At a 1000 cc's, it was a hell of a lot more powerful than the little 250cc Honda rebel I had been buzzing about town on. But being fearless, I jumped on and took it for a spin. I will never forget the thrill of that first ride. I was instantly hooked. The power was a massive turn-on, and it got even better when I rode past a whole slew of construction workers, who were building a bunch of new homes, and heard them whistling and screaming, "Whoo hoo!" and "Oh, hell yeah, Baby!" Sold.

The Harley gave me a whole new outlook on life and brought me to meet some of the greatest people on Earth. I thought strippers were colorful till I met all the bikers. I hit every rally and run I could and had more fun than I had ever known in my life. I still have the rally pins to prove it. A few of my great new friends, Smokin' Joe, the Wimpster and Queen Jackalene, became lifelong. Smokin' Joe was a really big guy, who was the funniest ever. He had an incredible sandwich shop near Neville Island in Pittsburgh called Maureen's. His sandwiches were legendary; gigantic and made on a whole loaf of Mancini's Italian bread with like a pound of meat on it. (If you never had Mancini's Italian bread, you have not lived. It is a Pittsburgh staple.)

One time, we were at a swap meet with some of our Pagan friends, and—in fun—I decided to turn Joe into *my* prospect. So, I took off my bra and put it on his head like earmuffs and said, "Do not take that off! You are now a prospect for Bag Lady Sue M/C." It was a riot. All the brothers laughed as I made him serve me drinks all afternoon.

Shortly after buying the bike, mom and I jumped on the Harley and went out for a couple drinks. A couple turned into a bunch for her (I wouldn't ever ride drunk with a passenger), and she was feeling pretty wild. We put on our helmets and headed home. Just as we got on the Interstate, mom says, "So, how fast does this thing go?"

WELL... *Let me show ya, mom.* I hit the throttle and opened the Sportster all the way up. Mom was loving it, until I heard, "Hey Suz, I think my helmet is falling off." I pulled over and got off to check her strap when I notice the damn thing is on backwards. Mom looked a bit like Gazoo from the Flintstones. I nearly died laughing! She sure was fun sometimes.

At the time I had no man, no child, a fast Harley Davidson and way too much time on my hands. I rode damn near every day and night, bar hopped all over the tri-state in all weather, including snow. Thus, I started my hard riding years.

DoDo

One night I came out of a bar and had to dust an inch of snow off "him." It was only 19° night so I bundled up in my furs, to the point I could barely turn my head, and headed out to Bike Night (every Thursday Night) at a badass biker bar on Neville Island called Mary's. I stopped in to get some whiskey and saw only one other bike out front. I had to know it would have to be someone like myself—brain damaged—to be out on a night like this.

I walked into the bar, took off my helmet, shook out my hair and heard, "Well, kiss my Dago ass. It's a girl!" That is the night I met the guy who would become one of my dearest lifetime friends, and surrogate dad, Dodo. Dodo was a really good-looking Italian man and retired city cop. At the time of our meeting, he was somewhere around seventy years old. He had thick, wavy, grey hair and one hell of a twinkle in his eyes. He always carried a 9mm, so he was pretty fearless.

DoDo

Dodo and I remained friends for many, many years. He even gave me away years later at my first attempt at marriage. We rode in on his bike, gown and all. I tried to back out of the marriage, but the son of a bitch wouldn't let me—Dodo, that is, not the groom! The ceremony was in a little park with a pretty lake, ducks, and all. We pulled up to park, I looked across the lake at all the people and said, "Fuck this! I change my mind." to which he replied, "Dammit, be a soldier and get your ass up there. He's waiting. You can always divorce later." Which we did.

Linda

As I would ride through my neighbor on my Harley, I could only image what my neighbors were thinking. One particular neighbor who lived two doors down from me was... I think... afraid of me. Her name was Linda Johns. Linda was a very conservative Christian woman with three beautiful young kids. I had never met her in person but when I'd see her outside, I always smiled and waved as I rode by.

One afternoon I was walking my dog Lumpy when she wandered right on into Linda's yard. I called her but she ignored me, which was uncharacteristic for Lump. So, I followed, yelling for her to come. We were almost on Linda's patio when all of a sudden the sliding glass door opened and she said, "Hi! Would you like to come in for a cup of coffee?" This caught me off guard, but I said that I would love to come in for a cup of coffee.

Then—out of the blue—she said, "I know what you do and it's ok."

This should have seemed really weird to me, but I wasn't offended. I'm not sure why I wasn't, but I knew Linda was a very kind person and probably didn't mean any disrespect by it. In fact, I truly think her statement was very sincere: she knew who I was and wanted to get to know me anyway. Even though we came from COMPLETELY different worlds, we became good friends. I felt really close to her and comfortable being myself with her.

Linda Johns

One time right after we met, I came over to her house to see if she wanted to go for a motorcycle ride and her young son answered the door. He must not have known what to think when this biker chick in a sexy tank top and the spurs clinking across their porch knocked on the door, because his eyes popped out of his head. He had never seen someone who looked like me. (I know this because Linda told me so.) I remember another time when I stopped at her house on my way to work in my nurses' uniform. She asked if I worked in healthcare. You should have seen her eyes when I explained that it was part of my routine. Classic!

Yet another time, I asked to park my Jeep in her yard when I was going out of town. Linda graciously agreed. That would not have caused a problem… usually. But on this occasion, she had just recently separated from her husband of twenty-four years, and the Jeep had a bumper sticker that said, "So Many Men, So Little time." I'm sure our neighbors had a good time with that one!

I found out years later that Linda was intimidated when I first moved into the neighborhood, but she prayed that we would meet. She said, "Lord, if you want me to talk to Sue, you're going to have to bring her to my door." Two days later, Lumpy wandered up on her porch.

Linda's love of God and faith in Jesus shined all around her. I had no way of knowing at the time the critical role Linda would play in my life over the next few decades. Even though I would wander in and out of her path over the years, I discovered that she ALWAYS prayed for me... and I mean always. Her good friend confirmed that they prayed together on a weekly basis for over ten years and Linda brought up my name every week.

Sarge

Later that year, I ran into Sarge when I was working at a bar called The Tennyson in Pittsburgh. He had been dating my friend Dusty when I met him seven years before that, and I hadn't seen him since then. I didn't think much about it at the time. My mom was there one night and remembered him from the Go-Go Lounge. He caught her attention and she asked me, "How are you not seeing this fine-ass man is into you?" That's the first time I really thought about it. After she brought it up, I remembered noticing that he had been coming into the bars I was dancing at pretty regularly for a while, but never said a word. It just didn't hit me. I honestly thought it was a coincidence.

Lots of handsome guys frequented my club, but Sarge had a quiet way about him that made him really sexy. He *always* dressed meticulously, even in his leathers. He had this leather fedora that he wore often that really made him look like a movie star. Standing

6'2" with dirty blond hair and deep, gentle brown eyes, Sarge just had a presence. He often wore black muscle shirts which showed off the incredible gym body, and he had some of the most amazing tattoos I ever saw. My heart always skipped a beat or two at the sight of him. On top of it all, he was a veteran. He was one classy badass and everyone respected him.

One night he stood at the bar just watching me dance. When he came up to the stage to tip me, I couldn't help but notice that the seams of his Levis were stretched to their limit. My, oh my. To make things even harder on me (pun intended), I was crawling across the floor on my hands and knees toward him. He saw me notice *it* and subtly brushed his hand over the front of his jeans right in front of my face. Wow. To me, there is nothing hotter than a man touching himself that way. It was getting hot in there.

Afterwards, we started flirting and he asked me to breakfast. I went. This started a 2+ year relationship. Sarge was beyond a gentleman, and truly a knight in shining leather. For only the second time in my life, I felt protected, adored, and truly cared for. He never tried to get me to stop dancing, and he never took one dime of my money. In fact, the day he asked me to move in with him, he gave me a dozen roses and said, "I will take care of you." He meant it. Sarge turned out to be one of the great loves of my life.

He had a house in a valley in the woods. It was a bachelor's pad to be sure, but it had potential. Before I moved in, his 1967 Harley FLH Electra Glide was in the kitchen along with his giant, red toolbox. He used his kitchen as his workshop and his big Rottweiler and Doberman would hang out with him while he worked. Over time the dogs did a number on the wooden kitchen floor. I don't have OCD, but I am a freak about my floors.

They were some seriously cool dogs, though. Sarge trained Jekyll, the Dobie, to obey hand signals. Boy, was he something.

One afternoon I was running both dogs loose in the woods down the road when this black dude came over and tried laying the wrap on me. When I resisted his advances, he began to climb the fence to come toward me. Lucky for him, there was an eight-foot fence between us, because Jekyll came running out of the woods. With one word from me, he was scaling that damn fence to go after this guy. The look of horror on the dude's face was the funniest thing I ever saw. He went running for his life.

It wasn't just his dogs who were protective of me, either. We used to party at a biker bar in McKees Rocks called Good 'N Plenty. (Before it became a strip club on my advice!) It was always a really friendly place with the usual crazy regulars and some great bartenders. Even the owner was a terrific dude. One night we were shooting pool with our buddy, Grizz. I leaned over to take a shot when some drunk jagoff came up behind me and leaned in like he was going to bite me on the ass. I didn't even see it... but Sarge

Sarge

did. I looked up expecting him to be impressed with the killer shot I'd just nailed, but all I saw was the look of *I'm gonna fucking kill someone* instead. So, I immediately went over towards him to see what was up when he grabbed a glass off the bar, dumped the drink on the floor, and started toward this guy.

I jumped in the middle and said softly. "Hey, Baby, what's wrong?" And Sarge said back quietly but intensely, "Move out of the way, Honey."

I said, "Whatever it is, not inside. Be nice now; this is our favorite bar."

He instantly calmed down and said, "Seriously, Sweetheart, please just move out of my way. I have to take care of something. I promise I'll try to be good." So still not knowing what was going on, I give him the floor and stepped aside.

The asshole walked into the men's room and Sarge followed him. At the exact same time, our big, bad, buddy Grizz walked over and blocked the men's room door by standing outside it with his grizzly bear arms folded across his chest. Suddenly, I heard a big BANG! Then a minute later, Sarge came out of the bathroom with his hand over his face laughing his ass off. A second later, the asshole comes out of the men's room with a huge pee stain down the front of his pants! We all just lost it. Poor dumbass, he didn't know how lucky he was.

Shortly after I moved in, Sarge had to go away for his two weeks' service with the National Guard. Me and my friend Donna Rizzo tore the whole kitchen apart and completely remodeled it, as a surprise for his return. For two weeks, we ran around like crazies to the local Home Depot-type place buying everything from saws to new wood flooring. The thing is… I had no idea how to do any of this stuff. But I still remember how surprised and happy he was. It was sweet. I surprised even myself.

The friends I made while we were together were amazing and some of the most colorful people I have still ever met. We had a lot of friends who rode, so we spent a lot of time during those years going to biker bars and strip clubs all over the place. Every weekend we made the rounds to meet up, laugh, drink, flash our boobs, and be wild.

Another lifelong friend I made during this time is a man named Michael whom I called Kikel (because he's Jewish). Kikel and I have remained friends all of these years. I met him when he and one of his buddies came into the Cricket strip club where I worked one night. Kikel had a huge crush on me for years and I adored him, but after getting to be my dearest friend and realizing my type at the time was big, badass, tattooed bikers with scars and bullet holes in them, he settled into accepting our friendship and turning it into one of the greatest real friendships of my life. (Kikel, by the way, was not a big, badass, tattooed biker; in fact, he was the total opposite.)

I remember when Kikel came to visit me during this time to meet Sarge. Well, it just happened that we were having a party at the house and had invited all our 1% club brothers and sisters from one of the more intimidating biker groups. Here comes my lil' five feet six-inch Jewish buddy, Kikel.

Kikel pulled into the driveway—which was full of Harleys—in his gigantic 1977 Lincoln Continental. (If I remember right, he needed a pillow behind his back to see over the steering wheel.) He gets out in his tennis shoes and bounces up the sidewalk onto the porch where there was one of the patch wearers in a Swastika embellished t-shirt that said, HITLER WAS RIGHT! WHITE POWER UNITE!

Kikel smiled and said, "Hi, Suzy!" then hugged me and whispered in my ear, "Am I going to get out of here alive?"

I howled! Not only did he get out alive, but he also had a good time joking with all the tough guys that night. They all liked Kikel, and so did Sarge.

The best part about Sarge was how much he supported me chasing the comedy dream. Sarge heard about a comedy competition which was to be broadcasted on a local TV channel in Pittsburgh. This would probably be considered a forerunner to the "Reality TV" craze because they were trying to make a comic out of a normal, everyday working stiff. Even though I wasn't exactly what they thought they were looking for, Sarge suggested I try out for it. So, I thought, *What the hell. Why not?* I wrote a letter to the station telling them about my life and sent it along with a picture of me as me and, of course, one of me as Bag Lady Sue. They called within days.

My audition took place two days later at the WDVE studio on the Northside of Pittsburgh. I got to the studio and the audience consisted of WDVE radio jocks Jim Krenn and Ray Tannehill. Just two guys. Even though I had been performing in front of large, live audiences since I was fifteen, I was terrified! Seriously, I think it was worse than my first time on the stripper stage with the Band Aids on my tits. But, admittedly, I love a challenge and spent every waking moment preparing. Well… I nailed it. I made it to the final two! In third place was a housewife, and—in the end—the winner was a Pittsburgh Police Officer. To be honest, I didn't even think he was funny. I do think, however, that it was more politically correct in that day to pick a cop-turned-comic over a stripper… even a seriously talented and funny one. Even though I didn't win first place, that competition was an awesome moment which changed the course of my life forever.

Shortly after this experience, I had the chance to be in a movie called *Blood Sucking Pharaohs in Pittsburgh*. I got killed with a jackhammer to the gut. The movie experience was really cool. When I went to audition, I dressed quite conservatively considering I was auditioning for the part of a hooker, and it worked. I was the only one there who didn't show up "in character" and I got the part. I read the piece three different ways to show them I could actually act. Fortunately, I had read a book about auditioning years earlier when I dreamed of running off to Hollywood like many young people do at some point, though I was pretty damn serious. It paid off.

I played the part of a hooker who gets murdered by some whacko. As I stood in a phone booth talking on the phone, this weirdo comes up and pulls me out by the hair, tapes me to a fence, and proceeds to kill me with a jack hammer. Then, after I'm dead, the dude shoves a parking meter in the hole and the camera pans up to the meter head which clicks "Expired". Genius! Though it was a "B" movie, it sure was fun to do. I learned a ton about the movie industry. You can find it online, *Blood Sucking Pharaohs in Pittsburgh*, a true cult classic.

My friend, Tom Savini, did the special effects for it. He also did *A Nightmare on Elm Street, Texas Chainsaw Massacre and Night of the Living Dead*. All of the gory stuff was very real looking.

After the shooting was completed for the night, I decide—rather than shower off all the blood—I would ride around at sunrise in my Jeep with the top down and my "guts" hanging out to have some fun. I still had blood on my legs and socks. What a blast! You should have seen the faces of the people in their cars on the way to work at 7 a.m., when they looked over at me. It was classic. I pulled up next to one car with two businessmen chatting away and said, "Excuse me, you have a Band Aid?" They could have shit.

Although I was never discovered for my acting ability, someone spotted me at a Rocky Horror Picture Show event one night in Pittsburgh. I was getting popcorn in the lobby of the theater and, suddenly, a gal came running up to me yelling, "Oh my God, it's Sandy Klienbacher from Blood Sucking Pharaohs! Can I have your autograph?" She was really loud, and everyone turned around to look. My few minutes of fame was really awesome. It was exciting to sign a few autographs and all, but I could not believe anyone actually *saw* the movie! Apparently, there are plenty of "B" movie buffs around and they are damn serious about their films.

War is Hell

The year was now 1990, and the First Gulf War was brewing. As a member of the National Guard, Sarge was put on call. If we declared war on Iraq, he would have to go. For three months we didn't know what was going to happen. The waiting was horrible. It was so hard on him, and on me, also. No one can truly understand what it is like for our troops and their families unless you are one of them. Suddenly, I was.

The stress of just waiting and not knowing anything all that time was hell. Watching the news and learning of our friends going over was awful. It took a toll on our friends, their families, and all of us. He finally got the call in December. Sarge shipped out right after Christmas Day. We tried to be happy for the holiday, but it was really hard. I said goodbye to him at the base and cried all the way home. We were both so damn sad.

Before he left, I gave him a stuffed bear to take with him, figuring he would leave it at the Pittsburgh base, but he took it with him to make me happy. I was thrilled when he sent me a picture of him holding Mr. Bear over there. Even though I didn't know if I would ever see him again, that small gesture helped ease a little bit of the fear.

The next three-plus months were the most stressful and depressing of my life. It got to the point where I had to force myself to stop watching CNN because I was having horrible anxiety attacks weekly. Once, I even called an ambulance because I was alone in the house and I swore I was having a heart attack. Back then, the news covered that war every single minute of the day. I'm convinced that forced the conflict to be settled quicker because people were aware, involved, and pissed.

I remember being glued to the TV trying to hear anything that might tell me if he was ok. I always hoped to catch a glimpse of him when they would show our troops saying hi to their families. We did get to talk on the phone now and then, and I still have the audio cassettes he sent to me from there on his little micro cassette recorder. I could hear the fighter jets taking off every few minutes over his head while he lay in bed trying to talk to me on the recorder. It tore me apart to hear how sad and stressed out he was. Only once did he ever let me know he was scared. I could hear him getting choked up. That just crushed me! That experience helped me to have an even greater appreciation for all the veterans and troops I've met.

I killed time (no pun intended) by embroidering one of his tattoos on the back of his denim jacket. The image had praying hands in chains in front of a hand of cards—aces and eights, the dead man's hand. The ace of spades had a skull on it wearing a black leather fedora like Sarge used to wear. It was one cool-ass tattoo. It took me two months to finish, but it was amazing! I gave it to him when he got back.

Finally, in March he received word that he was going to come home. I was so happy I couldn't take it. While he was gone, I kept in touch with the wives/significant others of the men in his Guard unit. Ironically, his old flame and my fav stripper of the time Dusty Rose ended up marrying one of his Air Force guard buddies. So, she and I hung together through much of it and helped each other get by.

I will never forget the day he came home. For the week before he was to come back, I collected plastic yellow ribbons and covered the entire house with them… probably over two hundred of them. Plus, I put them on damn near every telephone pole from the interstate to our house! Channel 11 news even came a did a story on it. They had asked me if they could be at the house waiting for us when we came back from the airport the day I was to bring him home, but I declined. I knew he would not want cameras on him when he came home. I didn't either. It was a nightmare that needed to end. I wanted our time to be private.

I was at the National Guard base for the homecoming. As the big jet came in, it did a flyover which made everyone cheer and scream with joy. When the plane landed and the door opened, I was so excited I thought my heart would burst. As he came out of the door, I rushed right up the stairs of the plane and into his arms. He carried me down. Looking back, I probably should have tried to contain myself till he got off the steps, but I just lost it. Apparently, that little scene made the news too.

I could tell he was really happy about all the yellow ribbons on the way down our street. When we pulled into the driveway and he saw the house covered in them, *he* lost it. I held him there for a good while and he let the tears flow. I could not really know what a relief it must have been for him to be home, until I watched him take off his shoes and walk in the grass in his bare feet. He hadn't felt the grass in months because, well, there is none over there. I just stood there and let him adjust to it all. I am really glad I didn't let the news crew come.

As excited as I was that he was home, I noticed he was different. He started going out with the guys more and riding all the time. Often, he stayed out late and came home smelling like beer. When I tried to get him to do something with me, he seemed to have other things he *had* to do. It was always the guys this, or the guys that. Eventually, I felt more alone when he was in the house

with me than when he was gone. I really tried to talk to him, be patient with him, and to understand, but he just seemed to drift further and further away.

One morning when we went to breakfast, I tried to talk to him and he just kind of sat there. That was the last straw. I was done trying. I got up, we paid the check, went back to the house and I started packing my things. The war had been hard on me too—in different ways, of course—and I just felt like there was now nothing I could do but leave. Worst of all, he didn't try to stop me. One heartfelt "please don't go" would have done it.

I moved out that day and went back to my mom's house. We kept seeing each other and swore we would remain faithful while we worked things out. One night I was at our/his house while he was taking a nap; the phone rang, and the machine picked it up. A chick named Diane left a message for him to call her. I knew every one of his friends, male and female, but this one I didn't know. I got that bad feeling. When he woke up, I simply told him who called to see if he would tell me willingly who she was. He did not.

I was really pissed. Knowing that he never strayed far from the strip clubs and biker bars, I figured I probably knew this Diane chic from somewhere. That night I went to do a comedy show and couldn't stop trying to think who the hell Diane was. Then it hit me… there was a bitch that tended bar down at a real shithole strip club on Rt. 51 called Sonny Days. It had to be her. So—six tequilas later—I stopped by Sonny Days after my show. I walked in, reached over the bar and grabbed this bitch by the tits/shirt, pulled her over the bar and asked, "Why the fuck are you calling my ol' man?"

This really startled her. "Oh my God, Bags, I am so sorry! He told me you two were over." So, I let her go and told her that if I found out she was lying, she'd better leave town because I was going to come back and disfigure her face. Then, I drove off back to the house hoping he was there. The rage in me was like nothing

I ever remembered before. I had stuck by him through that damn war and through all his head-trips and was still making love to him all the damn time, and this is the respect I got. Oh, hell no.

He was still out at some bar, so I very calmly put the dogs outside, and proceeded to smash everything I ever brought into that house... pictures, dragon statues, everything. I tore down the mirrored closet doors I'd put up, sliced up the pillows and the clothes I had bought him, and anything else that was a part of us. I shredded until my hands bled. Then last of all, I took that big-ass carving knife, laid that denim jacket I had embroidered for two months on the living room floor and stuck the knife in it.

Shortly after that, I heard his truck pull in. I went out on the porch. When he came up and tried to kiss me hello, I grabbed his arm, pulled his 220-pound ass into the house and said, "Who's Diane, Motherfucker?" I punched him with all my might right in the side of the face. He hit the wall, and I literally was in such a rage I pulled him by his shirt, dragged him into the living room, and pushed him on the couch, the whole time screaming, "Don't you dare move! After all we have gone through, how could you do this to me?" I am sure he was in shock because he didn't move or say a 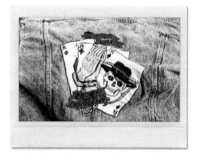 word for almost two hours. He saw the knife in the jacket on the floor and probably thought I might try to kill him if he did.

I was honestly pretty much out of my mind that night. And though I would never kill anyone, I surely would have fought him more if he had pushed back. To his credit, he did not knock me on my ass, which he could easily have done. He just let me go on and on screaming until I had nothing left. It had been almost a year since the war broke out, and I had been holding everything inside me all that time because I was worried about him and didn't want to burden him with my problems. Looking back, I am sure that was a mistake. We both needed to communicate with each other in order to survive it all in one piece.

Finally, I broke down and cried. He held me and we fell asleep on the couch. In the morning, I got up and left. My Harley was still in his garage, so when I came to get it the next day, there was a note on the door: "After seeing the house and all the things you destroyed, including my car alarm, and after cleaning up all the broken glass, feathers and things you ruined, I think it is best that we don't see each other for a while."

So, that was that. I left him be, moved into my own apartment, and the next thing I heard, he was prospecting for one of the major 1% biker clubs in town. I knew for sure then, there would never be another chance for us because I am simply not the *ol' lady* type. Never was, never will be. Nothing against the ladies that are, I am just too damn strong willed to be the kind of girl that could just sit back and not know from one minute to the next when my man will have to make a three-day run to who knows where, to do who knows what, with who knows who, while I sit home and wait.

Sarge told me years later that he wanted to come after me to bring me home, but the President of the club—who had known me pretty well—advised him against it. He told him that, undoubtedly, he would have to give up the club because it would never work for me. In fact, after the knifing incident, some of the club guys decided to nickname me "Slash." It wasn't funny then, but it is now.

Shortly after all of this, I decided to have my Harley custom airbrushed. It was something of a rite of passage from one life to another, I guess. I had Bag Lady painted on the front fender; on the tank, the puppet is holding a bottle of Cuervo Tequila in one hand and a big bloody knife in the other. That was in memory of all that had been.

My time with Sarge was the closest thing I ever had to actually being married. Of all the loves in my life—until recently—he was the best all around. I forgave him for the Diane thing because I know he had been through a ton of shit and had changed for a while. Even though I love men, and understand them on many levels, I am not one... and therefore lack the ability to think with my penis. However, even the strongest and most honorable of them are always one pussy away from fucking up their entire lives.

The Art of THAT Deal

Working as a stripper became a big part of my life. Those were some crazy times. When I hit the stage, I would dress in costumes to fulfill a particular fantasy for my customers: schoolgirl, teacher/secretary, nurse, dominatrix, you name it. It was a lot of fun. What girl doesn't like playing dress up? The dominatrix was my favorite outfit, of course, after Bag Lady. I loved dressing in all the cool costumes, especially the leathers: corsets, mask and thigh high boots. It made me feel so powerful and in control.

To add to the amusement, I even learned how to light my crotch on fire without burning myself. Ok, I did burn myself like two times, but only once was my fault. The trick was… I would line my G-string with paper, then hold a can of butane (a light, yet flammable gas) against the material and spray. It would leave a nice round wet spot in the center of the patch of material that lasted long enough for me to walk up on the stage. When I lit it, it would burn bright and steady. The guys would go freaking nuts! I would roll my pelvis to create a breeze and let it burn itself out. No big thing. Hell, I even let a few guys light their cigarettes off it! You could smoke in bars back then, like big people.

I remember the first and worst time I fried myself. It was a Thursday night, and The Cricket was always packed to the walls. When it was my turn to come out, the crowd was chanting "Light it up! Light it up!" So, I was hurrying to get dressed in my leathers when I realized I had no butane. *Fuck.* I freaked out and asked the other girls for hairspray, which also worked...not as good as butane, but in a pinch, you improvise. Unbelievably, four strippers and not one can of hairspray! So, I looked through the gold curtain from the dressing room for anyone I knew, and one of my buddies was there, so I had him run to the 7-Eleven next door to get me fuel. He came back with a can of lighter fluid because it they were out of butane. Oh well, the show must go on, so I squirted a wee bit of the shit on my patch, walked out on stage and lit the lighter.

All I heard was WHOOMPH as a gigantic fireball exploded up off the pussy so big it literally went above my head! My muffin instantly became a fire breathing dragon. Thank God I had my head back or I would have looked like Wile E. Coyote after a bomb hit him. Can you imagine *this* hair on fire? So, I suddenly realized there was no just letting it burn itself, so I start beating it out and the crowd went from, "Whoa, that's awesome!" to laughing their asses off right along with me. It left a bit of a scar there for quite a few years. The second time I had a wardrobe malfunction, there was a strobe light on, and I couldn't see the fire. Ouch! Don't try the shit when there are strobe lights.

One of the places I danced at in the '80s, The Edison, was an absolute shithole. This was the classic titty bar, the dive of all dives. I remember it had red light bulbs all around a 4 ft. x 8 ft. wooden stage. If you weren't careful when you crawled across it on your hands and knees, you would get splinters. Despite it's old, musty, dark, and dingy groove, the place—the patrons, and especially the dancers—had character.

We also wore G-Strings to cover our clams, so I personally always felt like I had something special left to give to my man even though I showed the world everything else. Believe me, that one-inch piece of material made a huge difference to me and him, whomever *he* was at the time. It also kept the dust and spiders out.

I went back to the same club recently, and the G-strings have disappeared! Times and people have really changed. It often makes me sad. I recently did a comedy show in a downtown Pittsburgh burlesque club that I used to strip in back in the days. Today it is a far cry from what it once was, and I am not sure that is such a great thing. Today it is totally remodeled and strives to be a classy place. There are twenty-plus girls in the rotation at any given time. Most—but thankfully not all—look and act like robots. Their faces are truly emotionless; they have no personality. Often their boobs are as fake as they are. The club is beautiful and is decorated with disco lights, big mirrors, three or four big stages, and all the bells and whistles of the typical modern day strip club. They've resorted to the canned music, Barbie doll outfits, heels they simply cannot dance in and are showing so much vagina. I felt like I was at an oyster bar, not a strip club!

My gosh, every time I turned my head, I felt like a damn dentist. "Dentist?" you ask. "But Sue, don't you mean a gynecologist?" No. I felt like a dentist because dentists see a lot of open, toothless mouths and can look all the way down to their tonsils. Each time a gal would lay there and spread 'em, I swear I heard the guy say AAAAAAAAAH! I remember thinking, *now where did I leave that tongue depressor?*

Being a stripper back in the '70s and '80s was very, very, different than it is today. We—or at least I—would roleplay on stage. For me, that made the job both fun and exciting. We would try to outperform the other chicks when we danced by trying to fulfil the guys' fantasies. The other gals and I would entertain the men, and sometimes even their wives, too! I remember many guys telling me they were going to bring their wives in to see my show because, as they put it, "She won't think it is so sleazy after she sees your act." I loved watching the women come out of their shells—once they had a drink or two—and realized they were the same as us… except we had lost our inhibitions a long time ago.

Performing was a lot of fun. My all-time favorite and most erotic act was my bondage show. I did the whole thing on the floor in the center of the stage, usually either to *Mama* by Genesis, or anything by Enigma. I had a big, sheer, beautiful white cape that made me look like a butterfly when I lifted up my arms. I could spin and make it into a sort of tunnel. It was truly beautiful. I wore the entire get up: white stockings, garters, bra, crotchless panties over my G- string and a long pearl necklace. The whole place would get quiet as I writhed seductively on the fuzzy blanket, peeling off my lingerie. First, I would blindfold myself with one of my stockings, bind my feet with a garter belt, and my hands with the bra over my head. I would throw the pearls over by head, so they ran down my back and let them slide into the crack of my ass. Then I'd lie face down on the blanket with my arms beneath me, reach under, grab the pearls with my hands still tied and, using my hands and wrists, pull them slowly down my back and between my legs. It was certainly a turn-on for many, and the guys *and* girls always told me they got quite hot from watching it.

Back then, being able to get that close to a gal's mostly naked body was simply magical for most guys. No internet porn or live streaming titty dancers in those days. Men liked being teased and more importantly, many knew how to tease back. It was really good, clean, glorious, fun! Nowadays, most of the clubs are fully nude. If a stripper isn't puffing sweet nothings in a guy's ear with her actual vagina while blowing him kisses with her labia minora, he thinks he's getting a raw deal! (No pun intended.)

In 1980 I was stripping at a bar called the Go-Go Lounge in McKees Rocks, which was and still is one of the toughest parts of Pittsburgh. Back then, it was run by mostly white bikers and some of the mob. I had only been dancing for a year or two at the time and was still very young. There was a girl there, older than me by about eight years or so, who I thought was absolutely the sexiest, most exotic dancer on Earth. Her name was Dusty Rose. I would sit outside the dressing room door when she was onstage, and just watch her... mesmerized. I wanted to learn to dance like she did. She moved like a snake and knew just how to make the men go nuts. On top of it all, she was a beautiful person. Dusty was dating a guy named Sarge, who was also incredibly sexy, but I really didn't much look at him because he was hers.

My mom was working as a bar tender at the Go-Go Lounge at this point in time. She often hung out with me at the clubs when I was stripping, but this was the only time we worked together. Crazy shit always happened when mom and I were together. One night, this badass named Ramey came walking in and just started shooting his gun up in the air! He filled the ceiling with bullet holes as we all hit the floor. All of the sudden, someone grabbed him and got him to stop. Believe it or not... that was that. There were no cops, no fights, no whining; just a whole bunch of "What the hell, Man?" That was all it took.

Of all the places I danced at around the country, the Go-Go Lounge was always one of the best. (Sadly, one night the place burned down, and we all lost touch.)

I worked with some amazing women in the business. Early on, I had the pleasure of working with the incomparable Honeysuckle Divine. Honeysuckle was a world-famous stripper back in the day, who became legendary for ejecting various objects from her snatcheroo. I personally got to witness her ping pong ball extravaganza. Imagine my surprise as a young teen as I watched her. I remember thinking, *Boy, when I grow up and stop dancing, maybe I can get a job as a counter gal at Dunkin Donuts, shooting doughnut holes through the air into cops' coffee cups.* Now, THAT would bring in some awesome tips!

"Eddie my Love" (her stage name) made more money than any other act I've ever seen. I was always fascinated at how Eddie worked the crowd. She would be dancing in front of one guy, shaking her ass, while piercing the soul of another man across the stage in front of her with her eyes. After she turned toward her initial target to receive her tips, she would move on to target number two—whom she had already softened up—and then eye up another guy across the room. She went back and forth across the room all night. It was masterful.

Another gem was Melissa Mounds. Melissa was a sweet little blond gal a few years older than me, who was about 5'2" inches tall with a 23-inch waist and 38-FFF breasts. I stripped with her in Poughkeepsie, New York. I remember her because while she was dancing some dickhead reached out when she wasn't looking and grabbed her tit really hard. It made her cry. So, I lost it, dove over the tables and punched him right square in the face. I was proud of that hit; it was a good one. He was lucky the bouncer threw him out before I *really* got ahold of him. That night earned me the nicknamed me "Taz."

I remember another instance involving "The Hedge Hog" Ron Jeremy (a.k.a. porn star) who was also doing comedy in Colorado Springs at a Strip Club called The Applause. He was a real piece of work. He grabbed my breast without asking, so I punched him, too.

I loved the customers but there were some real weirdos, too, like "The Show-er." He liked to sit right at the stage and have *it* out under the table. You could tell he was mighty proud of *it*, because every time one of us went over near him, he'd smile and look down as if to say, "Hey check out *Mr. It*! You want some, don't ya?" Well, had he tipped anything more than a buck, I and the other gals could have forced ourselves to keep tolerating this crap from him and *it*, but he was a cheap bastard, and strippers remember two types of men: Those that tip big and those who don't.

One night I had just about had enough of looking at Willy One Eye, so when the music stopped, I pointed at *it* and yelled, "Oh my God, he has *it* out again!" Needless to say, he left and did not come back on the nights I worked anymore.

Every Thursday night for over a year, the lineup was the same… I was on stage first followed by "Nunchuck Candy." Candy was quite the dominant type of girl, about thirty years old with spiky, punkish blonde hair and big natural tits. I admired her moxie and ended up becoming friends with her. As she would dance, she would swing authentic Asian nunchucks with such skill she could have been in a Bruce Lee movie! Nunchucks consist of two sticks connected at one end by a short chain or rope. The two sections of the weapon are commonly made out of wood, while the link is a cord or a metal chain. These bad boys are commonly used as a weapon in martial arts. Candy would come out onstage with her nunchucks and spin them like a black belt Ninja. Then guys would actually put a cigarette in their mouths, turn sideways and let her snap the damn thing right out of their face at lightning speed. I watched her do this a hundred times and never hit anyone.

Well, until one night when the dumbass turned his head just as she snapped the chucks. CRACK! She broke his nose. I assure you… you would *never* want to get smacked in the mug with a pair of these bitches.

She also had a huge wooden paddle about three feet long with holes drilled through it, which she used to whack many a poor dumb bastard on the ass. She would get a guy to come onstage—at the encouragement of his buddies—and assume the position (bend over, put his hands on a table). Candy would then take a whack. I saw more than fifty men receive a beating, buckle over from the pain, and then come back wanting more. Strange thing was… after a poor, unsuspecting fool would limp off stage holding his ass, even more guys would raise their hands hoping she would beat them, too!

Candy was a trip off stage as well. She invited me to have lunch at her place one afternoon, so I went. We chatted the afternoon away and realized we had to be to work soon. So, she said, "Why don't you just leave your car here and ride in with me and my friend Bill. He will be here to get me around 7." I agreed.

As we were getting ready for work, she said, "if you want to jump in the shower with me it's cool. Saves time." I thought since we always saw each other naked at work, what the hell? So, we are in the shower switching sides when, all of the sudden, Candy slides her very big soapy breasts across my back. AH OH! at first, I thought it was accidental, and then I realized she was being, shall I say, "playful". As I turned around, she kissed me.

I was not quite sure how to handle it, and I didn't want to be weird about it, so I tried to bow out lightheartedly. I knew she meant no harm. In the burlesque and the entertainment world, everyone is much more open to things. As a side note… I'm what you'd call "Strictly Dicky." It's nothing against people that are that way. In fact, when anyone asks if I have ever, I just tell them, "I tried it once but didn't inhale." That usually helps change the subject.

Her friend pulled up on time in his pick-up truck to take us to the Cricket. This is where things really got very weird. Candy was thirty, I was only about nineteen years old at this time. We jumped in the front of his pick-up and started off toward town. I'm seated by the door, Candy is in the middle, and Bill was driving.

Suddenly, without warning or any pre-trip *shit's gonna get real* from Candy, she turns to Bill and says, "Take it out."

Now at first, I thought I was hearing things until Bill says, "No."

Then Candy says, in a firm voice, "I said take it out!"

Bill says, "But what about your friend?"

Candy says, "She's cool don't worry about her." She proceeds to take off her high heeled shoe and hit him with it saying again, "Now take it the fuck out!"

I was now fully aware of what the hell was happening, and immediately glued my face to the passenger window. I started praying for God to get me out of this and to work in one piece. Candy is yelling obscenities at him and whacking him with her shoe while he is whacking *it*! Me? I'm shitting bricks. We're flying down the road at around 50 mph...*and he's driving.* I'm watching my life flash before my eyes, while this dude is white-washing his dashboard (!).

I wanted to punch her out right there but there was enough hitting going on. Finally, we pulled up to the club. I jumped out of the truck, went inside and waited for her behind the door. When she came in, I grabbed her and screamed at the top of my lungs, "WHAT IN THE FUCK WAS THAT AND WHERE DO YOU GET OFF INVOLVING ME?!!!

She said, "I'm really sorry. I should have warned you. Here, take this." and hands me a hundred-dollar bill. Boy was I pissed. I took the damn money, but I was still pissed!

There were some really fascinating customers along the way. I was doing the dominatrix show once at the Edison in downtown Pittsburgh, when a handsome, finely dressed man in a $2,000 suit came up to the stage. He sat down and handed me $20 with a note in it. I went backstage, opened the bill and saw that the note said,

"I want to be your slave." I showed it to my friend Little Chris, who had some experience in the wild world of prostitution. She said, "Oh wow, I know that guy! He is a millionaire and the head of a huge national company based here in town called _____ (respectfully, due to the stripper code, I cannot put in this book). He likes to be controlled, dominated, and even beat on. He'll pay you huge money to just act dominant and mess with his head!"

Now, mind you, I was like twenty-three back then and basically still pretty pure of heart. I had no idea what the hell to do with this whole thing. I expressed my concern in no uncertain terms, to which she replied, "Go back out there, lean over, grab his hair and whisper in his ear, 'If you can't fucking tip me at least a fifty, don't bother me with your wimpy bullshit again!'"

I said, "What? Oh, my goodness, I can't do that!"

Little Chris replied, "Trust me, damn it! Just do it!! He will go nuts, and you will make a fortune." So…when opportunity knocked… I went back out there, danced over to him, pushed his head down on the stage rail, threw my leg over him and dragged the heel of my thigh high boot very hard all the way up his spine. His next tip was a hundred-dollar bill!

This gentleman became my regular and over the course of the next few months gave me a small fortune. Yet, I never saw him outside the club…not once. All I did was "mind screw" him. Eventually, he did try to get me to meet with him after work, but I made excuses not to. I will tell you, that began my fascination—nearing obsession—with learning about Dominance and Submission (D&S). Long before *50 Shades of Lame, I* delved into the colorful world of kink. Had I had the presence of mind to write a book on the subject at that time, E.L. James would have likely sat in a corner and cried a while. Hell, maybe I will. The psychology of erotica is more exciting to me than the actual "feeling."

Through the years there and at all of the hundreds of clubs I danced in, I heard a bunch of really sad stories… far worse than mine. Occasionally there were good ones too. I always found each one fascinating.

One lady I worked with during that time was Darlene. Darlene was a bit older and incredibly talented. Boy, she could dance! She had wild dark hair, was perfectly thin and had silicone tits.

One night, a college punk kept messing with her and she finally had enough. But rather than bitch at or yell at him, she simply danced over to him in her sexy way, slid her hands through his hair, and then pulled his face into her knee. BOOM! That was the end of his crap. The bouncer threw him out the door by the seat of his pants.

Cricket Lounge

Two big lesbians served as our bouncers back in the day: one big black girl we called Mama, and a farm girl named Big Dawn. They truly loved all of us—well almost all of us—and would protect us. They didn't take anyone's shit. I would much rather have lady coolers than men… definitely less ego.

Big Dawn and I used to do this act called *Love and Torture*. After coming out in my dominatrix get-up, I would tie a guy's hands to a pole and blindfold him. I whispered in his ear, "I got a *big* surprise for you." Then I would walk off and Big Dawn would come out—all three hundred voluptuous pounds of her in a pink lace teddy. She would walk up to him and say, "Here's your big surprise," as she took off his blindfold. He would scream bloody murder as she took him down, laid him on the floor and jumped, crotch-first, right on his face! The crowd went wild, and everyone laughed till it hurt! We made a fortune with that routine.

I remember one particular night. I'd had enough of a dickhead that kept grabbing my ass. *So*…I simply danced down the runway, grabbed a full bottle of Miller High Life and bashed him over the head with it, never missing a beat. He hit the floor, and well, here came the lesbians… See ya! That was the end of that.

I met some amazing women during those years. There was Suzy Biker, whom I am still great friends with, who had her own Harley. She looked exactly like Dorothy from *The Wizard of Oz,* except with light brown hair, ivory skin, and huge, natural tits. It was funny because she looked about sixteen and onstage and had a sweet voice like a little girl. However, when she got off work and we were hanging out, she talked and swore like a gravel-voiced trucker.

Suzy Biker

Then there was a petite raven-haired beauty named Delilah with a perfect body, who—by the way—became even more perfect after she flew to California to buy a new set of tits. I have never seen any more real looking. I remember her doing a split between tables; one foot on one table, and the other on a second table. Now that is talent.

And then there was Skyy…Skyy was a tall, buxom, blonde, tobacco chewing redneck from Florida, who had more character and balls that anyone woman I'd ever met. She was *not* afraid to kick someone's ass if they tried pulling any shit. We became the very best of friends, and even spent some time touring together in later years.

I was always amazed at how many different kinds of men came through those doors. Every single type you could imagine from bikers to businessmen, millionaires to gutter bums. They all had one thing in common: they loved strippers. I went to breakfast with many guys, and even went on friendly dates with many others. One night we were all leaving the bar to go to breakfast at Ritter's Diner, which we did almost nightly. An acquaintance of mine from the bar came over to my vehicle very drunk. He hung on to my van door and said, "Hey, Bags, come party at our house!"

I nicely said, "No, Babe, not tonight. I'm going to eat with friends. Ya gotta get off my window." After the third polite warning to get off my van window, I yelled, "Dude, if you don't get off my window, I'm gonna drive off and drag ya!" He laughed. I punched it and my 1985 Chevy cargo van with the 5.0-liter V8. He spun right under the rear tires! All I heard was a quick scream and BUMP. I drove right over the crazy asshole. I have to say, there is no more eerie feeling in the world than driving over a body. Luckily, the van was empty and not as heavy as it could have been. Even talking about it gives me this tingly chill all over. My friends, who were standing around outside, were in shock. Half laughed, half just stared in disbelief.

Just then my one buddy yells, "Go, just go! He's ok, just get the hell outta here before the cops come!" So…I did. This poor dude went to the hospital because of some broken bones. But as I said earlier in this book, we used to own our stupidity, and when we deserved an ass kicking, we took it like a man, or a woman as it were. I felt terrible. Amazingly, this sweetheart even called me from the hospital where he still lay four days later and said, "Bags, I'm really sorry I was an asshole." Now, *that* is a *man* with balls. Injured balls, but still, balls.

As the years passed, I built a solid reputation for myself as a performer. I started to land some more important gigs and was paid more… a lot more. In contrast to The Cricket where I got my start in the early '80s, The Duquesne Club was at the other end of the spectrum. This was a very prestigious and exclusive, members-only private club where all the Pittsburgh elite hang out. I met many of the big sports stars and many of the guys in public office there during the times I performed for their events. They were almost all stellar guys. I have been tipped by some of the Penguins, the Steelers, and a few of the Pirates.

One night, Carlos Santana's bodyguard even tried to get me to go back to a hotel room with Carlos. When I said no, the dude got an attitude. I simply told him I didn't care if he was John Wayne's fucking bodyguard, I wasn't for sale. The rich and powerful never like being told no.

I stripped at many a celebrity's private party, too. I won't lay out names because, well…it's kinda the stripper code, as I mentioned before. I can say, however, that I did a comic strip-o-gram as a nurse for Art Rooney, Sr.'s last birthday party (Art was the founder of the Pittsburgh Steelers). They brought him to the engagement in a wheelchair, so we all thought my coming out as a nurse would be a riot.

Once they had me carried into the LeMont Steak house on Mt. Washington in a real casket for one of the county coroner's birthday parties. Six pall bearers hauled me down a flight of stairs with just my leg hanging out of it. We got inside and out I popped dressed in an Elvira-type get up, black wig, fishnets, corset, gloves and all. *That* was a trip. I'll never get over the feeling of lying in a real coffin… YUK.

Afterwards, I walked out onto the ledge and a took a picture—topless—with one of the Shriner's clowns; the city of Pittsburgh stretched out behind us. It was magnificent.

It was about the time I started to realize I might have a chance at fame and fortune. I was classy and talented enough to be hired by wealthy, *important* people, and I always believed I was more than just some strip club diva. From the time I could walk, I was an entertainer to my core.

Van Eden Ranch

Rocky Mountain High

Shortly after returning to Pittsburgh from Texas—before meeting Sarge—I had an experience which changed the course of my life forever. In the fall of 1986, my brother needed a ride from Pittsburgh to Denver for a court hearing. He had moved out west a few years prior and loved it. He also, apparently, started on his destructive pathway to the "Grey Bar Hotel" (a reference to a 2004 movie about Curtis Dawkins' prison time for crimes he committed under the influence of crack cocaine). Since Yogi didn't have a car at the time, he asked me to take him.

So, I jumped in my 1981 Jeep CJ-5 with my brother and my little miniature collie Lumpy Dog, and off across America we went. We made it all the way to Kansas before we stopped in the little farming town of Colby for the night. I remember waking up and looking out the back window of the hotel to see nothing but miles and miles of wide-open space. There were flat, golden, wheat fields and more giant rolls of hay than I ever could have imagined; miles and miles of them! Coming from Pittsburgh with her millions of green trees and rolling hills, this scene was far from common. But, still, it was beautiful in its own way.

It was cool to be on the road with my brother. I remember us watching how the locals began their day that morning in a Kansas diner with amazement. The people moved much slower than we were used to. I have seen mollusks move with more zest.

The place was filled with old country gentlemen in overalls and ballcaps. I will say they were not the friendliest folks. They were not un-friendly, mind you, just indifferent. Harvest had just ended. The only restaurants were little old diners with an amazing, home-cooking-type buffet that was as good as Mom's. I remember a post office, one gas station, but not much else. Back then Colby, Kansas, was a literal ghost town aside from the farming folks, and they looked at us suspiciously because we were outsiders.

We finally made it out to Colorado, and I dropped Yogi at his friend's house. Lumpy Dog and I then headed up into the Rockies. I stopped for gas about twenty miles out of Denver in a beautiful little mountain town called Idaho Springs. As I filled up the tank, I saw a sign that said, "Horseback rides this way" with an arrow pointing the way. Being ever the adventurer, I went that way. The narrow, paved road wound past a lovely old hot spring resort called Indian Springs. Just like everything else of any intrinsic value, it was stolen from the Native Americans back in the 1800s. The path continued through a little neighborhood of adorable small log cabins and mountain houses with gingerbread-like wood trim like you might see in Germany. After about a mile, there was another sign that said, "Van Eden Ranch two miles up this way." So, I went that way.

The road was dirt, rocky and bumpy as hell with big pine trees and aspen groves on each side. There was about a seventeen-per-cent grade at one point—which my Jeep took with ease. After about a mile and a half of nothing but up, I did get a bit concerned. I could hear the banjo theme from Deliverance playing over and over in my head as I kept looking for some wild mountain man to jump out of the woods and have his way with me.

The ride up was peaceful, beautiful, and seemed to go on forever. Finally, at the end of it, the forest opened up onto one of the most incredible mountain ranches you could ever imagine. It literally took my breath away! The ranch sat all by itself at the end of that long pine tree lined dirt road, about 9000 ft. up in the Rocky Mountains surrounded on all sides by national forest. The Van Eden Ranch had twelve lovely guest rooms, some on the front and some on the back side of the long building. The main lodge sat up on a hill surrounded by pines, except for the big front yard. Best of all, there was a big corral made out of rough-hewn logs and it was full of horses! Van Eden was the most beautiful place I had ever seen.

I walked up to the main house to see about a ride and met the lady who owned it. Patricia was a wonderful and mildly nutty, auburn-haired gal then in her early sixties. She was feisty and educated with a doctorate in Psychology. Her husband had been shot and killed by a ranch hand at the Indian Springs Resort a few years earlier, shortly after they had bought the place. Pat decided to stay. She and her slightly-off-kilter-son James ran the whole ranch. James was a big Baby-Huey farm boy who had a heart the size of Texas but was a little bipolar from birth, so he would snap now and then. He was Momma's only child born late in life which made him a spoiled-rotten brat.

When I first met them in the '80s, the ranch was a literal mountain paradise like something out of a movie with pine trees up to the back door, and a stream flowing through down the mountain. It looked untouched for a million years. There were tons of trout, mountain lions, bears, deer, and elk wandering about the land.

After returning home from that trip, I dreamed of going back one day to live on the Van Eden Ranch in Colorado. But I had just taken back my job working as a stripper and was settling into life once again in Pittsburgh. Then after meeting Sarge, I decided to stay planted in Pittsburgh for the time being. I couldn't have known at the time, however, how that one turn off an interstate would change the entire course of my life.

After the crushing break up with Sarge, I seriously considered going back west. But soon I started dating this redheaded boy with a kick-ass Corvette. Corvette Guy, it turned out, was gorgeous—especially for a redhead—but he wasn't good in the sack, so his time in my bed and life was extremely short lived. However, thanks to him tossing me the keys to the Vette frequently, I fell in love with Corvettes. The relationship didn't last too long, but it wasn't a total waste, either, because he introduced me to Scott.

I'm not sure how I never noticed Scott at the club but, apparently, he had seen me many times before. He later told me so. Scott was a fine-looking thing; five years my junior with dark, silky hair, dark brown eyes, a strong jaw, and a swimmer's body, which he wrapped in the tightest Levis possible. He had a sexy attitude to match. He appeared quiet and shy at first, so I never really talked to him much.

One night I walked into my buddy's garage where they were all lifting weights. Scott was there all hot, sweaty, shirtless, and sexy. And well, shit...this time I noticed. *But* at the time he was with his childhood sweetheart, and honestly, I just ain't that kinda gal.

Scott and I continued to run into each other here and there and ended up talking. He went on about his being married out of high school and how unhappy he was, which I now know is standard playboy speak for, "I really want to stay married to the safe, secure lil' heifer who waits for me in my cozy little barn, *but* I also want to run and play with the wild mare in heat that just ran like the wind across the pasture in front of me!"

I told him if he was unhappy, he should change things. Period. I had just made plans to pack it up and move out west… back to that beautiful horse ranch and Colorado, and no one was going to change that. He was pretty persistent about coming around and even running into me whenever he could. Over the next month we hung out and flirted here and there but I told him we couldn't screw around until after he made the choice to file for a divorce.

He and his wife didn't have kids, and to be honest, what was or wasn't wrong about their marriage was none of my business. This may sound harsh but, if their relationship was tanking, it started long before I ever came around. I believe things happen just the way they are supposed to. People meet and fall for who they do because it is part of some bigger plan.

Scott and I ran into each other one weekend at the Harley Drags in PA. A bunch of us rode to the local bar and had a few drinks together. He grew bigger balls this time, I guess, because he grabbed me on the way out the door and pinned me against the wall. He kissed me deep and hard and well… damn. What the hell? He told me he had it for me since he first saw me. He said he even used to go to North Park (our local hang out by the lake place) looking for me on his bike because he knew I rode out there. He was so incredibly sexy that it started to mess with me, but still, I resisted because he was married.

One day he called me and said he needed to talk to me. Scott came over to my house and started telling me his feelings. He was a hot-blooded German/Italian and did not give up easily. It was so hard for me to know what the hell to do with it all. I felt a huge desire for him, but I told him I was leaving for Colorado to go live on a ranch in the Rockies, and it would be pointless to start anything serious. Plus, I did not want to be a homewrecker. This went on for about a week or two, and then, in all honesty… I caved. We finally decided, "screw it" and took a road trip to

Niagara Falls. We just couldn't resist the connection we had. That time was incredible. This was long before he lost his damn mind, which looking back, I am certain I had something to do with.

I let him know how adamant I was about going back west to the ranch to chase my dreams. I had to be honest with him because I am always honest. I can't stand liars and pussies. I wish they would grow some balls and make a damn decision… even if it's wrong. You can have so much in life, but *no one* can have it all. Everything has a price.

About three weeks before I was due to leave for Colorado, he came to my house and said, "I am filing for a divorce and going with you."

Holy crap. I remember thinking, *I know the sex was awesome, but was I ready to live with this guy? Out West?* He was not in my initial plan. But Scott loved my passion to experience life, and he wanted a piece of that, too. I knew at the time that—no matter how it turned out—it was going to be a hell of a ride.

Scott seemed pretty certain this would be the right thing for him. I let him be a big boy and make his own decisions. Had I been as wise in the ways and minds of men as I am now, I *never* would have done it. But I was young, free, hot to trot, and… so was he. The adventure was just too irresistible to pass up.

I started selling all the stuff I had held onto for years. Everything that didn't have irreplaceable sentimental value had to go, and even some things that did—like the frog collection I started as a little girl. I stored all my pictures and videos at my mom's, changed the oil in the Harley, and was ready to go. Scott and I tore down an old trailer and made it into one we could load all our stuff, including my Sportster and his nice-ass yellow and white Harley full dresser, we were off. WESTWARD HO! We chased each other along I-70 across the country to the Rocky Mountains. Scott had never been west before. It was truly a thrill for us both!

I had no way of knowing that he really had not cut the emotional ties he had with his ex-wife, nor that when things got tough down the road—which they did—she is exactly who he would run back to. But in the moment, life was a thrill ride, and we were riding it with our hands in the air! I will never forget the feeling of looking over at his gorgeous face as he jockeyed past me on the road thinking, *Damn, I am a lucky bitch.* Off into the unknown we went, free as two birds across miles of wheat fields with plenty of time to think. I remember my heart being so full of joy it was about to burst. One of my biggest dreams was coming true. Thank you, John Denver!

We pulled into the ranch at night, so Scott couldn't see how incredible any of the scenery was until he woke up the next morning and walked out on the balcony in the crisp fall air. He was completely overwhelmed. It was the beginning of October. The elk had begun their rut a month earlier, and it was in full swing. You could hear the big bulls bugling through the mountains, and literally smell their musky scent in the air.

A couple days after we got there and unloaded the bikes, Scott and I took a ride on his yellow Harley up into Rocky Mountain National park. He was only about 5'8" but could ride his full dresser like it was a dirt bike. I've never seen anything like it since.

We saw a big herd of elk, so we pulled off the road. We hiked into the forest and sat in the pines right near them. It was wild. We made love right there on the ground. I later found out that the bull elk in the rut are actually spewing their semen out into the air when they bugle, and we humans subconsciously pick up the scent. *OH YEA.*

The party that started right then continued for the next five months. Still, between the beers we worked our asses off as ranch hands. We must have done well for a couple of "Greenhorns" because the owner decided to take some long-needed vacations and left us on our own to run the ranch for her. We turned that place into a good horse business, and everyone was happy. Life was amazing. Instead of watching TV, we road horseback every day into the mountains. I remember walking out my bedroom door naked in the morning with no one to answer to.

Our work was a joy, and Scott was one romantic son-of-a-bitch. We rode horses through the woods and would stop to make love in the forest or the meadow all the time. That Christmas, we even rode up to the meadow on horseback to cut our Christmas tree. Scott looked like he had just stepped out of a western movie in his cowboy hat, fur mountain man boots and woolen poncho. In the moment, I felt like he was the sexiest man alive.

There was a big teepee up in the high meadow that was hidden in the trees. We would pack up the saddle bags, ride up the mountain, park the horses outside, start a campfire in the teepee, grill ham steaks, and drink wine. Then we would lie down on the soft ground and make love for hours. One time, we even played *warrior kidnaps white woman*! He pulled a gun on me, tied me to the inside wall of the teepee and had his way with me. It was the hottest thing I had ever experienced up until then. I can remember it and him like it was yesterday. Every moment there was more incredible than the next.

Sometimes in the morning we would turn the horses loose to play in the snow. I loved watching them run; they would kick up the soft powdery snow with manes flowing and steam coming out of their noses. I will never forget that visual as long as I live.

To break up the tranquility, now and then we would go down the hill to the Indian Hot Springs. They had comedy night once a week, so it was the first chance since the competition at WDVE to show off my mad skills. The mountain people just loved my dirty sense of humor and inhibition because it was not common back then. Colorado was just like you'd imagine, laid back, open and free.

Scott took a job at the resort remodeling the downstairs, so at night we would sneak into the place and have the whole hot springs pool to ourselves. The huge greenhouse filled with decades-old trees and plants around a huge stone hole in the ground full of hot mineral water was incredibly romantic. Once in a while we would be joined by a couple of our wild-ass biker friends Steve and Lori, and we would drink beers and skinny dip the night away.

Scott

He used to stop his truck on the ranch road on our way back from town, shut the motor off and sing to me while the snow sparkled like diamonds on the pines. He sang just like Randy Travis. He would hold me in the front seat, and we would sit there for hours. At the time, I was crazy about him and he was about me. Yes, I loved him as much as I could for being in my late twenties. Life was free, fun, and great.

We had some really wild, fun times on that mountain. One night one of the wranglers named Todd took a horse into town with the intention of handing out fliers for the trail rides and rooms at the ranch. But instead, he tied the horse to a rail out back of the West Winds Bar. (Yes, they actually still had horse rails outside the bar back then.) After getting shit-faced, Todd fell off the damn horse on his way back to the ranch. We are on our way down the road to look for him when, all of a sudden, we see the horse walking up the road with its saddle sideways. No Todd! As we grabbed the horse, we noticed Todd coming toward us, drunk as shit, staggering along. There we all were on the road back to the ranch. We fed the horse a slice of pizza in order to get the saddle off, and then worked to get Todd's drunk ass in the truck. The horse knew its way back, but the wrangler was lost (see photo).

One night we got a massive snowfall—about three feet—and Scott decided to take one of the horses up the mountain to go hunting. I was at work at the Buffalo Bar down in town when I got the call… It was James, the owner's son, "Hey, Sue, we are rushing Scott to the hospital. He was riding bareback in the snow and the horse fell forward. When it came back up, it threw its head back

and smacked Scott in the mouth. He cut open his lip pretty bad. You can see clear through it to his teeth!"

Insert my laughter here. They picked me up at work, so I jumped in the truck and into Denver we all went. The E.R. doc was a hoot. He said to me, "Hey, come take a look at this!" Then proceeded to stick a pencil-looking object right through the hole in Scott's lip! EEEW. A few stitches and a bruised ego later, we were heading back up the mountain. I love riding bareback as much as anyone, but there is a time and place.

Yet another time, Scott and I went hunting for Bambi. It was not exactly the season for it, so we were sneaking about in the high meadow on the horses. Scott saw a herd of deer and had to shoot the only buck. His aim was stellar. One shot through the heart at about two hundred yards or more and, bang… Done!

I am not a fan of killing shit. Scott proceeded to dress the deer. His plan was to toss it over the horse's back and ride back down the mountain to the ranch just like they do in the movies. His horse, it seems, had a different idea. When it smelled the blood/death, it said, *Hell no… you're not putting that bloody thing on* my *back*, and it took off down the mountain! Boy, was Scott pissed. I, however, almost popped a blood vessel trying to hold back my laughter. So, since the snow was mid-thigh deep, he looked at me and told me to get off of my horse so that we could put this thing on it.

My response? "I'm sorry darlin, but you have a better chance of seeing Christ. Come now, Mighty Hunter, let's just tie the rope to my saddle, you jump on the horse with me, and we can drag it down." He was so mad that he decided to burn off his anger by dragging the deer one mile down the mountain all by himself, so… I let him. We hung it in the mini bunkhouse so the mountain lions and bears wouldn't get at it and went to bed. The next day, I realized that the long bloody trail it left in the snow could have spelled trouble, but we were lucky.

That spring, Scott was receiving visitors for horseback rides when three very large ladies came up to the trail to ride. I said I would take them. But halfway through the ride, one of the 200+ pounders fell off her horse! The horse took off back to the ranch. I bet he was thinking… *Holy shit, this chick weighs a ton and I'm OUT!* Well, my horse wasn't too happy with me either, because I let her ride him the rest of the way. Now I had to find a way to get her back up on the horse's back. Out on the trails we didn't have the steps available that we do when we mount up at the corral. The only thing available for us to use were a few fallen logs. Had anyone been there with a cell phone camera back then, this would surely have gone viral. Can you picture little me trying to get my horse to stand beside a log, while boosting a terrified, wobbly—but very upbeat and funny—large woman, onto the back of my horse? I literally had my shoulder under her ass and had to heave ho the woman into the saddle. I walked all the way back down the mountain on foot leading the horse and the chubby chicks. Working at the ranch sure had its moments.

I also learned how to clean a horse's wiener. When you geld a horse, you cut off the horse's nuts so he doesn't get boners all the time like a stallion does. This enables said stallion to automatically clean out his sheath of all the dirt and dust that gets up in there from well, just being a horse. So, on a gelding, it causes what are called "beans." Beans are tarry, asphalt-ish crap which, if you don't clean out, causes trouble for the poor whinny. To do this, you put some lubricant on your hand and forearm and slide it in and out inside the poor guys' pecker holder to loosen the crap off of him. I didn't mind this task, but the more horse cocks I got my hands on, the less attractive I found men to be. Best of all, the horses all just loved me. When I drove up the road, they would line up, drop out their big horsey wieners and whinny a fine, *Hello there, Bean Cleaning Bag Lady!*

Horses are amazing and funny creatures. They are so much like big dogs that the Native American's called them "Sunka Wakan" or spirit dogs. There was this one particular horse named Denny. Denny was a beautiful thirty-two-year-old Palomino gelding and the second smartest horse I ever met. In fact, he was a genius. For weeks, we noticed the grain supply was disappearing at a really fast rate. I knew it wasn't us taking all the grain. The horses were in the corral every night with a 5 ft. fence separating them from the food supply, and no small animal could consume that much grain.

We kept trying to figure out where all of the grain was going. One night we were all hanging out, drinking beer on the big deck beside the ranch house when—all of a sudden—we see Denny waking slowly up the road. Now, how the hell did he get out?

We watched quietly as Denny headed for the grain shed. The sneaky little bastard actually stopped outside the shed and started looking around to make sure no one saw him. When he got to the door, he stopped again. He looked to the left, then the right, paused, crooked his ears, looked around again, and proceeded to open the door with his teeth and went right in. AH HA… We found the culprit. So, I yelled, "Denny! Get the hell outta that shed!" and all we heard was bang, bang, bump! The door flew open, and Denny ran down the road and jumped back into the corral. We got a hell of a laugh out of that and, of course, had to start locking the grain shed door.

For nearly six months all we did was run trail rides, shovel horse poop, drink whiskey, ride our Harleys through the mountains, and screw around. In the back of my mind, I knew it was only a matter of time before I was going to get pregnant. Shortly after we moved into our cabin down by the creek, I did. I knew the night that it happened. Scott wanted to make love without a condom, so I warned him that we were going to make a child if we did. But he said that he liked living on the edge.

Two weeks later, I didn't get my period, and I just knew. I came home to the cabin, hugged him, and said, "Darlin', you just fell off the edge."

At first, like most men, he was both happy and shocked. Then reality hit him, and he became afraid. So, he tried to get me to go and have an abortion. I told him to go fuck off. There was no way at that point in my life I was not having this child. I said he was free to go if he liked, but I was going to make it work.

This was the beginning of some of the roughest times of my life. I was determined to have my baby and thought he loved me enough to support my decision. As it turns out, he was not the tough guy he so tried to make everyone believe he was. Rather than man up, or get lost, he convinced me to go back east where "he could get a better job to take care of us." In reality, he was running back his mom and ex-wife.

I didn't want to go back to Pittsburgh, but the thought of being alone in the mountains 9000 ft. up in a cabin in the woods, going into labor in December scared the hell out of me. So, against my gut feeling, I packed up our stuff and went back with him. Had I to do it all over, I would never have left Colorado.

Cheyenne

After packing up and starting the journey back home, I remember driving down the mountain into Denver heading East, crying the whole way. I didn't want to go back. I had nothing to go back to aside from a few good friends and I had made many great friends in Colorado. I was hysterical during the entire first trimester of my pregnancy because Scott pressured me to not have the baby. I knew all along I wanted to keep her, so when I first saw her little heartbeat, the game was over… no way I was NOT having that child.

I called Linda, in tears, on the drive back to Pittsburgh. Hearing how distressed I was, she offered to take me to lunch as soon as I got back. I'll never forget… Linda and Lois Kress met me at the McDonald's on Rt. 8 in Glenshaw and *brought me flowers.* I remember sobbing uncontrollably—not only was I emotional from feeling as if my life was crumbling before my very eyes, but I was also hormonal from being pregnant. They were so kind; they listened without judging and prayed for me. Even though I was still terrified, I felt a sense of peace. It's a good thing because life didn't get any easier from there.

Shortly after getting back into town, I found us a shitty little apartment in Shaler, PA. It was near a beautiful creek and park that had a waterfall in it, Fall Run Park. I knew when we got back Scott would be in his comfortable old surroundings and turn into a dick. I was right. Almost immediately, the fighting started, and Scott began spending more time away and stayed out most nights. Honestly, I didn't even like him anymore.

One evening shortly after we moved into the place, I had the strangest feeling he was up to something. So, I got in my car and drove to his ex-wife's house. There he was in the driveway hugging her. Needless to say, I flipped out, went back to our house and threw his shit out on the sidewalk. I wasn't mad so much, but just felt trapped… very trapped. Being stuck with someone you don't love anymore—especially when you're pregnant—and who obviously doesn't love you, is a real bitch. The thing I learned after it all was some people simply cannot love anyone but themselves, and they generally even suck at that.

So, after I kicked him out, he went to stay with his ex. She must have realized it was a mistake on her part to take him in and sent him packing. He, of course, came back to me. Scott begged my forgiveness and told me he would help me while I was pregnant if I took him back. So, after thinking about it, I did. No one can ever understand what a woman feels inside when she is pregnant. Just as no one can understand what goes on inside a man when "he" is also pregnant. Both are completely different, and under the best of circumstances, it is terrifying for both.

We basically acted like roommates who still found each other sexually attractive. The trouble was, he wasn't chubby and pregnant and therefore he could go out bar hopping at night with the boys. I was nesting and growing my little buddy, so drinking was not an option for me. One weekend that pregnant summer, Scott and I went to the Easyrider Rodeo in Prospect, PA to hang out and just be bikers. We were in a field chatting with our friends when I noticed Scott pull a piece of paper out of his pocket, look at it, and put it back. I felt some weird energy. When we got home and his drunk ass went to bed, I, of course, went through the pocket to find the paper. Normally, I do *not* check up on my man or *ever* go through his stuff. I also refuse to allow anyone to check up on, suspect, or accuse me of anything… since I am honest to a damn fault. I always feel that if we can't trust each other, we shouldn't be together.

I also know that if someone is a freakin' sneak or a cheat, you will find them out eventually. Your gut just knows. There was a name and number on the piece of paper… a woman's, of course. I didn't call, but I discovered where she lived based on her phone number. The name on the piece of paper was a unique one. I don't remember it, but it was a name few women had. I had enough friends in that area that if I asked around, I knew one of them would know this gal. I was also sure she didn't know about me, the pregnant girlfriend. Scott was a sneaky little prick, so I was sure he neglected to tell this chick when he asked for her number.

Here comes the weird part. Not more than two nights later around midnight, I had a hankering for some mashed potatoes and chicken gravy, so I went down to the local Eat 'N Park, a twenty-four-hour diner. Scott was out at a bar somewhere, as usual. The waitress came over and said, "Hi, I'm (insert the unusual name here) and I'll be your server. Can I get you something to drink?"

Well, I could have shit! So, I said, "Why, yes. A cup of tea, and do you know this guy?" as I pulled a picture of Scott out of my wallet.

"Yes, that's Scott," she said. "I just met him last week at a bar. He asked me out. Oh my God, why? Is he your man??"

And I said, "No, not anymore, but he is the sperm donor on this little project," pointing to my belly, "and we still live together. So, watch yourself, Hun, 'cause he's a real douchebag." How could

I be mad at her. He was damn good-looking at the time, and well, girls always hope for the handsome prince. We chatted for a while, and I knew she was truly innocent. So, I went home and again tossed his shit out on the street and blocked the door. He came home later that night, and I refused to let him back in. That was the end of that.

Scott still came around until the kid was born, and we still found each other a turn-on. In fact, the sex was really what our whole relationship was based on. Well, that and the memories we made living out in Colorado for the time. We just had that nasty, twisted, sexual attraction thing together. In fact, even though I despised him, I still gave him head in the delivery room when I was about fifteen hours into labor with the kid! Yep. I did. All the way. Ya see, they gave me a shot of this wonderful drug called Nubaine that made me high as shit, and I just got all warm and fuzzy inside and couldn't feel a single contraction. I looked over at him and well, he just looked good, I figured why not? I'll bet he still tells his friends about that to this day.

I will never forget the moment Cheyenne was born (named after the capital of Wyoming). I heard Scott say, "My God, Sue, look there she is! She is beautiful!" and I looked down to see her coming out of me. I swear she looked right at me, eyes wide open and clear. I felt completely connected to her instantly. It was as if she said, "We got this, you and me." Like she just knew everything I did not. I remember looking up to my left where Scott was standing, and for a moment, I saw right through him to the picture on the wall. It was as if he wasn't even there. I knew right then, he had to go, and she and I would be just fine. Looking back, had I tried to "make it work" with him, both her life and mine would have been horrible. Sometimes, we have to trust our guts and God. So, when she was about two months old, he and I had yet another fight and that was it. I threw his shit out the door and I was done... completely this time.

When I first got pregnant with Cheyenne, and her "Sperm Donor" (that's what I called him from this point forward) started criticizing my weight, I saw side of him I did not like and knew I never would again. It began as his little "joke" then turned into his way of trying to knock me down, make me feel bad and convince me not to gain weight. Like I had a choice! I realized later after I met his parents that is how his father talked to his mother. After giving him four kids was no longer the Vicky Secret model he'd married. Never mind that daddy was a short, squatty, little man with a huge chip on his shoulder. When he looked in the mirror, apparently, he still saw himself as a twenty-five-year-old buff Marine. He certainly was *not* that anymore. There was nothing I liked about that man from day one.

My point is that their son learned this as acceptable behavior because Daddy and Mommy played this game all his life. Dad dished it out; Mom took it. What Scott failed to understand is I was *nothing* like his mommy. I was the kind of woman who would not, and did not, hesitate to hit him over the fucking head or in the nuts with a beer mug when he got up in my grill!

After the Donor and I split, he moved into a row house across the river from Cheyenne and I in an even crappier part of town. When I could, I would take her over there to visit with him because I wanted her to know her "dad" like I never had the chance to do. I wanted this for her if I could swing it without too much drama. Cheyenne was only six months old or so and so I went to pick her up after she was with her dad. I don't remember what was said, but he and I got into a fight about some dumb shit, so I told him to fuck off and went to grab the kiddo and leave. His head and balls would have hurt less in the end had he let me go, but he wanted to be a tough guy.

He grabbed me from behind and held my arms against my sides. I don't like to be in bondage unless I consent, so I was just a tad pissed. We were wrestling about in the kitchen and I couldn't break his grip when I caught a glimpse of this big heavy glass mug full of beer out of the corner of my eye. I managed to grab it off the table and, with two strikes, bashed him on both heads. First his skull on the upswing, then the nuts on the down. I'm talkin' *ninja shit* here!

He let go as he dropped to the floor, so I ran for the living room. I picked the baby up off of the couch, grabbed the bouncy swing off the doorframe with my free hand, kicked open the screen door, and left. He got off the floor, ran out into the street after me and kicked in the passenger-side window of my little car. I yelled, "You little prick! You wanna play? How do you like this?" and I proceeded to start swinging the bouncy swing against the windshield of his nice Blazer. He started screaming "No! Please don't!" I got in the car and left.

He moved back out west shortly after and almost never saw Cheyenne again except for a couple times. To my credit, I never badmouthed him in front of her and tried to keep them in touch, but to be honest, I figured she and I would be best without the bullshit. *So*, I left it up to her to decide when she was older how she felt about him.

I never chased Scott for child support. He would send us $100 a month on occasion. I never went after him, that is, until one Christmas when she was about five. He called and asked me what she wanted. I told him a little mountain bike, which was about $75. He then said, "Well, how about I don't give you the $100 this month and just use it to buy her a bike?"

I hung up the phone and went to the courthouse the next day. Give 'em an inch…

Shortly after this incident, Linda invited me to go to church with her. I hadn't been to church for years and wasn't so sure that would be a good idea for me. I asked her, "Do I have to wear a long skirt and drive a minivan to be a Christian?" I was joking, but there was a little truth in my sarcasm too.

Linda bust out laughing! After she assured me that I didn't have to wear a long skirt and sing "Kumbaya" to go to church, so I agreed to go. Even though I felt awkward, I was in a desperate place at that time in my life, and Linda and her Christian friends had always been there for me.

One morning after the service had ended, a bunch of ladies got in a prayer circle to pray for each other and others in need. Linda prayed—to my amazement— and asked God to help me find a car. I laughed to myself when she said that. *No way God is going to help me get a car.* Afterwards, one of the women there praying with us came over and said, "Are you the girl that needs a car?"

I said, "yes, I am. Mine died."

She told me she had a car I could have. It wasn't pretty, she said, but it ran well. I thanked her but let her know I didn't have much money. She said, "I don't want money, just come and get it."

I was overwhelmed! My own family didn't love and care for me like that. And these people didn't even know me. They all recognized me as the hard-core biker chic who rode her Harley to church, and they accepted me anyway.

God hears everything. Talk to Him.

Motherhood

Although I may suck at relationships with men, there's one relationship where I thrive: being a mother. Motherhood is to me, simply the greatest gift I ever received and the most fun I have ever had. I have lived a completely full life right beside her, one I would have only half-lived without her. She made me want to experience life's adventures and lessons *with* her, and she gave me a reason to go on when many times I did not really want to. I can honestly say, I am truly in love with my child. I was from the moment I first saw her face.

Once I became a mother, something really troubled me. It became harder for me to understand my own mother—or any mom, for that matter—who doesn't feel like I do about her kid. My mom had some good points, but when I think back on the abuse I took and the neglect of my brother and me, I can't even begin to understand how a mother could do any of those things to her child. I recognized that Mom was never abused herself, but did she really not know how painful were the things she did, neglected to do, or indirectly allowed others to do to us? Worst of it all, she never quit treating us shitty until the years after her stroke. I tried through the years to justify my mom's behavior saying she was a spoiled, self-absorbed brat who never learned humility, but there's really no excuse.

It is easy to forgive someone if they *stop* the messed-up behavior that made them need forgiving in the first place. But "sorry" means nothing when the perpetrator does the same shit to you again and again and again. I see how Mom tried in her later years to become a better person and even a better mom, but it's a classic example of too little, too late. I was a good kid. I really was. Most of my troubles came from the insanity in my home. So, I ran away. Aside from the time I stole some stupid flower seeds, I can honestly say that was the extent of my being a bad kid.

All I know is I look at my daughter and my heart literally swells with emotion and adoration for her. She is half of me. To harm her, verbally or physically, would be like doing the same thing to myself.

I want to speak to the moms who neglect or mistreat their sons. I cannot begin to say how many literal hundreds of men I have known in my life that have a boatload of issues because their mother was either a slut, selfish, a narcissistic bitch, needy, co-dependent, or a physical abuser. Even worse yet is the woman who allows a strange new man into her kids' lives to dominate or abuse them. *No* dick is worth your children's soul, girls… not one. Trust me. If you do that, you will live to regret it. I was one of those kids, and I know it happens far too often. I have also fallen in love with men who came from shit like this. It's so sad, but I had to leave the relationship because the guy was simply too screwed up for me to help. You cannot fix someone, only they can. We can assist, but in the end, it is up to the individual to do the work.

Last but certainly not least, let us not leave out the really toxic, over-doting mommies who simply refuse to pull their tit out of their grown son's mouth to allow him to grow up and become an actual *man*. These are the ones who believe he is without fault or accountability no matter how heinous his actions.

There is absolutely no room for self-centeredness if you are a parent. At the same time, it is important to take time for rejuvenating yourself, your passions, and your marriage/intimate relationships. Those things are as important to keeping you a happy parent as anything else. Sadly, it is hard for many people to find the balance. But please try. It is so worth it down the road. If you don't take care of yourself, you truly cannot take care of anyone else. And if you don't, all you will be doing is adding more criminals to the system and degrading our beautiful country even further.

Dear God: kids need fathers and mothers… healthy ones.

I pray every day God allows me the time to watch her life happen. I love you, Cheyenne, with every ounce of my being. Thank you for being the best thing that happened to my life... ever.

Cheyenne

Gentle on my Mind

For several years it was just me and Chey. I dated a few guys but never got serious. I truly loved my time with her and made good money stripping, so we were ok. Mom would watch her occasionally while I worked. Still, having a little child and no help to speak of, was harder than anything I ever had to do.

When Chey was around two, I met a really sweet fella named Billy. Feeling stressed-out as a single mom, I had been sitting at my mother's house with Chey one night. I told my mom I needed a break, so I was going to run up the street to the local pub for a quick cocktail. I was sitting at the bar, which was pretty dead that night, when in walked the finest-looking man I had seen in a hell of a while. He walked past me, got a drink, and went back to shoot some pool all by himself. Suddenly, I had the strangest feeling and I got up, went to the pay phone, called my mom and said, "Hey, can you watch Cheyenne for another hour or so?"

She said, "Sure, why?"

I said, "Because I just met the man I'm going to marry."

Mom said, "No shit? What's his name?"

I said, "I don't know yet, but he's fucking beautiful. I'll tell you about it when I get back. Love ya!" I walked back to the pool room to put my quarters on the table. I smiled; he smiled; I said hello and it was on. I felt like I had known him all my life in an hour and a half.

I picked up Cheyenne from mom's, went back to pick up Billy and brought him home with me that night. *However,* he slept on the couch. In the morning, Cheyenne came running into my room saying, "Mum, Mum… Daddy!" I was not sure what she meant until she took me out to the living room and pointed to the guy on the couch. "Daddy" as it turned out, looked an awful lot like Scott from the back. He woke up and smiled at her and she ran right over to him. It was wild. He was so wonderful with her and so damn good looking it hurt.

Daddy Billy

Billy and I were together constantly and a month after we met, he asked me to marry him. I said yes but that since we were going to get hitched in a couple months how bout we wait to have actual sex? He agreed and, lucky for me, the honeymoon was NOT a disappointment. Playing house with him and Cheyenne was really wonderful…for a while.

Unfortunately, the marriage only lasted a little over a year. Billy liked his weed and—I guess—I wanted more out of life than he did.

So, in hopes of giving me what I wanted, he ended up going out to Colorado with the intention of me and Cheyenne following after. The trouble was… he was a hottie and there are not many of those in Idaho Springs, Colorado. He met some chick shortly after arriving. I don't know what I was thinking, because I wasn't really ready to be in a marriage with *anyone,* so we divorced amicably. Billy stayed in Colorado and ended up becoming quite the partier. He got married again and, sadly, got into trouble. He spent seven years in the Grey Bar Hotel and we lost touch.

To his credit Billy got out, straightened up his life immensely, and got back in touch with us. He said he wanted to be a stepdad to Cheyenne again and make up for lost time... if she would let him. She was beyond thrilled and they are inseparable to this day. I am so proud of him, and incredibly grateful for all the love he shows "our daughter." He is more of a father to her than anyone has ever been. For that I love and respect him deeply. She has brightened up so much knowing she has a dad who loves her. I love that she becomes a little girl again the moment Daddy Bill comes around or calls. It is adorable.

Daddy Bill

Prince Charming

A few years later, I remember going on a blind date. That would not seem very unusual, except at the time I lived in Pittsburgh, and the guy I went on the blind date with lived in Colorado Springs. We met on the internet back before cell phones, instant messages, and Tinder. There was this exciting new thing called the world wide web and a personals site called Yahoo. So being bored and curious, I began surfing around and that's when I saw his picture. It snatched the breath right out of me. This guy was all kinds of sexy. So, I read his page and he sounded great *until* I reached the bottom where he said, "No biker chicks, please."

Seriously? I simply had to respond to this arrogant jagoff in my best, *fuck you* fashion.

I wrote him back and my letter went something like this... "Hello, I saw your page and at first thought, *My what a handsome, classy, guy.* Then I got to the part about 'no biker chicks please' and well...here is my response: You narrow minded asshole! You have no idea what you're missing here. I may be a biker chick, but I am also educated, intelligent, real, passionate, honest, and sexy in ways your yuppie girlfriends will *never* know how to be. Your loss!"

The next day I got a reply from him, complete with an apology that said something like: "I am so sorry I offended you. You are right, I had no business assuming anything the way I did. I am sure it is in fact my loss. Please forgive me."

Well, well. Now I was feeling bad for my glaring response. After thinking on it and, of course, looking yet again at his gorgeous face, I wrote him back. "Apology accepted. My name is Suzanne."

His name was Joe, and he was Richard-Gere-handsome with a uniquely sexy voice and a slightly cocky, playful way about him that just drew me in. I could not help but like him. So, after talking and emailing for a while, he asked me to go to a Bruce Springsteen concert with him… in Las Vegas. *Las Vegas?* It had been my dream since I was a little girl to see my name in lights on the Strip. Because I felt that I could trust him after all the phone calls, and because I could NOT resist an adventure of any kind, ever, I agreed to go.

Joe being the Irish Catholic gentleman that he was, he bought my plane ticket and promised me my own room. I could hardly stand it; I was so excited.

On the flight to Vegas, I was so anxious to meet him that I couldn't help chatting with the folks around me about my adventure. They were all cool because they were on their way to Vegas too. By the time we landed, almost everyone on the flight was pretty excited for me and felt as if they were on an adventure also! I guess not many people would jump on an airplane back then to go on a blind date. It seems they found me rather fascinating.

Joe planned to meet me at the gate. This happened in the days before 9-11 so you could get through security without a boarding pass to meet your party as they exited the plane. I purposely waited so I could be the last one off, partly because I wanted to make him wait and partly because I was trying to slow my heart rate to a manageable level.

I didn't know this until later, but one of the guys I sat with on the flight approached Joe. He got off before me and saw Joe standing there, red roses in hand. He walked up to him and said, "You Joe?" Joe said yes in a puzzled tone, and the guy said, "You are gonna love this chick!" A bunch of others kept smiling at him with this *we know who you are* look as they walked past him on their way to baggage.

When I walked off the plane, my knees were knocking like a brand-new foal and my heart was ready to burst right out of my chest. Hell, I had traveled around enough to know how to handle myself should he turn out to be a douchebag, but there was nothing about him that made me think he would be. The moment I saw his him, I melted. His smile was absolutely gorgeous and so big it made his eyes all but disappear. He was even more handsome in person than in his pictures. We hugged and I melted into his arms, and we just stood there trembling and holding onto each other for a long time. I remember both of us were shaking so hard we could barely stand up. It was honestly like everything else around us just disappeared and it was just the two of us.

Joey was a very classy guy and a complete gentleman in every way. It was so different being with him than with anyone I had encountered in my life before. He came from old money and was raised with a strong faith and had a good family. One of his cousins is even a famous actor: the guy who played opposite Adam Sandler in Happy Gilmore, no less. He told me the first car he ever drove was a Rolls Royce. You would never know it, though. He was down to Earth, unselfish, and did not act entitled.

His brothers and a friend were in Vegas with him for the week, as well. Since I was up all night, I suggested he go hang out with the boys for a while so I could take a nap. He said they wanted to go to a strip club, but he wasn't going. I asked why not, and he said he didn't want to offend or upset me. At first, I didn't know how to respond to that. Then I said, "Get your ass out of here! Go hang with your brothers and go to the club! My goodness, what kind of women have you dated in the past?"

He was blown away that I was so cool. Well, I was actually a stripper at the time, so of course I was cool about him going to the strip club. I never understood why chicks get so weird about their guys going to see strippers. Men like to look at beautiful women, and as many different ones as their eyes can hold in a lifetime. it is just the way God made them, so as long as all they do is *look*, what the hell is the big problem?

Joey hugged me, smiled, and left to go hang with the boys. I slept like a princess for a couple hours. When he came back and woke me, he said the whole time he was there he wanted to come back and be with me. I knew that men are like rubber bands; let them go stretch out and they will generally snap right back to you.

That evening we went to see Bruce Springsteen at the MGM Grand. It was awesome! Joe was the perfect host and we had so much fun. I literally watched myself falling for him. The next night, we got dressed up and went out. He was dressed to the nines and looked absolutely gorgeous. I felt like Cinder-fucking-ella! It was incredible. I even remember the cologne he wore, Paul Sebastian, which became my all-time favorite. To this day, I always keep a bottle of it under my bathroom sink in case I need a man-scent-fix. I even spray it on my pillow sometimes.

We stayed at Harrah's and he took me to an amazing restaurant in Caesar's Palace called "The Palm." We had lobster, which again is not unusual, except that mine weighed three pounds and his weighed four! I had never seen one so big. The whole night was like something out of a fairytale. Sitting across the table looking at him was intoxicating. The way his mouth moved, the way his eyes stared into me, there was both a strength and an innocence in him and I wanted to have him. He was at that moment, everything I thought a man should be. At least everything I wanted a man to be.

We got back to the room, and he kissed me. I had never ever been kissed like that before. Never. He was slow, gentle and an absolute gentleman. All the way up till the moment I gave in, and then he showed me his strength and made love to me for hours. I felt like I left my body. I mean the right way, slowly and deeply, never missing a beat. The passion that flowed between us was the stuff of legends. My God, he was sexy! I wished that night could go on forever.

The next morning, we woke up and he looked in my eyes and said, "Marry me." Ah oh. I have to say if I hadn't already had Cheyenne, who was around six then, I just might have been nutty enough to do it. *But* he had to pass her "evil eye" test first. Cheyenne always had an uncanny ability to read people from the time she was a toddler, so I wanted her to meet him first. I just couldn't do something that crazy and be a good mom at the same time. I had honestly fallen for him and I hated so much to leave, but reality called.

About a month later I flew back out to the ranch in Colorado where I used to live to chill for the weekend. Joe had planned to come up and spend a couple of days with me. I was so excited to see him. I had planned an evening ride up into the hills with dinner and wine. He wasn't there for more than fifteen minutes when he got a call from his kids' maternal grandparents. I could hear the call. The grandparents basically told Joe to get on a plane, fly down to Texas and pick them up because they were being total brats and the grandparents couldn't handle them. Apparently, their bitch daughter was all they could take. He had just flown the kids down the day before, so he tried to make the grandparents a deal to keep them, but they were adamant.

He looked at me sadly, hugged me goodbye, got in his car and left for Texas. The red flag was as big as the Spanish Muleta swung in front of a bull. I knew there was no way I could marry a man who would drop me aside and jump like that for his apparently spoiled kids. To me, this should not have been so urgent.

Sadly, I later found out he had a pathetic ex-wife (a Gemini, of course) who still held him by his balls and twisted them by using their kids. I knew enough to recognize this was a battle I'd never win.

He was fun when he was away from the kids and we hung out together as much as we could. I did meet the kids once, in fact, just to be sure I wasn't wrong. I was not. They were absolutely adorable, but they had him wrapped completely around their fingers. And, since the ex-wife did too, there wasn't much room left for me. Plus, he drank a lot and had a bit of a temper when he did.

One night on one of my escape-to-Colorado weekends, we even got ourselves into a bar fight together. I was doing a show at a very cool little mountain bar called the Horse Tooth on Rt. 24 outside of Woodland Park, Colorado. (Unfortunately, it was lost in the big Hayman Fire in 2002.) Joe, little Cheyenne, and another friend of mine were there. I was done with the show and heading out to the car when some drunk asshat said something nasty about me. Well, Joe, being a crazy Irishman who was also a martial arts blackbelt, took offense and felt the need to defend my honor. So, he called the guy out.

The dude made two mistakes: one, he walked out the door first, and two, he pulled a knife on Joe. Joe did some Ninja shit and dropped the dude like a hot potato. One hit, and then he stomped on the guys' head with his Doc Martins on. Done. Cheyenne got quite a charge out of it all, especially when after that, Joey ran over and was like, "Shit! Let's go! I think I killed the guy; get in the car! Go! Go!" (He didn't kill the guy, I called and checked.)

Joe had a big McMansion in Colorado Springs, so we all spent the night there. After the kiddo went to bed, we had a few. It was nice being in that kind of environment. It taught me I am worthy of that life. Coming from a blue collar, welfare, middle class neighborhood, I was really liking all of this class.

We got together intimately a few more times. Each time it was as beautiful as the first. I never felt one tiny bit inhibited with him, nor he with me. He was open to my darkest, most erotic fantasies, and he became them as I became his. There is nothing sexier to me like a strong, virile man who is secure enough in himself to allow me to take control once in a while. Damn, I have so many outstanding visions of him, and I am so grateful for the times we had. Knowing him really changed my attitude about rich guys. I used to think they were all arrogant, snotty, dicks. Not all of them are. Some are of course, but so are some poor guys. Grandma always said, "Honey, you can love a rich guy just as easily as you can love a poor one." The rich are often just a bit more educated and more conservative with their dough, that's why they have it.

Unfortunately, there was too much clouding up his life and after a while, time pulled us apart. Still, we did still find our way to each other every couple of years if we were both single and it always felt like we just said goodbye yesterday. Still, we were just too different.

Kikel

Throughout our lives, every time some big thing happened in my life, it seemed Kikel was always there for me. When I found out I was pregnant, I was living in the cabin in the woods on Chicago Creek in Colorado with Cheyenne's sperm donor. Michael heard the fear and confusion in my voice, I guess, and jumped on a flight to Denver to come be with me for a few days. I was no fun at all, being newly pregnant to a guy who did not support my keeping and having my child and being exhausted and miserable. But Kikel just hung out with boring little me and held my hand. That meant more to me than he ever knew.

Kikel

One time he even gave me a really fancy sports car when he moved to Mexico because he couldn't take it with him!

When I married Billy, I contacted Kikel to tell him what was happening. He laughed. I couldn't get mad, tho, because I knew he would support me in anything I decided to do. Unknown to me he was on a plane the next day to Pittsburgh. The day of the wedding, Chey and I went to my mom's to get dressed. Mom said, "Hey, go up in the spare bedroom and get me that box off the bed." So up I went, and when I open the door, I saw no box, just a pile of blankets. I ran downstairs and told my mom I didn't see any box. She told me to go upstairs and look again. When I did, up jumped Kikel from beneath the covers… SURPRISE! I almost died! It was really awesome to see him.

A few years later, I got a call from Kikel again. His mom, sadly, had just died and he was looking to get away, so he said, "Let's go to

Vegas!" And we did. He flew me out, and we stayed in a suite at the Venetian Hotel. The best part was he took me on a helicopter flight over the freakin' Grand Canyon for a champagne picnic lunch! It is one of my favorite memories. But through it all, we never ever had sex. Not once. I did, in fact, try to jump him while we were in Vegas, because well, it's Vegas and I believed he had fantasized about it for like twenty years. But when it came down to it, we just didn't do anything but cuddle. I just love him.

Corvette Guy

Shortly before I met Scott (the sperm donor) I dated this tall, cute, redhead boy who had a kick-ass Corvette. I remember his dad just loved me, but his mom hated me because I was a stripper that rode a Harley. That image just didn't fit in so well with their "Better Homes and Gardens" set. I am sure the image of me pulling up out front of their house, with V-Twin engine thumping away, wearing my cut-off Daisy Dukes, cowboy boots and a deerskin halter just made her and all the Stepford Wives a bit cagey.

One time Corvette guy and I went to Ocean City. I'd heard about a killer biker bar called the Bearded Clam and wanted to go check it out. We followed the music and turned the corner to see a hundred bikes lined up on both sides of the street.

I yelled, "Hell, yea! This is awesome!"

He said, "Oh man, wait a minute, I'm not sure we should go in there."

I said, "What? There's nothing to be afraid of. Come on!" and grabbed his hand.

Just as we got to the front of the bar, the door swung open, and a dude flew out and landed face first on the street!

My date froze in his tracks and said, "I really don't want to go in there."

I replied, "What the hell are you worried about? Don't be a pussy, at least you know they have a GREAT bouncer."

After talking him down off the proverbial ledge, we went in. He had a blast! In fact, he kept the pool table for about two hours. That yuppie sure could slide a cue!

Boot

Another time, I was just doing the single mom thing and trying to find my way back to Colorado. I worked hard to make the transition from stripping to comedy, but at the time I was doing both. One night I was working at a topless club called the Evergreen Hotel in North Pittsburgh, when I met Boot. The Evergreen was a really cool place, very "Cheers" like—everyone knew everyone else. Boot was adorable and had the whitest teeth and biggest, most genuine smile ever. He shyly smiled at me across the bar, and my *dick-dar* picked it up in an instant, and… well, here we go again.

When I first walked up to him and said hello, Boot looked at me and said, "You don't know who I am, do you?" I told him he had a smile to die for and was cute as hell, but no, I don't recollect ever meeting him before. He said, "We really haven't met, but your daughter's father, Scott, used to be married to my sister."

OH SHIT! He was *Denise's* brother—the same Denise who Scott left to run off to Colorado with *me*. What the hell do you say to that one? We talked for a bit and, in the end, none of all that seemed to matter. We were attracted to each other big time. So, I really could not help but fall for him.

He was such a gentle soul and had such warmth about him, plus he happily became a stepdaddy to little Cheyenne. The next thing I knew, we were moving into his house. life was good. Ironically, we were moving into the family's house; the same house Cheyenne's donor, Scott, and Boot's sister Denise had lived in when they were first married back when I met him. It was also the house I caught him at after we moved back from Colorado when I was pregnant! You can't make this shit up.

So, Chey and I had been living there with Boot for about a month before any of his family realized just who the hell I was. They found out one sunny day when Cheyenne was playing out front in the yard. One of Boot's brothers pulled up and said, "Well, hi! What's your name?"

She replied, "I'm Cheyenne."

When the brother asked who she was with, Cheyenne replied, "My mommy and daddy. This is my house."

Boot's brother replied, "*Oh, it is?* Well, what's your mommy's name?" She told him that Sue's her mommy and Boot is her daddy. I later found out it didn't take long for him to put Cheyenne and Suzanne together and figure out that we were the *same* Suzanne and Cheyenne that his ex-brother-in-law, Scott, had been a part of.

I can only imagine the look on Boot's brother face when he put two and two together. To their credit—in spite of my part in Scott wrecking their family—the brothers accepted me and Cheyenne as though we were their family and became Chey's uncles. Everyone was great to us, all except the aunt. She thought I was Satan's mistress, I am sure. I think she always blamed me for splitting up her niece and Scott, though he made his own choices like we all do. To her credit, she kept it to herself, and was civil to me and kind to Cheyenne.

The house sat on the top of a hill in the very beautiful, country-like setting of Reserve Township, just north of Pittsburgh only about three miles out of the city. There were horses and farms all around us, and everyone was old-time family who knew everyone else. It was the kind of place where you could smell bread baking in one house and meatloaf roasting in another. Boot had built a lovely little playhouse for Cheyenne in the big-ass yard that matched the house. It was seriously almost perfect for a while. There was a big cemetery across the road from us where me and Cheyenne and our dogs spent many a spring and summer day hiking through the woods. The house was decorated for every holiday, and we had all the kids' parties there. It was really beautiful.

Trouble was, though he paid for most of the house stuff, Boot worked a lot, drank after work a lot, and fell asleep a lot. I started to feel like just a fixture, a mom, and a maid rather than a woman. Sadly, it became life-sucking and boring to the point where I had to leave, or I knew I would drink myself to death.

Then, one night I got a call from the owner of the very bar I first met Boot in telling me I needed to come down and see something. When I got there, he showed me a security tape of Boot sucking face with one of the bartenders whom I thought was my good friend. I went nuts. On one hand, I saw my out. On the other, I saw Cheyenne's happiness and all the safety and comfort of her and our life going down the toilet. I snapped. I got in my truck and went looking for that bitch. I found out where she was working at another place and tried kicking in the door to get a piece of her. She hid inside like the sneaky slut that she was, begging me not to kill her! Finally, my bros calmed me down, and I went home and started packing. The life I had there was done.

When it comes to long-term relationships, I'll admit I just never have been able to hang for the long haul. And I know why. When the unhappy times are more frequent than the happy ones, I'm *out*. Boot was a wonderful stepdad and very sweet to me, while it lasted. I spent four great years with him, and Cheyenne loved him and our life there very much. It was safe, secure, and comfortable. It was as close to "Better Homes and Gardens" as I ever came at the time.

Home on the Range

After leaving Boot, I saved up twelve hundred bucks, rented a 5x8 U-Haul trailer, and tried to explain as much as I could to my seven-year-old daughter. I called the ranch to let them know I was coming *home*. The day I was to leave, my brother showed up with his daughter, my niece Erica, who was also seven years old. He asked me to take her, too. My brother had been battling a drug problem back then, and I had my niece with us pretty often. I happily took her. We loaded her clothes into the trailer and in five minutes all of our lives changed.

I will never forget how I felt leaving. I remember crying, Erica was crying, and Cheyenne was crying because she couldn't take her other dog (Boot's dog) that she grew to love so very much. Later on, at the ranch, she would cry for a while because she knew her dad was gone, too. Fortunately, she adjusted quickly and was plenty distracted by the horses and all the wide-open spaces and fun she and Erica were having on the ranch. I tried calling Boot and keeping them in touch. Since she wasn't his blood—as often happens—he sadly didn't feel like making the effort to even keep in touch by phone. At the time, he was the only real father she knew growing up, mostly because he was there during the formative years from three to seven.

Some say I can't blame Boot because I left, but I think that we all owe children something when we take on the responsibility of becoming a child's stepparent. Yes, it is not easy to stay in touch after the spilt. There is often anger, resentments, and sadness, but our kids have those feelings too. So, I became both mom and dad again. Years later I asked my daughter how she thought I did. She gave me the sweetest look and said, "Mom, I honestly never missed having a dad. You were the best of everything."

Back at the Ranch

What an amazing feeling for me to be back on the ranch again! In the seven years I was away from it and my mountains, it was like my spirit had been asleep. That song *I left my heart in San Francisco* makes perfect sense to me now. I left MY heart in Colorado, and now I returned home to retrieve it.

My days were long and hard, but I loved every minute of it. I woke up at 5 a.m., fed the kids, drove the girls down the two-and-a-half mile dirt road to school, then back to work. I would clean the stables, feed, and care for the horses. Taking trail rides all day long did not suck. It was a hell of a workout, and my soul was at peace. I understood I was doing something that so many people dream about, but never get the chance to experience. On the rides, I also got to meet many different people from around the country and the world. It was never boring.

Around 2:30 p.m. I'd go back to get the kids after school, cook dinner, play mom, read stories, and tuck them in. Many nights, I would drive the twenty-five miles into Denver to case potential comedy gigs and hand out my business cards to whomever would take one. I had to keep going after the dream.

When the kids and I lived on the Van Eden Ranch, we stayed in a large, hundred-year-old, haunted log cabin made from rough-hewn logs which had been on the property since the turn of the century. The ranch sat at about 9,500 ft. above sea level, surrounded by one million pines. Though it had been improved upon over the years with electricity and plumbing, it remained sketchy, at best. The windows were likely the originals; the glass was wavy-looking and not insulated—even a little bit. The cabin had two big rooms, two small rooms, a kitchen and a "bathroom" on the first floor, and three small bedrooms upstairs. The fireplace in the main room was gigantic, but since there was no damper in the flue, the logs burned up fast. It was a hell of a job to keep the place warm. Back in the day before the kitchen was added, whomever lived there cooked in the fireplace just like you see in the old western movies.

Erica and Cheyenne shortly after arriving in Colorado

In the other room where I had my private apartment space with the girls, we had an old cast iron wood stove. The stove made things either too hot, or we would be freezing when it went out at four in the morning. I had to wake up and start the fire again nightly so the kids wouldn't die of hyperthermia in their sleep. I truly felt what it must have been like to settle the Rocky Mountains back in the turn of the century. As challenging as it was, I loved it all.

The lodge was also home to a at least one spirit, though I think more. One night I was sitting on the couch in front of the fireplace when I heard the tea kettle go off in the kitchen. I got up thinking, *That's odd, I didn't remember putting the kettle on.* I went into the kitchen to find the stove off and the kettle cold. Creepy. Another time I was sitting on the couch by the fire alone, and I heard someone coming down the old wooden steps behind me. I turned to see who the hell it was, and all I saw was the white shadowy silhouette of an Indian Chief. This caused me to freeze in my steps! I stared at it for a second, then it faded away. Oddly, it didn't scare me, just caught me off guard.

Dakota

After a time, chatting with the spirits got to be a bit one-sided and I was getting damn lonely up there all by myself. All work and no sex made Bag a miserable hag! So, one night I decided to go online to the old Yahoo personals and see if any mountain men had internet. The bunkhouse had a phone line that ran down from the main lodge, so I had dial-up. I fired up the idiot box, got on Yahoo, and there he was... I saw Dakota's picture on the first page, and he took my breath away. Instantly, I felt like this was gonna be something huge.

We wrote for a while and talked on the phone. Soon we were agreeing to meet in a little town called Bergen Park that was up in the mountains west of Denver. The place was beautiful; a park loaded with tall pine trees and a

Dakota

couple of log picnic buildings engulfed the town. Elk wandered freely all over the place. It was unreal for a gal from Pittsburgh, I can assure you.

I got out of my truck and started walking into the woods when I spotted *him*. He was a breathtaking Scorpio, who looked almost exactly like Kris Kristofferson in his younger days. The attraction was instant, mutual, and primal. I mean… from the moment we got near each other, there was a hunger and an ache between us that was tangible. We sat on a picnic bench a while, then went across the street and had lunch at a little mountain bar called The Whipple Tree. I sat there listening to his deep, sexy voice and looking at his handsome face. He had dark piercing eyes, and a gentle way of being. I fell for him instantly.

Dakota started coming up to the ranch almost daily and learned to love it as much as I did. Even though he was a city boy at heart, his mountain man shined through. Being that I was a city girl whose heart was captivated by the old west, we clicked… and fast. Kota dressed like he walked out of the Old West, complete with cowboy hat, boots, and jeans that showed just how fine he really was. At first glance, you'd have thought he was hiding his pet squirrel in there. Aside from being fine as hell, he was basically just a down to earth guy.

One sunny weekend when we first started dating, we jumped in his big pickup truck and went four-wheeling up near the town of Buena Vista, CO. (Patricia, the owner of the ranch, and some of the workers always looked after Cheyenne and Erica on the weekends when I needed sitters.) Dakota didn't tell me exactly where we were going, he just said, "I want to show you something awesome." I was thrilled to be with his fine cowboy-looking ass in his big shiny new GMC going *anywhere* into the woods. As we turned off the main road onto the dirt backroad, I had the strangest, strongest feeling come over me. I felt like I had been there before. There was no way I could have, however, because I had never been to this part of Colorado in my life. Still, the feeling was intense, and much more than your everyday déjà vu. As we headed further away from civilization and back into the mountains, everything started to look eerily familiar. So much so, that I finally said something. "Dakota, I swear to God, I have been here before!"

He said, "Huh? That is weird. You said you have never been up this way."

I said nothing more until we came up over a hill into a meadow, and I literally had chills run down my spine. "Stop the truck!" I yelled. I felt flushed and turned white as a ghost. He asked if I was ok and I said, "I swear to God, if there is a big-ass boulder with a little tree growing out of it around that bend, I have been here before." We rounded the bend and… son of a bitch… if there wasn't a big-ass boulder with a tree growing out of it! We both just sat there for a moment.

We left that site and went to an old ghost town called Tin Cup. In that moment I started having flashes of what I swear was my other life. I saw myself as a saloon girl in the old town. I hadn't seen the buildings yet, but when we pulled up, I knew exactly which building was which and where. They were very run down by this time, but still, I knew. I felt almost like I had come home. There was no way to really distinguish one from the other, until I saw an old photo of it in its heyday. That is when I knew I was right. I believe with all my heart I lived there back in the day. I swear it.

After ranting about my former life as a hooker in Tin Cup, I'm surprised Dakota didn't go running for the hills. But I'm glad he didn't. Dating a hot man while working a ranch is pretty magical. It was just me and him, and the critters all about. No distractions and plenty of ways for a man to be a man. Dakota was surely that. He was always there and ready to help me with everything from the horses to the firewood to fixing my truck. Watching him throwing hay around, all shirtless and sexy in that freaking cowboy hat, tight jeans and boots was more than I could bear.

Finally, one night he pitched a tent down under the pine trees by the stream, took me there, lay me down on a blanket, and made love to me by the fire. *My God.* He did everything perfectly. It was like I was living in some beautiful Zane Gray western romance novel. He was intense and passionate like no other. Even the darker side of the erotic just came so perfectly easy between us. There were no inhibitions at all, in any way, and each time we were together we discovered more about the secret sides of ourselves and each other. It was mind-blowing every single time we touched.

We both fell madly, passionately in love, and I swore I would never leave him. I truly thought we would be together forever. Things were literally like a perfect, romantic, erotic dream until about three months in and then… Ah oh.

In the fall, I entered a comedy competition at a comedy club in Denver, which was the only gig in town back then. I had come 1,400 miles west to chase my dream after all, so I had to start somewhere. I had been doing comedy back East for years, so I was ready. Over those first months, I had made a ton of friends in the little mountain town of Idaho Springs where I lived, and they encouraged me in my comedy career. I was on a roll! It all seemed too perfect, and I don't think I had ever been happier in my entire life than I was at that time.

I made it through the first two rounds of the competition. All of my new friends were completely stoked and stayed right along with me; they supported me through the three months of competitions it took to reach the finals. This was a huge step for me on the way to my big dream and I was, of course, inviting everyone I knew to join me in my journey. In fact, one of my wild mountain friends, "Al My Ho", went so far as to rent me a beautiful full-size bus for the final competition! I will never forget the feeling of rolling down that mountain feeling like I had finally started to make it. I arrived in Denver in style with a busload of crazy Rocky Mountain hillbillies and a lot of booze. I did not drink a drop of it, though, because I wanted to win the thing. When we got to town there was a line around the corner and down the street. I felt like I was going to a Hollywood premiere.

In the end, I won second place. My friends and I were surprised by this, though, since the crowd absolutely applauded hardest for me. I later found out it was fixed, because the guy that won was blowing the little gay manager. I mean… the little dickhead was literally reading his act off a piece of paper. Even the first year of my doing comedy, I never did that. I always felt that footnotes are for pussies! (Unless you're Rodney Dangerfield, who always had footnotes onstage under his foot, or so I hear.)

Regardless, it was an awesome moment for me. That is until Dakota wrecked it with a big fat helping of jealous insecurity. My being heavily cock-blind at the time prevented me from seeing any of said insecurities. But, that night of the comedy finals, they reared their ugly head. He had come with me to film it and support me, which he did well until he found out one of my exes, Vegas Joe, was coming up from Colorado Springs to see the big event too. The fact that my ex happened to be rich, handsome, and still my friend probably added to Dakota's insecurity, but that was his problem and not mine.

I learned a long time ago that when a man tries suggesting that I should not keep my male friends, or that I should *behave* in some way, I need to hold my ground. Too many men in my past manipulated or abused me for me to stand by idly and allow it to happen. My response is always, "Are you my dad?" They of course say no. I then say, "Well then don't act like my fucking dad, because I don't fuck my dad! If you are going to act like I'm a child, the sex is done right here, right now. You got that?" That usually gets the point across. Besides, I knew Vegas Joe way before I ever met Dakota.

So, on the biggest night of my life at the time aside from giving birth to my spawn, he snapped and started acting like an ass. The irony is, Joe never even got in to see me or the show because it was a sell out! So, all of his nasty attitude was for nothing. On such a night as this, or any other night, I was not up for any bullshit, so I simply got out of his truck, said a loud "fuck you" and began hitch-hiking back up the mountain. I made it back to the ranch, and he came after me apolo-gizing profusely.

I forgave that outburst and ended up dating him for two more years. Still, I would notice more and more of this insecurity crap along the way, and it really began to chap my ass. I loved Dakota and our little love affair, but I can't fix someone's issues. Only they can.

I was still trying to get my big break at the Comedy Club. Even though I had won in the competition, they still wanted me to do open mic nights. I later found out that they do this to all comics no matter how talented they are because they don't *want* them to grow out of the club and leave. Mostly they don't want to *pay* anyone they don't have to. When I asked the little manager, Timmy, about getting a spot opening for some national act and he replied, "You haven't paid your dues here yet." That, needless to say, pissed me way off. My thought was, *Who in the* hell *are you to tell me what kind of dues I have paid, Shrimp? You don't know me!*

So…the next time I went in for open mic night, I did *not* do Bag Lady. Instead, I dressed like a hot schoolteacher in high heels, skirt, blouse, and hair up neatly. I prepped the sound guy with my music and when I hit the stage, I simply said, "Good evening all. Many of you may know me as the Bag Lady, but tonight I am going to do something special for you all. I'm sure you'll enjoy it." Then, I laid down on the stage. When the song *Tequila* started, I flipped my legs over my head, the skirt flopped up and revealed my thong covered ass, and up comes Tequila George. George is a cool little hairy, sunglass wearing, puppet, that appears to be munching on my muffin to the music. All the while I'm pulling out things like a fish, a crab, baby powder, a feather duster, a fly swatter from "there." I closed the show by acting like he is "shaving" my parts with a razor!

The crowd went out of their freakin' minds! They were utterly hysterical so much so that the room was literally shaking. People were standing in their seats and the laughter was so intense that all the comics came out from the greenroom to try and see what the hell was going on. When I looked over, they were peeking out of the curtain and their heads all lined up one on top of the other like The Three Stooges. It was a howl. However, while the entire audience was laughing hysterically, it seems the shrimp lost his mind over this. He ran through the roaring crowd to the sound booth. Suddenly, the room went black. Everyone started booing the club and yelling, "What the fuck?" I knew enough about comedy clubs to know that a blacked-out room—when it's not caused by the power grid melting down—is a comic death sentence. So, I figured I would go out swingin'.

When the lights came back on, I stood up, grabbed George, and laughingly said, "Thank you all so much. Apparently, I upset the delicacies of the management, so you won't see me here again, but you *will see me*! My website is BAG LADY SUE dot com. Please look me up. Thank you so much and stay cool!"

I walked off the stage and went to get my shit from the greenroom. Here comes the shrimp cackling like a little hen. He started yelling at me, "You can't do that kind of stuff here! This is not a strip club." Well, *that* did it. I was going out in a blaze of glory. So, in front of all the comics and folks backstage, I responded:

> *Listen here you little fudge-packing prick, that was the funniest thing this shit hole has ever seen. If Jim Carey can come out on stage at a comedy club in Toronto fully naked with a tube sock on his dick on national television, I can pull a puppet out of my ass! So, you can take your wannabe comedy club and go fuck yourself! When I make my first million, you'll know because you will find a big steamy pile of horse shit outside your office door with my business card in it! Fuck you!"*

Sadly, he had quit by the time I cracked my first million.

I left the club and walked down the street to the local Martini bar to slug a few to calm my nerves. As I pondered the fact that I had just told the *only* comedy gig in town to fuck off, that few turned into six or seven. I didn't feel a thing at this point. When I left, I walked in a bit of a zigzag pattern back up to my truck, which meant I had to pass the comedy club. I got to it just as the doors opened and all the people from the show were leaving. I was surrounded by everyone and all of them kept saying, "Man fuck that place! You got robbed! We got robbed! That was hysterical! That was the funniest shit we have ever seen! Where are you gonna be next?" etc., etc., etc.

Fortunately, back then and still today, I never leave the house without always having a huge pile of business cards on me. So, I started handing them out to everyone. Then I got in my truck, covered one eye, and drove my drunk, angry ass all the way back to Idaho Springs.

The next morning, very early, my phone rang. It was my then-friend Rooster. I answered, basically still asleep. The conversation went just like this:

Me: (After clearing my throat) "Hello."

Rooster: (Very calmly) "Bag Lady Sue, please tell me you did not call Tim O' Shrimp a little fudge-packing prick and threaten to dump horse shit on his doorstep."

Me: (After snapping awake and levitating off my bed like the chick in the Exorcist) "FUCK THAT SHRIMP SON OF A BITCH!! WHERE IN GOD'S GREEN FUCK DOES HE GET OFF? THAT PLACE WENT WILD, ROO! COMPLETELY GODDAMN WILD! FUCK HIM, FUCK THAT CLUB AND FUCK…

Rooster: (cuts me off) "BAGS, STOP! Just stop, calm down a minute and hear me out. I want you to headline my club downtown. I am going to advertise the *fuck* out of you all over the city! Picture it… 'BAG LADY SUE, BANNED IN DENVER!' This town will go nuts, and so will the fuckers at the Comedy Club. Trust me on this and calm down."

Me: (softly) "Will you really? Well, ok."

And, just as he promised, Rooster began the mad campaign from print ads and fliers to literal gigantic screen ads in all the local movie theaters with my picture, and something like 'Come See Adult Comic Genius, BAG LADY SUE, BANNED IN DENVER!' everywhere. I even have a banner the Coors beer rep printed incorrectly that says, BAG LADY SUE *BAND*, in Denver. Hysterical.

Thus, began the meteoric rise to fame in Denver, which turned into… well, you know. That time still resonates inside of me to this day. When my friendship with Rooster ended, I was deeply saddened. All I will say is, people can change dramatically over time. Not always for the better. In the entertainment biz, there are a boatload of traitorous hacks who want to live off of the hard work of others.

Back at the ranch… even though I sensed that Dakota's time was coming to an end shortly (as my relationships rarely lasted more than two years), Dakota continued to come to the ranch as much as he could. He took such good care of me and the girls. He often went out of his way twenty-five miles to bring us McDonald's Steak bagels and hash browns in the morning before heading to his work. He had his own company putting in irrigation systems, so he scheduled us in almost daily. That was awesome because cooking in the old kitchen was rough. He helped me with everything he could and looked so damn good doing it. It was like living back in Little House on the Prairie.

Cheyenne and Erica loved Dakota and his son Rusty. The ranch was full of awesome, colorful people and the girls always felt so safe. And let's not forget the spirits… the kids knew they were around too.

One night, Dakota and I ran out to tend a horse. The kids were sleeping in the lodge where we had the fire going in the wood stove. We both had forgotten we left some wet wood on top of it to dry out. We were outside for about twenty minutes, when I suddenly got a strange feeling almost like I subconsciously *heard* someone tell me to go back in the cabin. By the grace of God, I listened. When I got inside the entire room was filled with thick smoke and the girls were sleeping in that room in their bed! Dakota and I grabbed them and carried them outside to get fresh air. I woke them up and said "breathe, girls… breathe!" They started coughing and were ok. Had I not heard the voice, they would likely have died from smoke inhalation. I know God was always protecting me and Cheyenne, even before I realized it.

We had days when there weren't any trail riders, so just like Scott and I had done years earlier, Kota and I would jump on the horses and head into the mountains. There was a big open meadow up behind the ranch and there was almost never anyone there. We would park the horses under a tree and lie down on a blanket and make love in the sun. It was just as I imagine it was back in the days of the old west…wild, free, beautiful, and natural. Best of all, he was the most perfect lover I ever had, and we were truly in love with each other. He made me feel sexier than I ever had before. He loved photographing me in and out of clothes, and he always told me I was beautiful with words and actions. Hell, I still have beautiful nude pictures of my thirty-eight-year-old self on the back of a horse I had taken on one of those mountain rides.

I was running the horse part of the business with this amazing gal named Veronica, who is still my friend to this day. Vern was a sexy, raven-haired, hippie chick who could ride a horse better than me. She had a playful, earthy, and gentle soul. She would constantly go braless to flaunt her fine set of tits. Nope, sorry guys, I never touched them but we did go riding bareback and bare-breasted— together—once or twice and, well, they are quite impressive.

Vern and I took riders out on the trail, cared for the horses, entertained the guests, or dudes, and helped run the B&B. Working a ranch comes with a constant list of things to do. Including drinking. A lot.

It is hard for most people to imagine what living that way is like. I often heard people ask, "How can you live way up there with no TV and be so far away from a store or a bar?" I suppose if I had to explain, they never would have understood. It is amazing what one can live without. I used to think I needed so much stuff to make me happy or complete. At the ranch, I learned what really mattered in life: health, hard work, good food, good friends, a good horse, and quality time with your kids. I miss living like that every day.

Although I loved my time at the ranch and wish it could have lasted forever… I knew it couldn't. I eventually left the ranch because far too much drama was being spewed among the folks that owned it. James, the son of the owner, was a sweet kid for the most part but learned very early that Mommy would give in and give him his way if he threw a temper tantrum. So, he used that ploy daily. Over the years James became a real asshole. He treated his mother like shit. He destroyed everything he touched at the place. He would start one hundred different projects, but never finished any. He acted like a complete whacko half the time. I once saw him jump on his mother's SUV like a gorilla and literally rip the wiper blade arms off the damn truck because she wouldn't give him his way. He drove a rented backhoe off the road into a creek in another fit of anger. The last straw for me was when James threw a knife and it stuck a horse in the backside. *That* was it; I was done! Time for me to go or… I feared I was gonna shoot the son of a bitch.

It saddened me to watch someone who had it all throw it away due to complete stupidity and a sense of entitlement. Worst of all, he terrified Patricia, his mom. She created a monster, and that monster took her prisoner. It reminded me of Frankenstein. The place went from a literal paradise to a complete abandoned dump over less than fifteen years. It broke my heart to go back each time and see how much more he had destroyed everything. Worst of all, the horses suffered. I found it funny that both of them were overweight, but they called me asking to supply hay for the horses.

Please… spank your kids' asses, folks. *Please.*

Honestly, the best memories of my life happened at Van Eden Ranch. From the days with Cheyenne's donor, to the last time I went up and camped alone there after it was abandoned, I truly found myself at that place. I hoped I would be able to buy the Ranch before they finally lost it but, unfortunately, I lack financial management skills at the time and was having too much fun to settle down.

Drunk on You

After leaving Van Eden Ranch, the girls and I stayed in Colorado but moved down to a little mobile home in downtown Idaho Springs near the Edgar Mine. It was a dump, but there was no drama. The trailer backed up to a hillside, and all that was behind me was rocky cliffs and mountains. I used to throw meat scraps out to the wild things in the winter, and eventually there was a coyote and a fox who came to my bedroom window and barked for a handout almost every morning at 5 a.m. I also had a mountain lion who slept on the roof.

Feeding time at the zoo was cool for a while… until I let my old Sheltie dog, Lumpy, out one evening and when I called her, she didn't come back. I was hysterical. She had been with me for seventeen years. So, I went out looking for her. When I saw the big cat's back-half as it ran around the wall in my back yard, I thought for sure Lumpy was a goner. As I walked down the street still hoping to find her, there she was… my poor, little, senile doggie was stuck in the neighbors' fenced-in yard. Whew.

Lumpy lived another eight months. One day she just looked at me and I swear she said, *I want to go now*. I made arrangements to put her down. Afterwards, I carried her up to the ranch meadow and buried her there. It was like losing a child.

The Beginning of the End

Living in the little town of Idaho Springs was quite nice. The only trouble was I still had to commute to Denver most times to set up shows, do the shows, and make connections with people in the business. The kids were too young to leave alone in the trailer, so I had to find sitters. Luckily, the mountain people are the salt of the earth and were always willing to help me. I was blessed to never have anyone try to mess with my daughter and niece. It's a good thing because I would have made them disappear. Apparently, that's pretty easy to do in the Rocky Mountains. I was surprised to see how many folks disappeared around here and have never been found.

Since I still hadn't made it big in comedy, I took a job working at a bar in town called the West Winds. I loved it. The place was like something right out of the old west. The building had been there since the 1800s and the floors and back bar were original. Many of the old ornately carved back bars with the big mirrors were brought out here from the East Coast by mule trains.

Once I started tending bar, things with Dakota got worse. During happy hour I always had people three deep at my bar, and everyone was having a blast. He seemed to be suspect of me and always checked up on me… in his own way. At first, I didn't much notice. But then he got me a flip phone and kept calling me every damn hour to see what I was doing and with whom.

I remember one time hanging out at the West Winds having some drinks, when he kept calling. The first time when I answered he asked, "Where ya at?"

I said, "Hanging at the Winds."

He asked, "Whatcha doin'?"

I said, "I'm drinkin."

He asked, "With who?"

I said, "My friends. I'll see ya if you come up later, ok?" He said Ok. End of conversation.

Ten minutes later, the phone rang again. It was him. He asked the same shit; I answered the same shit. Finally, the third time he called and asked who I was with and in front of all the girls at the table. I yelled, "I'm with your fucking replacement if you call me one more time!" and threw the phone out the open front door into the street! My friends lost it. We laughed our asses off.

Another interesting thing happened during this time. I met a man when I worked at the West Winds bar, who is still one of the best friends of my life. I was serving the locals cocktails one afternoon when a tough, sexy looking, old-school biker came in and sat at the bar. When I came over to ask him what he wanted, he had the strangest look on his face, and he just stared at me for a minute.

I said, "Is something wrong?"

Roy

He said nothing but threw what looked like an older picture of me on the bar. I thought who the hell is this guy and where did he get a picture of me? Turns out it wasn't me; it was picture of his ex-wife who could have been my identical twin! The man's name was Roy, and he had the thickest Long Island, NY accent on the planet. He was also a navy seal and serious badass. We became best friends from the first minute, though in another time we would have been awesome as more. He met a chick not long after this. He moved to town to live with her and stayed for many years.

But I was still with Dakota. I really loved him. He had a great family and a sister that became like my own. His one sister Wenda is still my buddy and looks just as lovely as she did the day I met her. I swear the bitch doesn't age. His mom, rest her beautiful soul, was one of the coolest ladies I ever met. I truly loved his family and was sad to have to end it, but his jealousy got to be too much. I was out there busting my ass to make it in comedy, so I had to be out and about mingling with folks—many of them men in the bars— and Dakota just didn't like it.

Three incidents happened around that time that finally did us in. First off, my mom came all the way across the country from Pittsburgh to surprise me for Christmas. I worked that night and was behind the bar having a ball. The place was packed, and I was running my ass off. I looked up from behind the bar and saw a woman that looked just like my mom. So, I thought, *wow… that lady looks just like my mom.* Then I realized, holy crap it *is* my mom! What a great surprise! I was missing her and Pittsburgh pretty badly since leaving that summer. I was glad she was there.

Rusty - Cheyenne - Sue - Dakota - Josh - Erica

I had told her about Dakota and how great he was, so of course he had to start drinking and ended up making an ass of himself. It was the holidays, so everyone was hugging and smooching each other and just having fun until my Indian friend, Benny, who was pretty buzzed, came up to kiss me for Christmas and tried slipping me the tongue. YUK! Rather than get on Benny, Dakota flipped out and got in *my* face. Not Benny's, *mine*! The trouble was, he made the mistake of jumping at me in front of Momma Bear, and she wasn't hearing that shit. She grabbed a bar stool and proceeded to try and hit him with it.

The place went wild! Some dudes broke it up and tossed Dakota out of the bar. Of course, the cops came and took Dakota to the tank to dry out. After another drink or three, Mom and I went to leave, and the cops grabbed her in the parking lot and nailed her for a damn DUI! She never even got in the car all the way. In the end she beat it, but she did still spend her first night in Colorado in jail. I ran around trying to raise her $1,500 bail, which I did in a matter of minutes. Thank you, my beautiful Idaho Springs mountain friends.

The second incident happened at Dakota's yuppie sister's wedding reception in his parent's back yard. I was hanging out with Cheyenne, Dakota, and his eleven-year-old at the time son, Rusty. We were dancing and having fun. Ok, we were kinda dirty dancing but something typical for any normal, fun, booze-available wedding. The yuppie sister decides we were behaving (I love this word) "inappropriately." When she says something to Dakota to that affect, he flips out! The next thing I know, he's leaving the party pissed and drunk.

Dakota grabbed Rusty, who was also the equivalent of *my son*, and went to get in his truck to leave. I'm watching this and think, *Oh, hell no, you don't! You're not driving my boy anywhere drunk!* So, I leaped like cat woman through the passenger side widow and grabbed the keys out of his ignition. Dakota now turned and ran after me as I walked down the street to throw his keys in the back of my SUV.

He is yelling, "Give me my keys!" I turn around to see the look of blind anger in his eyes, then I look down at my daughter—who was around nine at the time—standing beside me with a look of pure terror in her eyes. Being the protective mother wolverine, I calmly tell her, "Watch out, Honey." I move her aside, draw back, and with all I had in me, punched him right in the jaw! He literally went flying through the air into his mother's yard and hit the ground. I could hear the theme from *Rocky* playing in my head. He got up to try and come at me again, but his friends grabbed him and took him away, saving him from a second hit, which I assure you would have been done with my foot and been far more damaging.

Things between Dakota and me got more strained with his drinking and his jealousy. Eventually, I had enough. The last skirmish—and the one which put the nail in the coffin—happened one night when he parked his truck behind my house, snuck into my house, and hid in my bedroom. We weren't living together, and I almost shot him. It seemed he thought I was out with some other dude, which I was not, and decided to hide his truck out back of my house and let himself in. I came home, saw someone moving in my bedroom and went for the gun. He is really lucky I wasn't drunk!

Even though it almost killed me, I ended our relationship once and for all. I was sad really. If I ever wanted to realize my dreams, I knew I had to get out. In the end, I had to make a choice. I chose me and Cheyenne.

Dakota loved our time at the ranch, and he still called me now and then over the years. He always had a buzz on and told me so. I missed him for the longest time even though we couldn't stay together. He possessed a level of passion that very few are capable of, and with that amount of sexual passion comes passion in all things, including the negative. I do miss those days and him so much. He was probably the sexiest, most romantic man I ever knew. He always used to send me country songs over the voicemail that reminded him of us. I remember him every time I hear them still. This is true fairytale shit. I am so glad I had my time with someone like him, but it also raised my standards immensely.

I have often heard people say that you can't have it all. You can: but just not all at the same time! You have to pick what's really important to you. Sometimes this requires tough choices.

If the drinking doesn't kill me...

After I left the relationship with Dakota, I started drinking a lot more. I mean a lot. I was out being single and sociable and, well, I was having fun. Any inhibitions that I still possessed went out the window—not that I had many to begin with—when I was partying. I also found that my comic mind was quicker with a couple drinks down the hatch. After a while, though, it started to get out of hand. I started to *need* it to get onstage. I didn't used to in the beginning. During this time, I would try to stop at two or three and found that I just could not.

Worst of all, I started hanging out at the local pub in the afternoons while Cheyenne was at school. This wasn't so bad until I began staying there after she was home from school rather than being there waiting for her as I should have been.

I remember her calling me when she got home and only the dogs were there. She would say, "Where are you? When are you coming home?"

I would say, "I am up the street hanging with some friends, I'll be right there." Twenty minutes later when she would call again, I'd say, "I am really on my way," but I was still at the bar, having *one more drink*. Then she would call again, and I would make yet another excuse to stay for one more. To my credit if I deserve any, I usually did go after she called the second time, but either way, it was wrong. She deserved better, and I was being a selfish asshole. Cheyenne was only ten at the time, too, which I don't think is old enough to be alone even with good neighbors nearby.

Finally, one night I had a few more Bull Meisters than I could handle. I was wrecked! I remember sitting in my recliner and my heart went flippy—I thought I was having a heart attack. Fearing for my daughter's safety, I called an ambulance. They gave me oxygen to calm me down. Fortunately, I didn't need to go to the hospital, but it was enough to let me know that I needed help. I had to quit, or I knew I was going to die.

The sun came up, and I went to an AA meeting.

I remember sitting there in that room reading the twelve steps on the wall. Step 1 states, "We admitted we are powerless over alcohol and that our lives have become unmanageable." I was thinking. … *well, the first one is me for sure*! I was still drunk and feeling hopeless and ashamed of myself. I remember the people there were so awesome and kind; I felt they knew exactly what I was going through. I left there feeling better and vowed to keep going back to the meetings, and I did.

More importantly, I made some of the most authentic friends I have ever had. I noticed most of these sober friends actually cared about me just because I was me, not because of who I was or what I did. At that point in time my career as a comedian was taking off, and "Bag Lady Sue" was well known around town. I know that I THOUGHT many of my drinking friends genuinely cared about my life, but when I stopped drinking or when the weekend was over, 98% of them were nowhere to be found. Everyone wanted to party with the Bag Lady, but they didn't call to check on me and no one noticed I hadn't been around.

That initial AA meeting served as the first day of eighteen months completely sober… and the best year and a half of my life. I made more money and was in better physical and mental shape than I had been in many years. Best of all, I began to genuinely care about others outside of myself and my immediate circle. It was awesome.

I knew if I didn't consciously think about staying sober, and work on it daily, I would easily slip back into old patterns and habits. Addictions come in many forms. I always think of the old saying, "Too much of anything is no good for you." The hardest part comes in when you realize that you have to do some actual work to stay out of your particular addiction. That whole twelve-step program thing only works if you *do* the damn work. Often that means dealing with painful shit from your past. No one likes to feel pain.

Fear can also be crippling, too. It just seems easier to stay in the shit than it does to get off your ass and change things. Changing the way you allow your mind to *see* things is the biggest step. My guru, Anthony Robbins, gave a great example in his book, *Unlimited Power* (Simon & Shuster, 1997). This is not an exact quote but my paraphrase: *Some people look at a piece of Kentucky Fried Chicken and say to themselves, YUM Look how juicy and spicy this piece of chicken is and eat three or four pieces then wonder why they can't lose weight. Others look at the same piece of chicken and say to themselves, Good God, look at all the grease, fat and toxic chemicals in this crap, not to mention the "poor chickens" don't even have beaks they are so confined! And they won't touch it.* Control how you let your mind's eye see things, and you can control your behavior.

If you think you have a problem with booze or drugs, you probably do. Help is out there, so please, at least investigate it. Pray once a day for two weeks—I assure you God is listening—and ask for help. Step into an AA meeting just once or twice. Even if you decide not to stick around this time, the seed will be planted and eventually, God willing, you will come to the jumping off place and find your way back.

I am back in the program now and praying every day I can stay this time. My worst day sober is better than my best day drunk.

Hustler Magazine - Van Eden Ranch 2005

On the Way Up

When I was just starting out as a comic back in Pittsburgh in 1991, I had gone with some friends to a Sam Kinison concert. Sam had been my most notable and most recent inspiration, and I just adored him. The night of his concert, his flight was delayed. The opening comic went up, and when he was finished, there was dead air for a really long time. Someone from the stage staff had made the announcement that they were very sorry, but Sam's flight was delayed, and he was en route, but it would be a while.

My friends start egging me on to go up and do some comedy for all these thousands of pissed off folks till Sam got there, so… I did. I went to the stage and told one of the security people that I was a comic and would be happy to do some time to fill the air till Sam showed up. The security guy came back to side stage and said, "C'mon up!" I have to say, I was seriously terrified and wondered just what the hell I was thinking. My heart was seriously about to explode in my chest, my knees were shaking, and I couldn't have been breathing harder if I was running the Olympic torch up the side of Pike's Peak! Being up there was truly awesome. Before that, I had only played local bars around the Burgh and Bag Lady was still just a strip show.

I wasn't up there very long when someone from backstage yelled, "He's here! Sam's here!" So, I bowed out and that was that. Sadly, I never got to meet him, and I'm sure no one ever even told him my name. Hell, I always wondered how my life might have been different if they had.

Doing comedy at the bars around Pittsburgh was fun, but I knew there was more for me. I always dreamed of seeing my name in lights on Hollywood Blvd. or the Las Vegas Strip, so dive bars and strip clubs weren't going to cut it.

After the debacle at the comedy club in Denver, I wasn't sure where to go from there. I headlined at Rooster's and a couple small clubs for a while, but I knew that wouldn't get me where I was going. I spent many nights looking for any bar or nightclub in my area which had a stage. After promising the manager to pack out the place if they let me perform, I would canvas the area like a damn prostitute hanging flyers and inviting folks to the shows.

And then… finally… I caught my big break.

I remember the day I got the first call from a cool dude named Possum who saw me at one of the biker-friendly bars called Kermitt's Roadhouse up in the Rocky Mountains of Colorado. (Best green chili on Earth!) I was in the shower the day Possum called and answered the phone nude and wet. He explained who he was, and that he had seen my show when he was out in Colorado. He said he thought I was just amazing. He organized a little biker rally in the Midwest called Thunder in the Sand (now called Redneck Revival) which he would like to hire me for, but didn't think he could afford me.

I damn near dropped the phone! Thanks to my quick thinking, I said, "Well, I am a bit expensive, but maybe I can work with you. What is your budget?" What I never told him—or anyone back then—was I had been making a shitty little $200 to $400 a night around Denver on weekends and an occasional Wednesday night and was starving half to death.

He said, "I can do like $2,500 for the weekend for two shows."

I said, "Well, I'll tell you what. If you throw in a room and food, I think I can do it for you." He agreed and that was the start something really awesome.

I will never forget the first time I saw the Conesville Event Grounds. I flew into Des Moines, Iowa, because I didn't have the money to fly to the closer airport. I remember my friend John G. from Minnesota picked me up on his full dresser and hauled me and my bags across the state to the rally. I had been around the biker world plenty through the years, so that wasn't an issue. I had even gone to a nice rally at a place called Conneaut Lake Park in PA, as well as the big Easyrider Rodeo there a few times.

But I had never actually been one of the big-name acts before! I was out of my mind excited when I saw the mile-long row of campers, tents, and vendors set ups. It looked huge. There was even a big, tall crane that did a Honda drop, and get this... a giant backhoe with the bucket welded up to look like a dragon, complete with flame thrower, that ate Jap bikes. It was an absolute circus for big biker kids like me.

Suddenly, I had that chickenshit feeling I had the night at the Sam Kinison concert. What the hell had I gotten myself into?

In addition to Thunder in the Sand, Possum and his wife Pam ran another rally in Conesville, Iowa at the time called Hog-Wild Rodeo. There were thousands of people at these events—all friendly, fun, and open—and my goodness, the bikes were awesome. The men were hot and clad in leathers with long hair and cowboy boots. The chicks all scantily dressed, many with their tits just hangin' right out! Hell, there were even guys walking around in thongs. I felt like I had just found Xanadu!

The stage floor was huge and stood about neck high with big speakers, lights, and a crow's nest. The backstage area was fenced off and had security. Security? For me? Wow. Now *that* made me feel like a damn Rockstar, just like in the movies. Best of all, I was treated like royalty by everyone. There was no feeling like it, and I knew instantly this was what I had dreamed of all my life. I'd found my place in the universe. Screw Hollywood; I was home!

My next big rally was The ABATE of Indiana Boogie. The Boogie was off the hook. The twenty-five thousand people strong, old-school, biker party was held in yet another cornfield. When I played for the first time, the event was already in its twenty-fifth year. My gosh, it was incredible! Best of all, I was booked with Lynyrd Skynyrd. I had always loved them and was so psyched. Hell, when I was fourteen or fifteen, I ran away from home while listening to *Free Bird*, so this was beyond incredible for me. That was the point when I felt like I'd about made it.

The promoter put all the entertainment up at the swanky 5-star resort on a lake, and I decided I would head out to the pool for a swim. (Mind you, I was sober about five months at the time, damn near lived at the gym, and was in the best physical shape of my life.) When I got out to the pool the only other person there was this big furry biker-looking guy I felt I had seen somewhere before. So, I asked, "You one of them Skynyrd guys?"

In the finest southern drawl, he said, "Yep. Who are you?"

Excitedly, I said, "Hi! I'm Bag Lady Sue, I'm opening for you all tonight!"

He paused, looked me up and down twice and slowly said, "Bag Lady Sue? The fuck you are." So, I jumped in, swam on over and made a new friend. It turned out to be Billy Powell. After our swim, I got to meet the entire band at the resort bar and had an amazing time getting to know them. I clicked most with Billy and another member, Ean Evans, who was—by the way—a damn babe. Sadly, they both passed in the same year. I have often thought of writing to the rest of the guys. I am sure they remember me.

That night, I got into a fight with their stage manager, or whatever manager, when he tried to have me leave the backstage after I had a damn heat stroke performing before the band in 90° heat with 99% humidity. Ok, it wasn't really a fight. All I had the strength to do after passing out backstage while lying on the floor with paramedics putting ice bags on my pits, tits, neck, and snatch was to raise my arm to flip him the bird… but he got the point.

Going backstage with the bands was—and still is—a big kick for me. The first couple of times I was actually shy about talking to them, as if I was some little peon and they were gods. I mean… come on, I grew up listening to most of them so seeing them standing right next to me, sharing the same stage, or having a drink with them, was surreal. Better yet, they were coming up to me after my shows saying how great they thought I was. Can you imagine? The guys from Lynyrd Skynyrd told me I was awesome. Wow. It was hard to wrap my head around at first.

Still, none of that ever compared to the real down-to-Earth people that became my fans. I remember realizing I have fans.

Opening for Lynyrd Skynyrd

Holy shit! If you had told me this back in junior high school, I would *never* have believed it. I have kept in touch with many fans and they with me through the years. I have shared many laughs with them, and I have also shared their losses. Many come across state lines to see my shows in other parts of the USA. They are the biggest reason I have reached this place.

In the biker world, word of mouth is everything… good or bad. If you suck or screw over one of the *family*, you are disowned and not ever trusted by the rest. But when you have honor, and are open and real, we will do anything we can to help you. I always say we bikers are good to children, animals, and veterans because most of us are one or all of them. So, we relate.

We look out for one another too. I remember a situation involving my dear friend Wade Musso's mom. (He's one of the Iron Skulls M.A.) His parents—in my eyes—are the equivalent of the Beaver's parents, Ward and June Clever. They are some of the kindest folks I know. One of the managers of Jackyl was rude to Wade's mom and I caught wind of it. Since we were sharing a dressing trailer backstage, I felt compelled to go through the door—half dressed as "The Bag Lady"—at this guy and jump in his face. My exact words were something like, "Listen, fucker! You better rein it in and go apologize to Mrs. Musso, or I am gonna call you out on stage. Remember, I go up before you all, have a microphone, and about 3,000 friends here. Don't be a dick!"

The Daytona rally was always a blast, too. One year at the Broken Spoke I opened for Brett Michaels. (Brett is originally from the Pittsburgh area too.) He went out stage right with his bodyguard, stood on a picnic table, and watched my entire show! I could see him out of the corner of my eye, and he was howling the entire time.

Last time I went to the Daytona Spoke, however, things were starting to change. When I saw my friend Richard from The Kentucky Headhunters, he grabbed me after their set was done and said, "Hell, Bags, you gotta come see this!" He took me backstage and showed me a sign that said:

"ANYONE USING THE 'F' WORD FROM THE STAGE, WILL BE GIVEN ONE WARNING. THE SECOND TIME YOU WILL BE REMOVED FROM THE STAGE!"

This is at *fucking* Daytona Bike Week. I think soon they will need to change the name to Daytona *Bitch* Week.

Sex, Drugs, and Rock-n-Roll

In the beginning, I played at rallies in Iowa and Illinois more than any other states. Gotta love the Bible Belt! Who ever thought my dirty sense of humor would be so popular in the Midwest? Midwesterners are the most fearless, amazing, and resourceful bunch of folks I've ever met. If you ever look up all the amazing inventions this group has come up with, it will blow your mind. They are true survivalists, to be sure.

I've performed at many, many of the big (and even smaller) rallies over the year, but some stick out in my mind more than others. Hog Rock, for example, is one big Debauchery Fest, and always a good time. I had the opportunity to work with many, many amazing artists who are less known but no less unforgettable. They, kinda like me, just never got the *big break...* at least not yet. A true entertainer never lets go of the dream. We can't; it is just in our blood.

And then there's Sturgis. At the beginning of my career, Sturgis gave me some wonderful breaks and opened the door to many other shows across the USA. For one, I was seen by the number two guy at Hustler Magazine, and he asked if I would let them interview me. Of course, I said yes. They wrote a three-page article about me and it was fantastic! My fees went up $1,500 across the board after that.

The Sturgis Rally is always pretty ridiculous, but one particular year was more so than others. I remember vividly the first time I walked down Lazelle Street: My buddy Katie Patron and I pulled into Sturgis, parked the short bus, and headed down to where all the action was. I was wearing one of my fur halter tops, and—not more than fifteen seconds after we hit town—a couple guys saw me and yelled, "show your tits!" So, I figured… *what the hell it's Sturgis*, and released the ladies.

Immediately I was grabbed by a cop and told I was under arrest. At first, I laughed and pulled my arm away. "Oh, yea sure." But then the officer grabbed me again, tighter, and I thought what the hell is this!? "You're kidding me, right?"

He said, "Nope" and took me to the paddy wagon, which was literally parked right off the main street. Apparently, the unadvertised law is that you can be arrested for showing your tits unless you have something painted on or stickers covering your nipples. I remember thinking, *what kind of double-standard bullshit is this?* So, I sat in the wagon surrounded by three or four cops while the guys and Katie waited outside of the opened door.

Then one of the cops said, "I am going to go thru your purse, is there anything in here I should know about?"

"Just a dildo," I responded. Hey, it got a laugh but nothing like the one that was coming. I told him to go ahead because I figured I had nothing in there to be worried about. Or so I thought…

"What is this?" he asked, as he suddenly pulls out a small piece of cigarette cellophane with some black shit in it.

I absolutely lost it and began laughing. I told him with all sincerity in front of his other cop friends, "That is nothing. Seriously, you really should just put that back." He persisted so I said, "Ok but…"

just as he goes to open it, I said, "Please don't spill any, because that it is the hair from my old man's nut sack. I shaved him last night and I am saving it up until I have enough to make a coat."

He dropped it like it just exploded and caught fire. His cop friends lost their minds, and so did all the guys who were standing outside. My fine was $105… or $52.50 per titty. Katie and the guys collected that amount going up and down the street within a few minutes. If you ask me, it was worth every dime.

Hog Rock is—bar none—the most awesome event I have ever played. In my opinion, it is surely the best rally in the USA, and, honey, I have played just about all of them at least once! Even the R.O.T. in Texas can't touch Hog Rock for its all-around *real* biker good time and honest to goodness freedom.

Playing Hog Rock makes me feel like I have a huge family of like oh, 20,000 people. I joke with friends about being a comedy Rockstar, but at Hog Rock, I can honestly say I feel like I really am. The rally is held twice a year at a beautiful, private campground on the Ohio River in southern Illinois: the second weekend of June and again in early October. Goodness me, you will see things there that will boggle your mind. It reminds me of Woodstock for bikers with bands all day and evening, hypnotists, snake charmers, helicopter rides, amazing bikes, booze, dopers, broads, and the friendliest half-naked people you'll ever meet. It is like a big kids' carnival! Now and then you'll see naked guys just strolling about with wieners so big the horses shake their heads. Chicks walk around with pickles in one of their many orifices, but hey, it's all in good, drunken fun.

Hell, I even have a friend who has a pecker piercing. I've seen him walking about with everything hanging off it from a cowbell—yes, a real full-sized cowbell—to a damn disco ball. Yep, a real disco ball hanging from a chain! He'd spin it while his ol' lady shined a flashlight on it. *Saturday Night Fever* couldn't touch this shit!

Tim and his family, the organizers of Hog Rock, are really cool, really smart people! Grizz, is a big furry country boy; Tony, a sexy, dirty, biker; and Bundy, the resident cowboy—complete with horse—have been watching my back there for about thirteen years.

For example, the first time I was there, I got myself in a little bit of a jam. My girl Skyy and I were selling DVDs and pictures after the show from the trunk of her car. The crowd got so big around me that I had to jump up on top of the car

Skyy

and sign autographs from the roof! Everything was cool… until the people started surrounding the car, pushing and squeezing up against me. They meant no harm, but I was quite the damsel in distress. All of a sudden, just like in the movies, here comes John Wayne "Bundy" on his trusty steed. He rides right through the crowd, scoops me off the car and away we go. It was soooo cool!

Management, location, and the wonderful, colorful, uninhibited people who attend Hog Rock combine to make it so incredibly awesome. The only rules? No club colors, no weapons visible, and no bullshit like robbing or assaulting your fellow partiers. Honestly, that leaves a lot of room for the imagination. Some of the shit I have witnessed there has even made *me* blush, if you can believe that. I could write an entire book on Hog Rock. If you ever get the chance, just go!

My Warrior

I have never slept around on the road, though I could have plenty of times. There were those two times, though: a one-night-stand with a gorgeous, twenty-six year old, four tours of duty, tall dark and handsome soldier named Kevin, and the "I don't speak good English" German tourist in Alaska, whose name I don't recall. After all, I did it for my country. Oh ya, and there was a magical night to remember with a friend who is a famous country singer, whose name shall remain my secret forever. He was as hot as the night itself. Aside from that, I just never jumped in bed with guys. For me, it didn't seem like it would be fulfilling no matter how great the sex might have been. I need to know and trust someone for me to give myself in that way. I can't help it, and I'm glad I'm like that. So are the men I've loved.

In all the years on the road, there was really only one guy that I could have pounced on from the moment we met. I'll call him Warrior. It was one of those struck-by-lightning things. I saw him and WHAM! He was a fun-loving, absolutely breathtaking, raven-haired soldier that had done numerous tours in Iraq and Afghanistan. The first time we met was at a huge rally in the Midwest. I was on stage thanking our veterans when a friend of his brought him to the stage. It was the end of my show, so I took him up with me. I introduced him to the huge crowd and gave him a "Bags for President" shirt. The people applauded vigorously, and I know it made his day. Warrior is a Special Forces/Green Beret/Airborne Ranger, AKA a certifiable badass.

I adored him because he was authentic. He was also the first soldier I ever gave a shirt to that actually took the time to send me back a picture. I can't tell you the excitement I felt when I saw the picture of him wearing "Bags for President" and holding his SCAR (Special Operations Combat Assault Rifle) in Afghanistan. When I received the email with the picture, I was so blown away and so touched that he would send that to me I cried off and on for half the day. I remember running around with the picture showing everyone I knew. I was so honored. The next year I looked for him at the rally, but he wasn't there that time. I heard from a mutual acquaintance that he had gone back to Iraq for another tour. Then I didn't see him for a couple of years. But when we met up again the lightning was there, just like before.

We kept in touch every now and then on Facebook, or we would run into each other at a rally, but nothing ever happened between us because he had a girlfriend and *homie don't play dat.* Over the next few years, it seemed that when he wasn't overseas, he would find his way to one of my shows. Sometimes with his gal, and sometimes alone. We always got pictures together, and he would

post them all over his social media page. I felt so proud when I saw them. He was always in the back of my mind. In time, we grew close and talked now and then but nothing more. Then a while back he wrote me online and told me

he and his girlfriend had split up. I honestly felt bad. I thought they were good together, but I guess no one on the outside ever truly knows the real story of anyone else's relationship.

A few months later, I got a letter from him saying he saw that I was performing one state away, and that he was intent on riding up to see me. I was beyond thrilled! It was a seven-hour ride for him, but he thought nothing of it. He just wanted to see me. He was so full of life and that energy radiated from him in buckets!

A few days before the show, he called and said he had something to tell me that he had been waiting years to say. He told me that since the first time he saw me—which apparently was long before we ever actually met—I had been his biggest fantasy. He said he wanted to show me just how big, and that if I would let him, he was going to spend the entire weekend making love to every inch of my body, like I had never been made love to before. Oh, Dear God…

So, for the next week until the rally, I felt like a little schoolgirl waiting for prom night. I flew into my gig, rented a beautiful little B&B in the country, and tried to keep the butterflies from punching a hole in my stomach. I waited to hear his bike pull up. When he walked in the door, I lost all reason and accountability. He was more handsome than I even remembered, and there he was standing right in front of me. He came over to me, reached out, gently held my face in his hands and said, "My God, you are so fucking beautiful. I can't believe I am actually here with you right now alone. You can't know how I have waited for this moment," and then he kissed me like I had not been kissed in literally thirteen years. We were both shaking and instantly filled with fire.

Warrior

I wanted to give myself to him right there, but I had a show to do, and of course, "The show must go on!"

My childhood friend, Dee, whom I hadn't seen in thirty years, had also driven up to see me and took my things to the club so I could ride with Warrior. I jumped on the back of his beautiful bike, wrapped my arms around his big, strong body, and we flew away. The smell of his skin, his long wavy hair in my face, the feel of his leather, and the warm night breeze blowing over me was intoxicating. The ride went by in a minute.

The show was fun, but I'm not sure how I managed to get through it. All I could think about was how it would be to finally see him and feel him on me and in me. Doing the show was incredibly hard, no pun intended. I kept looking over at his handsome face from the stage awestruck, while he laughed at my silly ass with a smile that could stop time. He sat beside the stage with Dee watching over me like he was the freaking secret service. I don't think I remember feeling so safe in forever. Knowing he was such a true badass, yet seeing him be friendly, kind, and wonderful to my fans turned me on to no end. I loved that he had nothing to prove; he just was.

After the show, we rode back to the farm on the bike, and my heart raced all the way there. When we walked in, it was on immediately. He gently undressed me, then he did exactly what he promised me he was going to do. His warm, full lips slowly found their way from one end of my body to the other, and he took me over. I had not wanted to give myself to someone so much in forever. I melted into him, and when he finally put himself inside me, it took all I had not to pass out. I got lost in his long, silky hair and dark eyes as his body rocked over and over on and in me for hours like waves on the ocean. I swear to God, he made love to me for literally two entire whole days. We were lost in each other completely. Not once did either of us need any help staying in the moment. It was unreal. I don't remember feeling that alive, passionate, and adored in so many years. We were like two wild animals, and I honestly felt like I was in a grown-up fairytale. He made me feel so beautiful, and he was a magnificent beast. We barely slept. We just made love over and over again. We only left the bed to eat and shower, and only left the cabin once to go to Waffle House and Dairy Queen, for lack of a better place out in the sticks!

In my whole life, I had never encountered such a magnificent creature. We talked about his time in the war. He told me how, throughout his life, he'd always wanted to be the best at whatever he did, even when it meant all the things that come with war. He spoke about many of the things he went through over there, but you would never know it by the way he carried himself. He said he had PTSD, of course, but had made his mind up to learn how to accept the things he went through as part of what he had to do—both to survive and to save the lives of his brothers. I don't think I have ever felt such respect for a man. We hated to say goodbye, but knew we had to…for now.

Thank you, Veterans

The rallies had some redeeming moments, too. My best memory came years later at Sturgis when I received a letter from a Vietnam veteran I had crossed paths with at the Broken Spoke Saloon (near Bearbutte) one afternoon. It changed the course of my comedy life once again.

Here is the letter he sent me:

Back in 2010 while at the Broken Spoke, I was standing in the back watching Eddie Money when a lovely wavy-haired blond walked up to me, put her hand on my shoulder and said, "Thank you." I looked at her and asked, "For?" She responded, "You're a Veteran." Eddie Money was singing his tribute song "Another One's Coming Home," and I was standing in the dark crying quietly alone. If I failed to get it out that night, you are very welcome. I was pretty distracted and was planning on doing something terribly drastic after that final trip. Thank you for appreciating an old soldier. The only reason I knew who you were was afterwards I went over to the Drag Pipe Saloon and you were playing there. Also, I had previously went to Red Lodge Montana to ride the Beartooth and saw you there as well. I have thought about telling you many times since, but I just heard that song and it reminded me. Still Riding…Thank You. Scott

I have never been so moved before! That letter touched my soul. From that moment forward, I decided to make reaching out to and helping our veterans a priority as much as I possibly could. I started making time to thank all our veterans at every show, big and small. I also began telling people that if they had a son, daughter, brother, sister, neighbor, or friend that was active military, to send me their APO/FPO address and shirt size and I would send them a care package. I never missed one and still send them, even when I am broke. To me, that is a very small price to pay for my freedom.

I have held/hugged many veterans and even broke down and cried with them when they let it go in my arms after my shows. One Vietnam vet in Iowa lost his son in Desert Storm. No one will ever understand what hell most of them have had to face.

Over the years through all of my travels, I've met so many amazing people. You know who you are; please know that I will never forget you.

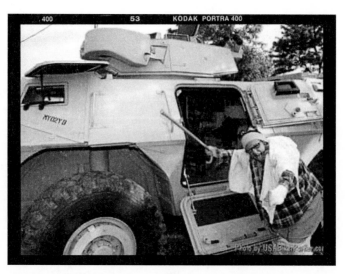

Bag Lady Sue Supports our Troops!

Alaska!

I remember wanting to go to Alaska since I was about twenty-one. I would watch John Wayne in *North to Alaska* when I was a kid and think about how cool it would be to be able to go into the wild like that, pan for gold, and live off the land. I also heard John Denver sing about it and watched one of his specials on Alaska. That was all it took. Ok, that and my seeing a copy of Alaska Men magazine…Good Lord!

So, one day I was sitting home on my computer and I thought I would surf around the personals in Alaska and see if there really were a bunch of hot single men up there. Apparently, there are in fact plenty. However, one of the great Alaskan sayings is: "The odds are good, but the goods are odd." That suited me just fine because I'm not exactly normal, either.

I met a guy via email and mentioned to him that I was a comedienne looking for places to perform in Alaska. He was cool enough to write me back and turn me on to a friend of his who owned a couple of bars in Fairbanks. The guys' name was Dave Lambert. So, I called him and sent him my website. He invited me up to play both of his bars: The Greyhound Lounge (now closed) and the Gold Rush Saloon, which is still there and still run by him today.

On the plane ride from Denver for the first time, I was thrilled to death and honestly a bit scared too. Hell, I didn't know anyone up there. It was so far away, and all I heard for years was its a wild-ass place where the men outnumber the women twenty-five to one. (That last part is what got me on the plane.) I will never forget the feeling I had when the plane took off from Seattle. *My God,* I thought, *how big are my balls?* Single gal, alone, with no gun, heading into the wild unknown. What I forgot to remember was this was not the first time I grew a pair and headed off into the great unknown. This was just the first time I was doing it in Alaska.

When I looked out the window of the plane during the long flight, I remember thinking we were flying over the ocean. It was a clear night and I could see the stars, but I hadn't seen a light on the ground for at least an hour. So, I asked the guy sitting next to me if we were flying over water and he said, nope, that is just wilderness. I could not even imagine such a naked place. A place where there were literally no humans, at least none who had electricity. It is hard to conceive how big Alaska actually is.

After two hours of still not seeing one light below, all of a sudden, I saw something strange out my window beside the plane. It looked like a huge, smoky white ghost stretched out across the sky. I kept staring at it. Then I realized the damn thing was moving. Holy shit! I frantically grabbed the poor dude next to me again and said, "What the hell is that?" He looked over me out the window and said, "Oh cool, that's the Northern Lights. Do you know how lucky you are to see those your first trip?" My heart jumped in my chest, and then I felt an amazing peace come over me that I can't describe. I felt like the pioneers must have felt when they first saw them. I was in awe.

I landed in Fairbanks at the smallest airport ever and was greeted by Dave. Dave had the most wonderfully genuine smile and eyes that twinkle so bright you can see them through his wire glasses. He dropped me off at a nice efficiency apartment on the University of Alaska campus and told me he had a surprise for me when he picked me up in the morning. *Well, how sweet,* I thought, then I hit the bed and was out cold immediately.

Rarefied Air

Bright and early the next morning, here comes Dave with his constant, contagious enthusiasm, and off we go to… I still didn't know where we were headed. Finally, we pulled up to a tiny little airstrip in the middle of nowhere. The next thing I know, I have a headset on, and I am in the tiniest airplane I have ever seen. It was literally an engine mounted to a metal frame, wrapped in a thick canvas Army-tent-like thing with a couple of windows shoved in. This plane, and I use the word loosely, looked like he built it himself! It was an old two-seater, one seat in front of the other. It was so loud that you could only hear each other talk through headsets. The pilot was a crazy mountain man, who seemed amused that I was terrified, but he was very reassuring to me as he fired up the plane. I watched the little propeller begin spinning and felt my heart start pounding. It was not like taking off in a jet. Not one little bit! We rolled down the runway for oh, about five seconds and then popped right up off the ground into the air.

Up, up and away we go, over the tundra and out towards the Alaskan Range. They are snow-covered mountains about an hour out of Fairbanks, at least via this particular mode of transport. It is jagged and fierce looking; it comes right up out of the tundra from almost sea level and shoots skyward to an altitude of up to 20,310 ft. at Denali Peak or Mt. McKinley, as most call it. That may not sound big to some Coloradan's, but our mountains start at 5,280 ft. and go up from there to 14,440 ft. So, when you are looking at that "big" mountain peak, it is not even half as high or big as Mt. McKinley!

At that moment, I *was* living. Every nerve in my body and mind was shooting off at one hundred miles an hour. When we flew next to the mountains, they looked enormous. We were right in front of them climbing higher and higher. It was cold, and the mountains were still thick with snow. I could smell winter in the air even though it was April. My heart was already pounding as we flew along the front side of the mountains. Then this maniac decides to give me Dave's money's worth and flies me right over top of them! We were honestly so close to touching them that I… swear to God… could have hung by my feet from the wheel strut and scooped snow off the top of the mountain with my hand. I mean, I was right next to them and they were gigantic! Honestly, it was unbelievable. I had never felt a high like this before—never in my whole life. It was at that exact moment that I fell in love with Alaska.

On the way back in, I saw a couple of moose and a few caribou under us, though not the giant herds I expected from all the Alaskan wildlife shows I saw on TV. We were still an hour out from the airstrip when I noticed I was getting really sleepy. I mean *really*,

like someone gave me a drug, and BAM! I was on my way out. I am yawning like crazy and couldn't understand why.

So, I told the pilot through my headphones, "Hey, buddy, I feel like I am going to seriously fall asleep. I wonder why?" to which he replies in a somewhat concerned tone, "Oh shit! I was wondering about that…hey, put your face out the window."

To which I replied, "Excuse me, but what the hell did you just say?"

He said, "No, serious-ly, open the window there beside you, stick your face out and suck some wind. You need some fresh air. It seems as though carbon monoxide is getting into the cabin from the broken  heater hose. Damn it, I thought I fixed that damn thing."

Whaaaat? Well, ok then. So immediately, I stick my face out the tiny window and begin to huff in the fresh clean 15° April air. Just then it occurs to me that this pilot—who, by the way, has my life in his hands—is still sucking in the carbon monoxide because his head is *not* out the damn window. So, I lean back in and through the frozen snot on my upper lip exclaim, "Hey! Why the hell don't you have your head out the window, too?"

"Well, someone's gotta fly the plane," he replied. That, my friends, is Alaska.

My first show was held at The Greyhound. The place was packed with true Alaskans, and boy, they can party. After the show, we were all hanging out at the bar getting our drunk on when I asked about the big night club across the street (now Kodiak Jacks). One of the girls said, "Oh, fuck that place! The owner is a tool!"

So, I suggested we all take off our clothes, run across the street naked and moon the assholes right in their front door! So… about seven of us did just that. What a howl! Out the door we ran across the four-lane highway, stood in front of the door, asses lined up and yelled to the doormen, "Want some ass!" Then, we ran back to The Greyhound, put our clothes on at lightning speed, and sat down to start drinking. Not ten minutes later, in walked the cops. They asked who here was streaking?

I jumped right up and said, "Holy shit, Officer, about ten minutes ago a bunch of people ran through here buck-ass naked! They came in that door and ran out that door. I almost crapped a brick!" No one else said a word, they just tried desperately to keep from cracking up. After the cops left, we waited approximately fifteen seconds and lost our minds! That was seriously one of the hardest things I ever got through with a straight face.

Years later, I took Cheyenne back to Alaska with me. I will never forget the first time we saw Mt. McKinley, Denali, or *The High One* as the natives call it. There is simply no way to truly describe it other than to say it is truly gargantuan. The distance from Fairbanks to Anchorage is about three hundred and fifty miles, and on a clear day you can see the mountain from both places! Cheyenne and I drove the trip from Fairbanks in the north to Anchorage in the south, and I could hardly take my eyes off that mountain. It just draws you in and holds you.

The area around the base of the mountain is Denali National Park. It is hard to imagine the scope of land size. You can only drive in so far and then you have to hike back in. Or, you can take one of the many bus trips back into the deep wilderness of the park. Some of the buses go twelve hours in, though they travel extremely slowly as the road is so narrow. In some spots if a bus is coming from the other direction, it has to stop and wait till the other bus passes, as there is a thousand-foot drop off the edge.

Edge of Bering Sea - Nome, AK

We took an eight-hour trip and saw so many animals. Big Horn/ Dall sheep, caribou, moose, and on the way back, even saw a grizzly. He was a big old bear. He was just strolling along the sideroad and came right near the bus. What a thrill for Cheyenne and me. It was surreal to be so far from any civilization. Except for the bus, there was just nothing except the few of us in the incredibly vast wilderness with all the wild things.

As we rode back, I remember thanking God for my life and for the ability to give this incredible gift and many others to my kid. I hoped I would be able to instill in her the fearlessness that I managed to find and carry on my path. I hoped I would have the strength to let her go when her time comes to explore and find her own adventures. I thought about Pittsburgh, and how many of my friends actually have never even left the city and surrounding areas. Some never even took the four-hour drive to New York to visit Niagara Falls, one of the seven natural wonders of the world. They wouldn't drive one state over, let alone have the balls, the freedom, the drive, or the ability to jump on a plane alone and head to a place like Alaska. People are this way in every city in America. They live only three to five hours away from something amazing, yet—in their whole life—never make the trip to see it! It boggles my mind and is sad as hell.

You just have to do it—and take the kids when you can. It is the best education they will ever get, not to mention it will open their minds to other humans and ways of life outside of their safe little circle.

Nome, AK

Nome was—and still is—a rip-roaring town on the edge of the Bering Sea, in N.W. Alaska. The gold rush of the early 1900s made it one of the many booming towns up there. Like many others, it managed to survive. Unlike Anchorage and some of the other more "civilized" towns, it has kept its bawdy, rowdy heart. I have been there twice. Both times during the *Iditarod*, which is the last great race on Earth. It is over a thousand-mile-long sled dog race through the Alaskan wilderness in the frigid, winter conditions every March. It began in honor of the dogs and mushers that ran serum 647 miles from Seward to Nome in five days in the middle of winter to save many lives during a diphtheria outbreak there back in 1925. (For more amazing info, search for Iditarod or 1925 serum run.)

Iditarod mushers and their dogs are the last of the really supreme athletes. You cannot imagine what they go through with absolute pleasure to win this thing. These folks and their dogs have

the world's biggest balls. Screw the reality show dipshits, the ungrateful, infantile NFL players, and most sports jocks.

I have a great tee shirt I love that says, "What runs over one thousand miles in 8 days, eats raw meat and sleeps in the snow? Sled dogs!" I love it. I have met these dogs and some of their owners, and I can tell you they are the real thing. One of my dear friends, Lance Mackey, is a four-time Iditarod Champion… not to mention he also won the Yukon Quest four times, as well. Both are incredibly grueling races for man and dog and are just a few weeks apart.

Lance and his dogs have won one after the other a few times. The Iditarod goes from Anchorage to Nome in March and the Yukon Quest goes from Fairbanks to Dawson in the Yukon Territory of Canada in February. If you get a chance, read his book: *How Dog Mushing Saved My Life* by Lance Mackey. It is terrific!

Cheyenne and I first met Lance Mackey, a crazy Gemini, in Fairbanks, at the "Northern most Denny's" one afternoon and started chatting with him. We were lucky enough to have him invite us to his home in the Alaska backcountry. When we were there, he was still building it so we had to use an outhouse. Cheyenne and I got to spend the night with him and his eighty-four dogs. Had he not been married at the time, I would have ridden him like a snow machine, but I'm not into married guys. He was a true gentleman who, at the time, was quite in love with his then crazy wife.

There was just something sexy about this guy. I think it is partly because he is so damn good to his dogs. He lives for them. There were even four that got to live inside full-time. I know because one just about slept on my face. Lance is an amazing man. He has beat throat cancer, frostbite, a miserable marriage, and just keeps going. I ran into his wife once in the Anchorage airport, but I didn't say anything to her because, to be honest, she was past shitfaced at the time. She threw the whole, "Do you know who I am?" card to the bartender. I know better than to try and reason with an obnoxious drunk—or any drunk for that matter—so I just sat there and observed. They divorced soon after that, so I never actually met her.

People often wonder if dog mushing is cruel. Being someone who absolutely adores dogs, and who will not hesitate to punch the shit out of anyone I ever see hurting animals—dogs or horses especially—I can honestly say these dogs are born to run. I have mushed them myself, and they are in heaven. You can see joy in their eyes and even hear it in their bark as they pull at the leads, straining to go the moment they get hooked up to their harness-es. It is sad that more dogs don't get the chance to run their asses off like sled dogs do. Most are forced to lie around the house or ride in a truck with fat, lazy owners who never really walk them. Sometimes they will chain them to some doghouse alone for years! To me *that* is animal cruelty.

I took Chey back there again years later. When Lance saw her, he went goofy! She was no longer the cute little fourteen-year-old he met years earlier, but now a gorgeous young woman. Men truly are dogs… they can't help it; it's just how God made 'em.

I have mushed a sled in small races three times. Once in Fairbanks, where I did a three-mile split. That is where the musher took control of the team for the first half of the race, while I sat in the "basket." My buddy Kathy neglected to inform me that, while sitting in the basket, I would be getting sprayed with dog pee throughout and likely have to dodge a couple of flying turds as well. Sled dogs don't stop to pee and poo… they let it fly in flight. Then she and I switched, and I got to bring them in. I was hooked!

I even got to race against one of the Green Bay Packers' second-string quarterbacks. I don't remember his name but, hey, what do you expect from a die-hard Steeler fan? I didn't win the race and I didn't care. My fourth-place finish was still a huge thrill. Another time, I had the chance to race three dogs in a three-mile competi-tion in Nome. I won third place. I had to run my ass off during that race. One of my dogs only had three legs… imagine that? There are few thrills like racing a dog team across the frozen tundra, all the way to the finish line. I competed for three miles, and I cannot imagine what it must be like to go over a thousand!

Alaska is an incredible place. During my trips I have seen wild musk ox, wolves, lynx, moose, caribou, and grizzly bears. In fact, I've observed just about every animal in Alaska, except wolverines and polar bears. I would have to go further north around Barrow to see polars but hope to get up there next trip. The wildlife in Alaska is incredible, and some of it can even kill you. For example, do *not* mess with a moose. Yes, they are stupid cute and look like they could be as gentle as a cow… until they are not. I almost

got stomped in Yellowstone by a mother with her calves. Boy howdy, that was a close call.

Another time, I was driving out Chena Rd. on my way to a beautiful hot spring at the end of the road, located about fifty-five miles outside of Fairbanks. I had been warned and was watching for moose, when—out of the corner of my eye—I saw something. It was a lone wolf taking a drink from a lake. I swerved off the road and stopped the truck. We just looked at each

In the Race! Anchorage, AK

other for a few seconds, eye-to-eye. It was intense. I turned away to grab my camera, and when I looked back, he was gone. Just instantly gone. I have also heard them howl in the wild, and eerie is not adequate to describe it. Magical is more like it. It sent chills down my spine and my heart raced so fast I thought it would burst.

I truly love everything about Alaska. Best of all, I have more friend's numbers from Alaska in my cell phone than any other state, including Pennsylvania. I'm not sure why that is; I think because it is really such a small place, despite its massive ground size.

I got to meet the girls from the reality show called *Flying High Alaska*. Great chicks. Ariel and I partied together in Nome, and boy, she can party. I am seriously concerned for her liver. She is, however, one of the sweetest, most delightfully real women I have ever met.

Years back, I did a show at Eielson Air Force Base for the troops and got to meet and party with a particular captain of a certain Alaskan crab fishing show. He was doing a book signing, and we met through a mutual friend of ours who had set up the show for us both. I hadn't really watched this show, so I had no idea how sexy the Captain was, and when I saw him my first thought was thought was, *Boy I'd like to give him some crabs!* (Kidding). I was in a relationship at the time so *that* was out, but I still needed to mess with him.

When I came out on stage as the Bag Lady, the Captain was sitting along the wall with his friends. During my comedy gig he, his friends, and all the troops were laughing hysterically. Near the end of the show, I headed over to him in full-on Bag Lady and said, "Hey sexy, ain't you that crab fisherman guy? You want to catch some crabs? I got some special fucking crabs for you right here, Baby!" as I grabbed my crotch. Then I told him, "The salmon are runnin', Fucker! Get down here!" as I proceeded to grab his head and try to get him under my dress.

Well, apparently, the Captain is a bit shy when he is sober. He damn near crapped his drawers, at least until I stripped out the bag lady duds, shook out my hair, and jumped in his lap. Then he was all over it.

After the show we all headed into the bar and proceeded to get rip-roaring drunk together on shot after shot of Crown Royal. He and the rest of my Alaskan friends were a blast! We partied like rock stars. We were all having so damn much fun, I wished the night would go on forever. He and the guys wanted to go to the *Alaskan Bush Company*, a far-out, totally nude strip club in Anchorage, and they wanted me to go. The trouble is, I am not a fan of looking at other chicks' gashes, so I bowed out and went back to the house. I had some tea and crawled into my big cozy bed.

Somewhere around 4 a.m., I heard a knock on the door. The conversation went something like this:

Captain: "Hey, Suzi Bags, are you up? Can I please come in and sleep in your bed? There's no more room out here."

Me: "I'd rather ya didn't."

Captain: "But, Suz, come on. I mean, there aren't even any blankets or pillows left. Pleeeeease?"

Me: "Oh, geez! Fine, come in, but I swear, you better behave!"

Captain: "I will, I promise!"

So, I moved over, gave up a pillow, fluffed my remaining one measly pillow, (I need at least four to be really cozy) and tried to go back to sleep. Next thing I knew, I'm getting spooned!

Me: "Come on now, knock it off and move over!"

Captain: "But can't I just cuddle ya? I'm cold."

Me: "You're a damn crab fisherman on the Bering Sea. My ass, you're cold."

Captain: "Well, yes, your ass is a bit cold."

Me: "Go the fuck to sleep!"

Captain: "Shit! Ok, fine!"

Barely five minutes went by, and here he came again. This time he not only tried spooning me but forking me, too! I say this because sticking into my spine was his hard-on, which I might add was comparable in size to an oosik, (For those who have not been to Alaska, an oosik is the Eskimo name for the extremely large penis bone of a walrus.) Now I was getting pissed. Ok, in all honesty, I was more pissed that I had a new boyfriend and couldn't jump on his moby dick and ride off into the midnight sun than I was that the Captain was poking me in the back with *it*. But I digress.

So, my honor and respect of my new beau made me remain rational in the face of excitement and danger. So, I yelled, "STOP! Now, I mean it!" to which he yelled back "Ok! Fine then, dammit!"

I figured I had gotten through to him, finally, and off to sleep I went. Sometime after, I am not sure how long, this giant meat hook of an arm slid under my side and scooped me up and set me smack dab on top of him… dead center on the *oosik*! I swear he dented my tailbone. Thank God, I had shorts on because, had he hit the bullseye, I am afraid this monster would have run clean through me.

So, I freaked out and started whackin' him while saying, "Now, I asked ya nice to knock that shit off. Ya didn't listen. Now, get your ass out of this bed!" I was acting cross but laughing inside the whole time because he was just plain adorable and didn't have a mean bone in him. Oh, I said *bone*… ha, ha, ha, ha. Seriously, at least not towards women. Of that, I am sure. In fact, I am certain that the Captain truly loves women. I figured he has probably loved a whole bunch of them because he was a sexy man, and—at the time, a huge celebrity thanks to the show—so I thought it best to save myself.

God, I love Alaska! It is just so full of amazing, colorful, and unique people.

I have even gotten to meet some real "Eskimos" (the nickname for native people from many different Alaskan tribes). I must say, they are some of the kindest humans I have ever met. Their art is just amazing, and what they can scrimshaw on a piece of walrus ivory is unbelievable. Sadly though, like many of my Native American friends in the lower forty-eight states, they drink a lot. The government gives them money every month from the pipeline, and so many of them get caught up in drinking their lives away. It is heartbreaking to see how much spirit is being swallowed up by booze.

Sadly, I just lost one of my best Alaskan friends, Willy Wood. Willy was a beautiful Native American Alaskan man, whom I had known since the first time I went up in 2004. He inducted me into the Polar Bear Club. One night after partying at one of my favorite bars up there, the Gold Rush Saloon, Willy and I left and headed to his house. On the way, we pulled over and parked the truck by the Chena River. Willy suggested we jump in. I looked at him like he was out of his Eskimo mind, then I realized he was, in fact, a native and used to doing crazy shit like this. It was April and there was snow all about and even still a bit of ice on the shore.

We walked through the ice-cold mud. He stopped and took off his jeans (which made me really happy) and went right into the frigid water like it was nothing! There he was floating around like a duck. He started mocking my chickenshit ass, "Come on, it's warm! Seriously, Suz, if it was that cold there would be ice on top!" So, in I went, hair and all. THAT was the coldest water I had ever felt in my life. I swear... my heart wanted to explode. I jumped back out while he just laughed and kept floating. I have a picture of us all wet in his truck, but it is blurry because of the damn fog, I guess.

I was crazy about Willy. I spent the night with him more than once, and each time he was a pure gentleman. Willy had a face that reminded me of the moon: the blackest eyes, silkiest hair, and skin as soft as a velour blanket. I guess we always had a thing for each other, though we had not been *together*. I lived here, and he lived there, and as much as I wanted to move to Alaska, I knew Cheyenne wouldn't hear of it. She always won that kind of argument. So—for the time being—we were content to just be cuddle buddies and friends.

The last time I saw him was on New Year's Eve a few years back. I was doing a show at the Gold Rush Saloon in Fairbanks. Willy worked up on the North Slope of the Brooks Range, so he was away a lot. But if he knew I was coming to town, he would never miss my shows when he could help it. When he walked in, I was so happy! We partied with all our friends like we always did, but this time, he looked at me and said, "Of all the times you have been here, we have never been together. Tonight, I want you to be with me." I had known him easily ten years. I decided it was time.

My best buddy, Dave Lambert, had gotten me a beautiful suite at the Regency Hotel in downtown Fairbanks complete with a hot tub. As the taxi drove us there and he quietly held my hand, I felt such a great peace come over me. We cracked the champagne, lit some candles, climbed into the big hot tub and just lay there in the quiet holding each other. It was beautiful. Slowly, he began to kiss my face so gently, then he started softly pressing and sliding his cheeks and his nose against mine. In between, he would kiss my lips, then go back and forth alternating all of it rhythmically like a slow beautiful dance on my face. It was like nothing I had felt before. The heat of it all consumed us, but never once did I feel rushed or like there was a goal. We just lay there in the water and kissed for what could have easily been two hours. I had to keep adding more hot water! I will say he was a beautiful man inside and out with a heart as big as the state he lived in. He was my first and only real Eskimo kiss (which is nothing like what you see on TV). I think of him so often.

I got the call last year from my friends telling me Willy died. They found him at his gold mine in the cabin in the woods. He had been drinking a lot. I am not sure exactly what happened, but they think he had a heart attack. I will miss him so much. God, he was just precious. When I go back up now, Alaska will not be the same without him. He was adored by everyone, and I know he is missed by everyone, too. See ya on the other side, Darling. Thank you for the kisses, the memories, and for being my spirit friend.

On one of my trips I had the chance to play a club called Ivory Jack's Saloon. It is outside of Fairbanks, in an area called Goldstream. It's an absolutely beautiful, very large, log cabin bar out in the woods with an attached liquor store. They serve Alaskan sized portions of incredible grub. Personally, I think it has the best eats in the state—bar-none.

Ivory Jack's is run by a guy named Dick Ellsworth and his amazing wife Jonie. Dick is truly one of a kind. He is the most benevolent and funniest men I know. I swear he missed his calling… he should have been a comic. Never have I seen a wit like that on a man. Both of them work their asses off every single day. Dick works, and therefore lives, in hospital scrubs, the crazier the print the better. He's a Yankees fan, so I had some custom scrubs made for him with New York Yankees material. I think he liked them a bunch!

Dick filmed my first ever television commercial as the Bag Lady for Ivory Jack's. It's a freakin' howl and is still getting played all over the state. Man, how I love these people with all my heart.

Every time I went there, he and Jonie treated me like a Rockstar. It's likely that they lose a ton of money because I eat them out of King Crab! I am sure he is pleased that I quit drinking because I cost him a fortune in Scotch back in the day. In fact, one time when I took my best friend Sandy Beeche up to Alaska with me, Dick gave us his truck to use so we could get around the state. One night we wanted to go out and watch the northern lights, so he gave us a bottle of Chivas and a couple pounds of King Crab legs to go.

Beeche and I parked out in the woods, popped the bottle open, and watched the northern lights put on their incredible show for us while we stuffed our faces with King Crab. Trouble was, we unknowingly dropped a few shells on the floor between the seats, which of course no one realized until later in the spring after the thaw.

I remember getting a call from Dick., "Hey there Bags. Any idea why my truck stinks like dead fish? I have been driving around for a week trying to figure out what the hell is going on. Finally, I looked under the seats and found all the old rotten crab leg shells and dried up French fries you goofy broads dropped in the truck back in March! It didn't start stinking till spring set in and the sun baked the shit. Nice job there, ya dork!"

I had to laugh. Thank goodness Dick did! That's the kind of folks who live in the Great White North. Shit that pisses off the average douchebags down here rolls right off Alaskans like water off a duck's back. People love life and find joy in just about everything up there.

My buddy Lambert and his lovely wife Ann did—and still do—take care of me when I come up, even though he closed the bar. Alaska friends are the kind who loan you a truck, feed you King Crab, give you a fabulous hotel to stay in and buy you expensive booze. At least Dave and Dick and their ladies are those kinds of friends to me.

There is another kick-ass cool club I have played many times out in the sticks called The Howling Dog Saloon. There is just no place like the Dog. The Dog is the kind of place that has bras and all kinds of weird shit hanging from the ceilings and on the walls. There is even a red carpet on the stage that was under the Pope at one time or another. I played with a very talented and crazy lady who is an Alaskan celebrity named LuLu Small. LuLu and I met years ago at the Dog and have played together many times. She is somewhere around her sixties with wild-ass red hair and a foul mouth that could scare a sailor. She's a lot like me! I love her.

LuLu picks an axe like Stevie Ray and writes her own hysterical lyrics. She also uses a can of hairspray in place of her fingers on the frets of her guitar and simply rocks out! We have worked together many since, and I think she is truly one of the greatest performers I ever met, not to mention a truly wonderful human being. It is sad that she never got picked up by a label because she is absolutely brilliant. But, like me, she has a vagina, and her lyrics are a bit off-colored, so we are the last ones to get any help in this business. Look her up online sometime. I love ya, Miss LuLu. www.lulusmall.com.

If you get messed up at the Howling Dog, which inevitably you will, there are cabins out back you can sleep it off in. I stay in them every time I played there because I generally ended up shitfaced. At least I did when I was still drinking. Only trouble is… after the bar closes all there is a common bathroom, toilet, and shower that you share with whoever else is staying there. You also have to walk a good forty yards in the cold from your cabin to use it. Brrrr! I think the slogan "What happens in Vegas, stays in Vegas" was stolen from the Hollow Dog.

Do you remember me mentioning my one-night stand with the hot German guy? It happened there. I had finished doing my show and went over to the bar for a drink. The place was packed and there were some fun foreign guys there, so I had to say howdy. One of them was tall, dark and Playgirl hot with a thick accent who barely spoke English. We clicked instantly and hung out till the bar closed. They were staying in some of the other cabins out back near mine and were flying back to Europe the next evening. So, one kiss goodnight led to the kind of sex you see in the movies where they slam each other up against a wall, rip each other's clothes off on the way to bed. The next day the place looks like it was raided by the FBI. I have to say, it was pretty wild. We were safe, but I know now why I have never been the one-night stand kinda gal. It is fun for a few hours and then what? Nothing. But in truth, a one-night stand was on my bucket list, and there is no better place for some debauchery than The Howling Dog Saloon… especially with a hot German that I knew I would never see again.

I also have amazing friends in Wasilla, Kenai and Anchorage. Most recently, I got a call from a guy named Fred Becker, who manages Denali Harley Davidson in Wasilla. Fred saw my show many years ago when I was performing at the Brown Bear Saloon, a very cool little hole-in-the-wall on the Seward Highway about forty miles south of Anchorage. The Bear sits almost in the middle of nowhere with deep woods behind it and the ocean inlet across the street. It's a biker hangout for sure. On show night, I had to get dressed in the trees, so I came walking out of the woods in full Bags. I saw him and his bro in the parking lot on their Harleys. I waddled on over to see if I could mess with them a tad. Apparently, I made an impression because he never forgot my silly ass and looked me up last year to see about having me play an event he was putting on.

Denali H.D. is one of only four dealerships in the whole state. The other three are owned by one woman, who is in my opinion an absolute Rockstar: Dia Matteson… a black-haired beauty with lips like Snow White, a brain like Steven Hawking, and tits like Marilyn Monroe. She bought the shops from her dad and runs all three of them like a *boss*. A very, very cool boss. Best part is… she is barely into her thirties! We have become great friends and I played at all three of her dealerships, from Kenai Peninsula to Anchorage to Wasilla, in one summer.

When I returned to Alaska that fall, I played in Fairbanks at my favorite bar on Earth, Ivory Jacks. Low and behold, who the hell shows up to surprise me, but these maniacs—Fred and Dia! They all jumped in an airplane in Anchorage and flew up to see me. That wasn't the real surprise, though. Fred—nutjob that he is—dressed up exactly like Bag Lady Sue in the airport bathroom. They then grabbed an Uber and walked in my dressing room unannounced. I lost my mind! It made me cry. I honestly have never seen another Bags that looked so much like the original… *ever*. Apparently for weeks prior, Fred and Josette (his wife) searched high and low

to find the exact outfit, or as close as they could. They imitated the boots, the hat, the socks on the hands, and even the freakin' shawl. When they walked in, I was literally five minutes from having to go onstage. It took all I had not to start crying like a baby.

I have taken my daughter, many friends and a couple lovers up to Alaska with me. I am glad I could give others this amazing experience. Cheyenne always had a blast but is not a fan of the cold, so we went in summer. Twenty-plus hours of

Fred as "Bag Lady Sue"

daylight is cool but sadly, you can't see the northern lights then. I think I am going to drag her back for that. There is nothing like it on Earth.

One of my best trips up there was one I took alone. It was a bucket list trip for me. I drove down to Seward to kayak with the orcas in Resurrection Bay. I floated by playful otters and watched bald eagles fly over my head as I paddled down the pine tree lined coast away from town. It is thrilling and scary to be out on all that water in a little plastic boat that flips on a dime knowing that lurking beneath you are Shamu's hungry cousins.

On a serious note, orcas do not like the taste of—or usually eat—humans. Usually is the key word. I'm sure compared to organic seal, we taste like bad ass. I have to admit, after seeing their dorsal fins out on the bay in groups of two or more, it gets real... very quickly. They did not approach my kayak, but knowing they were probably watching me scared the shit out of this old lady. And yet, it was the best thirty bucks I ever spent. My next bucket list kayak adventure is floating the Kenai Fjords with the humpback wales.

Life is short; make it happen! Alaska is, without question, my Heaven on Earth. I hope you all get to see it before your time here is through. Trust me, it will change you forever.

Lance's sled - Fox, AK

The Storm Rolls In

At this point in my life, I was still battling alcohol. The more success I was experiencing, the more money I made, the lonelier I was. I went through a lot of ups and downs on the way to getting sober, and they weren't all peachy. Many tears were shed, and there were times I would pull into a bar parking lot crying because I was one second away from going in and getting shit faced. But I would call an AA friend, and they would always talk me out of it.

So, eventually it got easier, and life came together better than ever. The promises you would hear in the AA rooms started coming true. In that year-and-a-half I remained sober, I made more money, had more fun, and remembered more of what I did than any year before or since. There were many great meetings, and I tried to go to a new one at least once a week.

Some friends had told me about a meeting which was mostly bikers called Putt-n-Sober and said I should check it out. I put off going till one beautiful summer night in late June 2005. I had no idea how that night would change my whole life. I was sitting home on my deck and kept hearing a voice in my head saying, *Go to the biker meeting. Go to the biker meeting.* So, I jumped on the Harley and off I went.

Putt-n-Sober was held in a big warehouse building in a pretty sketchy area on the north side of Denver. When I walked in, even I was a bit intimidated. There were some really rough-looking folks there, so I sat with my back to the wall and watched the goings on. The place was packed with bikers of all ages and walks of biker life: young, old, 1%-ers, yuppies, the whole gamut, and—honestly— they all seemed none too friendly. But hell, I was there so I figured I'd stay and see how it went. Suddenly, the door across from me opened and a warm breeze blew in and hit me right in the face. It was the kind you get when you are standing outside at night and a storm suddenly whips up out of nowhere. You know how you can smell the freshness of the rain coming and feel the electricity all around you? That was how this was for me.

When I looked up, I saw the most beautiful man I had ever laid eyes on in my entire life coming through the door. He literally took my breath away. He was 6'5" tall with messy dark silky hair, warm green eyes and lips like Elvis. Oddly for a biker meeting, he was wearing Khaki shorts, sandals, and a polo shirt. He certainly did not fit in with the crowd, but he did not seem out of place either.

I couldn't take my eyes off him, and my heart raced in my chest like my Harley was inside it! He sat down across from me, facing forward, so I was looking at him from the side. He seemed quite restless and kept tossing his gorgeous black hair back off his face. It was all I could do to not sit there with my mouth hanging open with drool pouring out the corners. Suddenly, he stood up and started talking, and that is when I noticed the wedding ring. SHIT! Oh well, so much for that. I was not one to *ever* mess with a married man. At least I was until then...

Apparently, he was there for his stepdaughter's one year sobriety "birthday." When he spoke, my heart just melted. What he said and how he said it was beautiful, and all I could think of was how sad I was that Cheyenne didn't have a man this great as her stepdad. It made me cry, so I decided to go outside. I was standing in the corner alone by the soda machine all weepy, when—out of nowhere—this girl came up to me and said, "Are you ok?" I said, "Yeah, I'm just a little sad. I just heard this guy say really beautiful things for his stepdaughter, and I wish my kid had a dad like that."

She replied, "Oh! That was *my* dad." I could have shit right there! I had no words. Then she said, "He is so amazing! I don't know why he is with my mom. She is such a bitch to him all the time. She doesn't appreciate him at all."

I thought, *no way is this happening right now*. I mean *What are the odds*. I said to her, "What? That's your dad? Wow, you are really lucky to have someone care so much about you." So, we talked a while and she began to fill me in on things at home, and all I could think was, *Wow, this broad must be a real piece of work if her own daughter thinks she's rotten.*

I gave her my card and we chatted about me being in showbiz, then she told me her dad was an amazing singer. Just then she looked up behind me and said, "Oh wait, there he is! I want you to meet him. Dad, come here, I want you to meet someone." I turned around and he walked toward me. I swear to God my knees were knocking. Not only was he gorgeous, but when he smiled at me, I saw the damn sun and it was nighttime.

He was the friendliest guy ever, and we ended up talking for a good hour in the parking lot. I didn't even see where his daughter went. It was cool that we were both in the entertainment biz, well… I was, and he was trying to be. He told me that his wife never supported his dreams of singing or having a Harley. She didn't even keep a clean house, but he loved his kids. All he did was work to give her money for bills, and she didn't even work. As I listened to him, I couldn't wrap my head around that fact that so often some miserable, usually unattractive cow gets a man like this and keeps him as her beck-n-call boy. *Why?* I mean, what is it? Sure, pussy is awesome, and I have been told mine is stupendous, but even I wouldn't use it to keep a man just for his money. Not one who I couldn't share laughter and joy with, no matter how good-looking he was. But that is me.

Despite the fact that I was incredibly attracted to this dude in every conceivable way, I knew—good or bad—that he belonged to someone else. I figured I'd better go. I hugged him a friendly goodnight, hopped on the bike, and that was that.

Until ten days later on July 4th...

I was working a gig in Salida, CO, for the Independence weekend, which is also my birthday. I had taken my niece and my daughter for a mini vacation when I noticed I had missed a call from an unknown number. When I went to check my voice mail, I was glad I was sitting down. The message said, "Hey, it's Storm. We met last week at Putt-n-Sober. I have been thinking about how great it was talking with you and was wondering if you would like to meet for coffee or to sing some Karaoke? My wife is cool, she won't care. Anyway, here's my number call anytime."

What the hell? I didn't know what to do or think. I have to be honest, for the last ten days I couldn't stop wondering why this woman's own daughter would say the things she'd said about her mom and stepdad... and I couldn't stop thinking of him. I just sat there. I wanted to call him so much, but part of me thought better of it. I mulled it over for a good while and then, I'll be honest, I caved. I was single and had no one to answer to, and what the hell would be wrong with having a gorgeous friend to hang out and sing with? That was my first mistake...

The next thing I knew, we met for an evening of Karaoke at a bar in Golden. We stood outside in the warm July air and talked and laughed for what seemed like forever. It was so easy; we finished each other's thoughts as if we had been best friends for years. Then, he got up and sang for me, and that was the last time I ever had possession of my soul. I fell for him instantly.

At first, we became fast friends and hung out together as much as we could. I guess we just made each other feel the best of our true selves. I was lonely, and he was in an unfulfilling marriage. As time went on, it became clear this A) was not your average attraction, and B) I was in deep shit. Still, when someone makes you feel like you are on a constant life high, it is only natural to want more of them. Addiction is addiction, be it to alcohol, drugs, or a person.

Over the next month, we got together every chance we could. I have never laughed or fell so hard in all my life. He told me he felt

Storm

like a man when he was with me but a wimp when he was with her. I was screwed.

I had to play the Broken Spoke Saloon in downtown Sturgis for Bike Week at the beginning of August. Storm had just been laid off from his job at the Rocky Flats Nuclear site. So, I mentioned that it was too bad he can't come to Sturgis with me. He said, "well, hell, yes I can!" And off we went. It was the best time of my life… at first.

We drove across Wyoming singing Fleetwood Mac and old Gary Puckett tunes at the top of our lungs. We laughed and enjoyed being free. Knowing some of his life story, I am pretty sure he had never felt like that before. I could see it in his smile. My God, what a smile.

One evening, I got him up on stage at the Broken Spoke Saloon to sing for a huge crowd. He sang *Man in the Box* and, as always, sang it better than the original. Watching him made me feel such awe, and—for the time being—I forgot he was still married. In my heart, I had found the true mate to my very soul, though my head knew deep inside that this was going to end painfully.

For the moment, however, I just didn't care. No man had ever made me feel what he did, and we had not even had sex, NONE! We got to the Spoke and it was around 95° out. So, I got ready for my show in the beer cooler. Storm was there to help and right before I went out to go onstage, he grabbed me and kissed me deeply and passionately. It was the first time in my whole life I was kissed while in full Bag Lady. HOW SEXY!

The show went amazing, especially considering I threw my cigarettes out the window on the drive up and was a nervous wreck. There were a bunch of the Hell's Angels there for the show. Apparently, they also thought we were pretty great because when we left, Storm respectfully asked if we could go past, and after a few nods of their heads, they opened up an aisle for us through the crowd so we could leave. I will never forget the feeling of walking down a row of H.A.s and seeing them smiling and even clapping for the old Bag Lady! It was awesome, and I was honored and so very proud. I know Storm was also. As we walked, it started to rain, so he put his jacket over our heads. Years later after we split up, I found a statue of two lovers hiding under a leather jacket kissing. I still have it today.

When we got back to the room that night, he sat on the bed and played guitar for me and sang. At one point I saw tears in his eyes but said nothing. I know he was fighting an inner battle that I couldn't help him with. We laid in each other's arms. It was beautiful.

When we made love for the first time, it felt like we were one soul split between two bodies. There was not one part of this man I did not want to consume. The smell of him made my head spin: his hair, his skin, everything. His scent was intoxicating, and his green eyes were intense. It was as if he literally climbed into my soul. I sat on top of him and looked down at his incredible face and I was lost. When I put him inside of me, I swear to God if he would have died right there, I would have died with him, and he made me believe he would have done the same. I had fallen in love with him that much.

I was going crazy inside because I could not understand what the hell was happening. I just knew he believed in me, my talent, and my work with all his heart, or at least he acted like he did. So much so that I hadn't a clue otherwise. I was so alive, and even if just for the short time we shared, I also believed in him. We had everything in common. People noticed and would comment about that to us all the time. No matter where we went, even strangers saw it. "Kismet" I believe they called it. He was pretty much me with a dick. We just had this "thing."

I remember walking around Deadwood in just my white chaps, cowboy boots, a white lace thong and bra with most of my backside showing (it's a Sturgis thing), feeling on top of the damn world. He was right beside me watching over me, being so open and friendly and he seemed so damn proud to be with me. He kept telling everyone who I was and to come see my show. Never once did he promote himself. He just reminded me all the time that I was beautiful. Our times together were, even today, the best I have ever had.

After Sturgis, I told him he had to go back to her and make a choice. I did not want to be in a triangle with him and his wife. I had to walk away, but my soul felt dead. He left and I drove back to Denver alone. I didn't see him or even talk to him for about a week. Then he called me and said, "I left her, I am coming to be with you." Of course, I was selfishly thrilled. Remember this man had become the love of my life! In my eyes, he was perfect.

Deadwood

Within two weeks he was back. He said he felt like his soul was dying when he was with her, and he showed up with his duffel bag and the things he could bring. The storm had blown back into my life. (Storm is not his real name, just a nickname I gave him for the chaos he created when he blew into my life.) I knew it would not be that easy and there would likely be much more drama ahead, but to be honest, all I wanted was to feel that high again. Sharing life with him was like being on a beautiful drug, and I was addicted. I remember him standing behind me in front of my mirror holding me and saying, "My God, look at us! You are so damn beautiful, and when I am with you, I'm strong. I'm the man I was meant to be. I feel like there is nothing I can't do. I can see it in my face. I look so healthy! I feel invincible. Look at us… do you see it?!" I did see it. Happiness makes us look and feel so much different than misery does.

I had another gig in Iowa, so he came with me. As we drove along interstate 80 across the wide-open prairie, that sense of freedom filled our souls again—just like the first trip to Sturgis. This time we wrote a song together called *Backs Against the Wall* about a soldier going into battle. I think it is magnificent. I copy-wrote it. Maybe someday I'll find someone to record it. Toby Keith or Trace Adkins would be perfect. Hell, I need to look into that.

We went to a big rally in Conesville, Iowa, called Thunder in the Sand (now called Redneck Revival) and performed with my friends Skin Kandy. They let Storm come onstage in front of the huge crowd and sing *18 and Life* by Skid Row. He nailed it so much so that chicks were throwing their freaking bras at him! He lost his mind with joy. I had never seen someone so high after a performance. Little did I know, I had pretty much created a monster.

After we got back to Denver that Monday, he had called his soon to be ex-wife about seeing his kids and that is when the shit started. She had his balls and was not about to let them go. Looking back, he may not have really wanted to give in to her. He had no idea how to fight back, and I could not make anything better. All I could do was let him go and figure it out himself. He tried going back and forth between lives for a brief time, but we both knew I couldn't be in that with him. I didn't feel like he loved me as much as he said or acted like he did. If he had, nothing would have stopped him from figuring it out.

There is an old song by Percy Sledge called *When A Man Loves A Woman* that kept playing over and over in my head. It's the truth.

Honestly, I had fallen so deeply in love with him, that even after I knew I had to walk away—and did—it took me almost nine years to get over the whole damn thing. After we parted, I felt a lot like the walking dead. My body functioned and my work mind, but my soul was asleep for years. My momma's mind worked, too, because I had to go on for Cheyenne. Still, the point is, I *did* walk away.

What I eventually learned much later in life was he was a textbook Narcissist. It would take an entire book to clue you in on exactly *what* that means, so instead, I will just say, *please* search for it! There is a guy named Richard Grannon who has some incredible videos on the subject. It is worth your time if you have ever been, or never want to become sucked into the toxic pool that is loving one of these maniacs. I left mostly because I watched things between him and his wife (a.k.a. now ex-wife) over the months we hung out and realized it was kind of a toxic game they played.

I walked away but he would come back, and I would let him in. Then I would know he was still addicted to her and the shit, and send him away, again. Then I would miss him and his laughter and the way he made me feel, so I tried to reach him. It was like a drug or alcohol addiction. I hated that I wanted him so badly because he was not mine to have. In the end, I definitely ended up paying dearly for my stupidity. But I would almost take the pain again for the times we shared. At that time, I had never felt so alive with anyone, and I know no one ever made me laugh so hard and so often. I loved myself when I was with him.

The trouble was, I had no idea at the time that he had a ton of shit he never actually got around to facing about his life. I am pretty sure his ex-wife hadn't, either. Even though he divorced her, it seemed they were still both hooked on the drama between them. Apparently, she knew how to mind fuck him into submission using his kids, her snatch, and whatever other means of guilt and shit that she could use to keep the meal ticket handy. He was not without guilt as well, and I am sure he put her through a ton of shit in return.

I think that so many people do not truly know what *love* is. I see it often: women like that break a good man's balls so badly that he becomes a shell of what he once was and then… she doesn't even want him anymore. Chicks that use their kids to manipulate or control men, in my opinion, are scumbags who should be taken out and shot by a firing squad. They cause many generations of garbage to be passed down from their kids to others and their kids, and so on. It sucks. If the bad times outweigh the good, move on. Kids deserve healthy family relationships whether *you* like him or not.

The trouble with people like this chick is she didn't want him, but she didn't want anyone else to have him, either. It is like a child with a toy. They will let a toy sit on a shelf for a year and never give it a second thought *until* some other child wants to play with it, then… holy hell, look out. It's mine, mine, mine! Suddenly, that is their favorite toy again. That was him and her. She'd make him miserable; he would jump the fence, cheat, and then she would take him back and punish him. Addiction. On top of all the garbage between the two "grownups," don't even get me started on what kind of hell and damage it lays on the kids.

I don't know her story, but I am sure it is equally a mess. I know he came from some really bad stuff in his childhood, and I am sure now that is what made him Narcissistic and also kept him in her clutches. Better them and their kids than me and Cheyenne. Trust God when he doesn't answer your prayers. There is a reason.

It took a while before I honestly could even look at other guys. I mean, I had been heartbroken before, but I *always* managed to appreciate looking at men. This time I felt nothing at all. Antonio Banderas could have ridden up on a big black Friesian stallion with an 8" cock, a bag full of money, and a white flag of surrender flying from his flag-pole-sized weenie, and I would barely have noticed. I was in bad shape.

Thank God, I had Cheyenne. She needed me to be all that for her. Otherwise, I might well have just lay down and died. It is hard to imagine being so sad for so long that you simply do not wish to go on one more moment. It is a strange kind of pain because it spreads through you like a virus and consumes your entire soul, but no one else can *see* the broken parts, or *feel* what you are feeling. It is horribly lonely. I will never forget what that was like. I also now understand how and why so many people, including our veterans, make the ultimate decision. Until you feel that level of loneliness, pain, and darkness for a long period of time, you simply cannot understand how someone could take that road. Now I understand.

My Wing Men

Eventually, being that sad for that long got to be more than I could bear, and I got the ridiculous idea that I should kill myself. Seriously. I had the most amazing life, but I simply could not see anything in my future. All I knew was I wanted to stop hurting.

So, I got a fat life insurance policy, made arrangements for Chey to go back East to my mom should anything "happen to me," and I drove up to the mountains fully intent on driving my truck off a cliff on Hwy 103. I was so lost in my misery that I couldn't even think of what that would do to my precious child. It was *that* dark inside of me. Looking back today, I am terrified that something like that could get away from my rather intelligent mind. Trust me, no human being is worth ending it for. If you understand that darkness, please find help.

On the way up I-70 I began to cry and pray. I said, *God, if You are really there, You need to help me. You need to take this pain away and show me how to go on or I swear I am done!* Suddenly, I remembered there was a bike rally going on at Copper Mountain

Resort, so I thought I would take in one last party before I checked out, and I passed the exit for Hwy 103. When I got to the resort, I parked my truck down at the bottom of the lot and started walking up to the event. Still praying, mind you, I said, *Please, God, please tell me what to do.* Just then, two long-haired guys on new Harley Road Kings flew past me. I rounded the bend just in time to see these two gorgeous men taking off their over shirts to put on their vests. One was literally shirtless and the other was only wearing a white tank top. They were both breathtakingly handsome... no, screw that, they were ridiculously sexy! So much so that I stopped in my tracks, looked up at the sky, smiled and said to God, *Damn, You're good!* He knew how to get my attention, that's for sure.

So, even though I lightened up some for a moment, I was still pretty down. As I walked past them, I said, "Hey, excuse me, how the hell do you get in this place?" They looked at each other and then looked at me, and at the exact same time said, "Come on, we'll show you."

Well, ok then. One got on one side of me, the other got on the other side, and we walked into the rally together. From that moment they never left my side, not for one moment except to pee, of course. Even though neither of them had any idea how terribly sad I was or what I had set out to do that day, they became my wingmen simply because they stayed by my side. The blonde's name was Harley, and Michael was the dark-haired fella. I will never get over the connection we all had that day. It literally saved my life.

That night when I got home, I called Harley to say thank you and see if they would be open to hang out again the next day. He said that would be awesome, but they had something to do in the morning. His exact words to me were, "You are probably going to think we're weird, but we go to church." I'll grant you I was a bit taken back because to look at them you would not expect the word "church" to come out of either of these guys' mouths, but I did not think it was weird at all. In fact, all of the sudden, it made incredible sense.

He suggested I come with them, but I politely declined as church was simply not my thing. But he had told me where they were going, just in case I changed my mind. I said good night and told him to call me after church.

That night I had the worst dream I had ever had of Storm and me. I literally woke up crying hysterically just like I did the night I dreamt of my dad. I jumped out of bed, put on the first thing I could find to wear, and headed for the door fully intent on going

My Wingmen

directly to the local dive bar up the street and drinking myself to death. I had simply had enough. Just as I got to front door to leave, inside my head as clear as day I heard, *Go to church!* It was so clear that I yelled out, "Screw church!" as I grabbed the doorknob and opened the door. Again, I heard, *Go to church!* I stopped crying and just stood there for I don't remember how long. Then I turned around, put on a nice dress, fixed my hair, and went to church.

I pulled up to Faith Bible Chapel in Wheatridge, Colorado, and felt very out of place until I saw their Harleys out front along with a few other bikes. I thought, *Ok, this isn't so bad.* Then I found the guys, and they hugged me warmly. I felt like I belonged there and was surrounded by them and their friends. This began a years-long friendship which was one of the realest I had ever known.

Eventually, Harley fell in love and moved to California, but Mike and I spent a year-and-a-half together almost daily. I even took him to Alaska with me, not once but twice! We had the time of our lives, but we never became more than friends. Michael's faith was so strong, and sex just wasn't something either of us needed to share. He was like my brother and his family was mine as well. Michael was a great man, and a true Christian. I often felt Jesus come right through him to me. We lost Michael to cancer in 2017. If there truly is a Heaven, I know he is there. I cannot thank them enough for taking the time to care about a total stranger in the worst time of her life.

South Carolina and Scotty Joe

Thankfully, I still had to travel for my work, and that was a wonderful distraction. I had met a guy when I played Myrtle Beach Bike Week the year before who owned an awesome indoor/outdoor venue, kind of like the Broken Spoke Saloons. It sat on the edge of the woods in the low country on the outskirts of Charleston, SC. (It was owned by the same guy that would later hire me the following year to open for Kid Rock in Ladson, SC.) He had called me and asked me to play his bar, so I jumped at the chance to once again get out of Denver—and as far away from Storm's memory as I could.

Even though my mind was toast, I was still in incredible physical shape. I was even rockin' six-pack abs. I had remained sober and working out like an animal. Back then I stripped out of Bag Lady and ended up in a little pair of white, lacy booty-shorts and a bra. That night, after my show ended, it started raining so we all ran inside the bar building—me in my lacy lingerie. As I blew through the old, rickety screen door, I heard the sexiest southern accent on Earth as thick and slow as maple syrup say, "Well, I'll be damned. Where you runnin' to Honey? Come on back here and let me buy you a drink!" It stopped me in my tracks, and I looked up to see the finest looking 6'6", blond-haired, country boy I'd ever seen. He smiled, I smiled, and well, hell. I told him, "Thanks, but I don't drink," and turned to run off.

He was a persistent fella and would not let up until I agreed to at least talk to him a minute. That damn accent was kicking my ass, and he had a cocky sexiness about him that came off as confidence. So, I stopped and chatted a bit. His name was Scotty Joe, and I could see how, if I stayed, I might have gotten myself into some trouble. Finally, after a few minutes I stood up prepared to run off again. As I was leaving, he walked behind me yelling, "Wait! Come back."

I was settling up with the promoter and getting ready to catch my ride back to my hotel when Scotty came over to the other side of the bar. He tried to get me to hang out for a while. I told him I really needed to get going back to my room, so he offered to drive me. I said, "I don't even know you and you've been drinking, so I just can't. Thank you, but I'm sorry. Please understand." His response was, "But I have a Corvette. A nice one. Hell, I'll even let you drive! C'mon, now. Don't be *skeart*." (That is, apparently, is how you say "scared" in a thick southern accent.) Part of me wanted to let him, but more of me was still so damn damaged from my last affair, I couldn't even see the adventure in it.

However, I gave him my card and said, "If you want to get to know me, here you go. Bye now," and I had the promoter drive me back to town to my hotel. I remember lying in bed that night unable to stop crying. I was as lonely and sad as I had ever been. All I could do was pray for relief.

The next morning the pain was still there. To make things worse, on the way back to the airport I heard the song by George Jones, *He Stopped Loving Her Today*. No other song to this day has ever wrecked my heart like that one. I think it is the saddest, yet greatest love song of all time. However, if you are even thinking of suicide and that song comes on, SHUT IT THE FUCK OFF! At that moment, my mind changed "He" to "I" and "Her" to "Him." I almost lost it.

When I got back to Denver and turned on my phone, there was a message from Scotty Joe. I was glad. It sure made me feel better. He called me sexy in that fine accent, and I got all tingly inside. I liked that.

I've always heard it said that when you are trying to get over someone, get under someone else. So, I figured I might give that a chance. I called him and we hit it off instantly. By then end of the conversation he was making reservations to come to Colorado to take me skiing. I told him not to come out if he was doing so simply to get laid, as I was not that gal and could not in good conscience promise that would happen. After all, I did not know this guy past the five minutes we'd talked in South Carolina. He swore he wouldn't push the issue, so I agreed to the weekend ski trip.

Scotty flew into Denver after the snow started falling. I picked him up, and we headed straight to the mountains. We reserved a gorgeous, swanky B&B in Breckenridge on the side of a mountain and—honestly—had the time of our lives. His country ass had never skied before, so you can imagine the disaster I got to witness as he rolled over and over down the mountain looking like a big blond snowplow. He wiped out twenty-three times on one trip down the hill. I counted. I commended him for being persistent! The back of his Carhart jacket was so frozen that it curved up and stuck out like the tail of a duck. He was funny, witty, cocky and sweet all in one. Being a true southern gentleman, he kept his word on the *not trying to screw me* deal, which of course made me want him even more. All I will say is… my, my, my.

Life suddenly became exciting again and, though my heart was still pretty cracked, I decided to make myself start to live again. We kept in touch pretty regularly over the next couple of months, and I got to know a lot about him. He grew up in a little town called Kennett, Missouri, and went to school with Cheryl Crow. He wanted more from life, so he moved to South Carolina and worked managing a big steel company. He was a redneck country boy deep down even though he had made good. Very good. I liked that he was so real… despite apparently having a shitload of money, a nice new Corvette, and a big-ass house on a golf course. I honestly don't think I would have liked him had he not been so down to earth, regardless of how rich he was. Money, fortunately or unfortunately, had never impressed me, though I sure as hell liked driving that damn car!

We did the long-distance thing for over a year and whether in South Carolina, Missouri, or Colorado, we always had so much fun together. Our kids even got to know each other. His son was a couple of years older than Cheyenne, so he flew us all down to spend a week in South Carolina with him. I hadn't been with a man who had a beautiful home, a lot of money and class for years. It was nice to be spoiled, treated like a princess, and shown off. He always made me feel like he was very proud to be with me. I loved that.

The first time I went down to see him, he had to go to work. He kissed me goodbye, tossed me the keys to his souped-up 2006 Corvette complete with Borla Cat-Back exhaust, Bose stereo, pop top and nitrous, and said, "Go on, Baby, have yourself some fun." So, I did! I felt like Julia Roberts in *Pretty Woman,* sans the hooker part. I was thrilled! Needless to say, I spent every day on the beach on Isle of Palms mingling with the wealthy, and it sure didn't suck. I found out not all rich people are dicks. Most of them were so nice and very benevolent, just like many of my biker friends who aren't so rich.

In the evenings we would go out to dinner and happy hour with his golfing buddies, who it seems all got a hell of a kick out of me. I felt like a trophy girlfriend!

I will never forget the one time Cheyenne flew down with me when she was around twelve. She was super impressed with the opulence of it all—especially the big fancy house on the golf course—and the fact that he *never* let me pay for anything. The Corvette, of course, gave her a thrill too. I think that trip and the experience of knowing him profoundly raised her own standards.

She and I took a drive one sunny afternoon to the beach in our bikinis and lounged about on the sand like rock stars, drinking virgin Strawberry Daiquiris and Piña Coladas. Later, we drove through downtown Charleston so I could show her the old mossy oaks and grand southern mansions. All the boys were checking us out! I will never forget her big smile and how very pleased she was with it all. I remember stopping at a light in town and seeing a really cute but sloppily dressed teenage boy loafing with his friends on the corner smoking a cigarette. They looked over at us, smiled and waved. We smiled and waved back.

Then I looked at my daughter and not being sure where it came from said, "Honey, I want you to think hard about something. You are a teenager now, (she was almost thirteen) and boys are going to come and go. You will have crushes and loves. You are going to have to make some choices that will affect everything that happens to you for the rest of your life. You can either fall for a boy like that, who hangs out on some corner in beat-up clothes partying with his friends and have *that* life, *or* you can choose a guy who has work ethic, class, and focus; someone who wants to make something of himself and have *this* life. It is up to you."

She thought about it for a minute and said, "I want *this* life, Momma." I was quite proud. I have never treated anyone as less because they don't make a bunch of money or because they have issues or because they don't choose to live the way I do, and I have never allowed my daughter to either. But I also learned almost too late that I deserve to be treated well and with absolute respect. I also earned the right to live an exceptional life. That doesn't mean the guy has to have a fat bank account or a Corvette. In the end, it is what lives inside of someone that matters first and most, though Grandma always did say, "Honey, you can love a rich guy just as easily as you can love a poor guy." Money isn't everything but having it and a good man together doesn't suck. It is amazing what that kind of lifestyle does for your self-esteem.

Being with Scotty in his world taught me and Cheyenne so much. I am grateful to him to this day for all the great moments and memories but most of all for reminding me I was worth being cherished, spoiled, and adored. He was definitely a man's man, and for me that was a huge turn on. It also allowed me to feel like a girl again rather than just the tough-ass biker chick I had become struggling on my own.

Eventually, we both realized I couldn't move to South Carolina and he couldn't move to Colorado, so we stayed friends and moved on. He found a really nice gal and got married. We still talk now and then. He sure is a peach.

Looking back on the relationships I have had, I am grateful that *I learned to accept the things I could not change, had the courage to change the things I could, and the wisdom to know the difference.*

Today I am pretty certain my and Cheyenne's life is so much better for it. We should trust our gut when it tells us to walk away. Yes, it is hard. Yes, it is sad, and yes, it is scary. Loneliness is a bitch. But I have come to learn that it is far better to be lonely for a time than to stay in something that literally sucks the soul from you.

Scotty's Vette - Ladson, SC
2006: Opening for Kid Rock

Raising Chey

Over the years Cheyenne and I have had enjoyed our life as a family. Doing comedy on weekends and making great money all these years has given me the ability to give her all she needed, including time together! We have traveled all over the USA from Alaska to Florida and Pennsylvania to Hawaii. She has learned more this way than any school can teach her. She is my greatest joy and reason for living and always has been. She attended college, doesn't drink, smoke, or do dope. She loves and respect all animals, helps the homeless, cares about our troops and—like me—is a huge patriot. I am so proud of her; I can't even stand it.

Cheyenne is a class act all the way, and she thinks I am just the bomb. How lucky am I? Very. She even went up on stage when she was little and introduced me at some of my rallies. Fearless little thing she was. She still is fearless but cares a little more these days about what people think of her. I told her the story my Grandma told me when I was about her age, and I think she is starting to understand. I think part of the reason Cheyenne turned out so great is because she had nothing to really be curious about. We have always had a very honest open friendship while still being mom and daughter.

I used to ride Cheyenne on my Harley with me from the time she could straddle the seat. I remember strapping her onto me with a wide elastic belt, because she would doze off on rides sometimes. The wind and the road lulled her right to sleep. Looking back… that was a bad idea. This is how I know we both have angels.

Cheyenne has been more like the parent than I have many times, I'm afraid. Not because I was a crappy mom, but because she is simply a Capricorn child, and they are the "Benjamin Button" of the zodiac (based on a short story by F. Scott Fitzgerald about a man who ages backwards). They start out mature, serious, and organized then get more childish with time. I even bought her a tee shirt once that said, *It's Hard Raising My Mom.* People used to ask me how my dirty comedy would affect her. Apparently, she gets it and never acted like a goof the way mom has. She's genuinely more grownup than me. I would like her to be wild and adventurous enough to make some of the crazy memories I have, but that's not her personality.

Unfortunately, though, Cheyenne was exposed to some drama at a young age that most children don't have to experience. I remember an incident that happened while I was dating Dakota. Cheyenne was at the wedding with me when things got really crazy, and I punched him in the jaw and sent him flying through the air. After we left the party that evening, Cheyenne and I pulled over on the side of the road to chill a minute. The situation had escalated very quickly, and I knew she would need a minute to debrief and catch her breath.

I asked her, calmly, "Ya ok, Pup?"

She said, "Yes, Mom, but that was scary."

"Yes, Baby, I know, but you know Mommy's got you, right?"

She answered, 'Yes."

I said, "I think that was kinda fun watching him fly through the air, huh?" She smiles. "Ya hungry? I feel like a cheeseburger. How's that sound?" Cheyenne and I enjoyed our cheeseburgers that night and were able to shake off the drama from earlier that evening.

By God's grace, I found the right way, the right words, and the right times to reassure Cheyenne that I will ALWAYS have her back, and that she is never alone. Also, by God's grace... she turned out amazing.

I wanted her to always feel safe coming to me with ANYTHING, knowing I would not judge or be mad. Most of all I made sure I never called her names or said anything to make her feel less or small. Don't get me wrong, she did get her fanny whacked a few times, and I used a guilt-trip now and then. And just like any child, she had to learn some things the hard way.

Life's Little Lessons

There was one particular incident that happened the week before Christmas in 2004 that shaped *both* of us for the rest of our lives. I had been working at a little neighborhood bar in Golden, Colorado to fill in the gaps between comedy shows. At the time, those gaps were long and happened more often than not. One night I went to work, and the place was closed. I mean really closed. No warning, no explanation, no paycheck... no nothing. I was flipping out, especially because Cheyenne's birthday is on Christmas. I had bought her plenty of gifts and all the goodies for her birthday but was counting on that money to pay our bills.

Throughout her life, I never told her when things were bad, even when they were at their worst. A few years prior to this we lost our house because I got hurt lifting an air conditioner into a window and was unable to work for almost a month. We ended up "camping" for a few days in a tent until I could find us a new place to live. I didn't feel the need to tell her how extreme the situation was—it would have ruined her camping trip. Personally, I believe little children shouldn't need to worry about grown up things… especially things they can't do anything about.

So…Chey woke up that Christmas morning and after she opened all her stuff, I *suggested* she pick one small thing that we could give to a little child who has nothing for Christmas. She acted like a selfish, ungrateful little hag and well… I just lost it! I grabbed by her little hand, put her in our SUV, and off to the Denver Rescue Mission we went.

Cheyenne needed a lesson in humility. The entire way there I ranted loudly about how very lucky we are and how hard it had been for me to keep our nice house, in a nice neighborhood, with a closet full of fancy clothes, blah, blah blah. We turned onto Lawrence Street and pulled into the parking lot across from the mission—which was empty, aside from the makeshift cardboard "houses" that people put up around the perimeter. There were at least thirty people mulling about, and another thirty or so in line for the hot Christmas breakfast.

I looked at her—her eyes now filled with tears—and said, "Cheyenne, I know you don't understand this, but mom lost her job, and we could seriously be a month away from ending up here if I don't figure things out. I knew full well that by hook or by crook, I would NEVER let that happen, but she didn't. We sat there for another twenty minutes or so in silence.

Out of the corner of my eye, I noticed a guy coming slowly toward us on her side of the truck. He saw me and made a gesture, as if asking if he could approach. I nodded yes. He came right up to her window which was half open. This startled her. I smiled and said, "Merry Christmas," expecting him to ask for some help. He did not.

What he did say is this: "Merry Christmas, kiddo. I think I know why your momma brought you here today. You wanna know why I'm here?"

Chey, still rather taken back by him, barely nodded but looked at him the whole time.

He said, "three months ago, I had a great job, a really nice house where I lived with my two kids, my pretty wife and our dog. I lost all of that because I like to drink. I have a problem with alcohol and couldn't stop drinking. I got my third DUI and went to jail. I lost my job, and finally my wife had enough of me and told me I could not come home anymore. Now I am here.

"You have a really nice truck, and I'll bet you have a nice house, too. You have a pretty mom that I know loves you so much, and she doesn't want you to end up like me. You better be nice to your momma and most of all... be thankful." Then he turned and walked away.

I yelled, "Thank you and God bless you" out the window and he turned and smiled. God shows up for us more times than we realize. That day changed her. From then on, she never let me pass a homeless person on the street without giving them whatever we could. She is still that way today.

Even when times were hard, I always made sure that Cheyenne had everything she would possibly need. Growing up, I remember surviving off powdered milk, canned pork, and government cheese. My mom used to fry spaghetti to make "garbage sandwiches." I promised myself my daughter would never have to do that. I think that's why I am so addicted to good food now as an adult. I'm a shopaholic when it comes to food, and always made sure our cabinets were stocked with all kinds of healthy foods and goodies too. It's amazing that Cheyenne and I don't each weigh a thousand pounds.

The Limelight

Being the daughter of "Bag Lady Sue" also provided opportunities for her that many other children never experience. I have a video of her and my niece Erica when they were around five years old dressed like Ann and Nancy Wilson of Heart. I did their makeup, gave them big 80's hair, and they got up in front of a crowd and sang *My Heart Will Go On* from Titanic. Their performance was perfect!

My Mini-me

Cheyenne first introduced me onstage when she was around eleven or twelve. Later, in her early twenties, she even held my ankles when I did the puppet at the HogRock Rally in front of around 10,000 folks.

Throughout the years, though, we've had many amazing times together. Chey and I also had the opportunity to go to the Florida Keys together. She has always loved the beach and Florida was her first one, so I take her back there as often as I can. I had always dreamed of going down to the Keys, and since it was on the bucket

list, I figured it was time to check it off. I initially planned to set up a show during a big biker event there called Phil Peterson's Key West Poker Run but couldn't make it happen. I tried to score something with the Hog's Breath, or Sloppy Joe's but still no luck. So, I did some research and found a nice 200-seat theater that is owned by some wonderful gay guys. Trouble was… after they found out who I was they wanted to price the tickets too high. Unfortunately, they didn't know enough about marketing to bikers, so I scrapped the idea.

I still wanted to make the trip, so off we went. I rented a gorgeous convertible in Ft. Lauderdale and got a flat tire seven minutes out of the airport. I bought a can of fix a flat after the car rental company told me I had to pay for a new tire. Yeah, like that was gonna happen. So, after we hit Key Largo and I knew the tire was good, I let Cheyenne drive. I wanted her to experience what it's like to be blowing down the coast highway with the wind in her hair and the salty smell filling her nose. She loved it so much! The Florida Keys are just lovely.

On our way down the overseas highway that connects Key Largo with the other Keys, we felt like Thelma and Louise without

the drama. There are actually 1500 islands in the Florida Keys, but most are too small to notice. We stopped on Islamorada Key when we saw a sign for hang-gliding trips out over the ocean.

I pulled onto their property which sat on the edge of a beautiful cove. I got out of the car and was greeted by a sexy thirty-some-thing boy with wild beach-boy, blond hair and an irresistible smile. He and his also cute friend Chris Greendale ran this amazing hang-gliding experience over the Keys. (They have since moved from the Keys and are now in Miami at Hang-gliding Miami. check them out!)

Cheyenne lost it when she saw the hang gliders and asked me if she could do it. Naturally, my first instinct as a mother is to try and talk her out of doing something I perceived as horribly dangerous. Lucky for her, my normal way of irrational thinking kicks in and I tell myself, *You only live once,* and say, "Sure, Baby, go for it!" Eric ended up taking her for free because he is awesome. I told him I was the Bag Lady and promised I would make them my Y.O.L.O. poster children and promote the hell out of their business, which I did. But the real truth is likely that Cheyenne is smoking hot and that is why they offered her a free flight. Gotta love men.

Here's how it worked: the guys had this big-ass *kite* and hanging from it is a thing that looked like couple of squid tubes that two people can slip into side by side. The instructor and you get in and are attached to an actual Hang Glider. *Not* a Parachute. This is not parasailing, folks, this is real-life hang-gliding. Cheyenne and Eric got suited up, put on their helmets, and got into the swingy-thing. They were now dangling from the kite, which is sitting on the back of the boat.

I, Chris, and their dog got in the boat and out onto the water we all went. I was trembling like a snow-covered cat, but Cheyenne was psyched out of her skull! I am praying under my breath the whole way out to sea. All of the sudden, Chris hits the throttle and the wind picks up and is blowing through my hair. We are cruising along and once we get up to speed… POOF the kite pops right up off the boat and up, up, and away goes my precious baby. She is getting smaller and smaller the higher they go. The line reels out from the rigging on the boat just as if you were flying a real kite. They are now hanging from the thing swinging back and forth like a pendulum. Once they were 1500 ft. above the water, Eric cut loose from the boat. The kite stopped in midair for a moment and suddenly the world went silent. I literally couldn't hear a sound.

I watched my only child flying around on the currents of air like an eagle. They circled, dove for a bit, and then stopped to float around. It looked so amazing, but I sat there like a chicken-shit, not wanting to even think about trying it.

After about twenty-five minutes they began coming down slowly and gently. As they got closer and closer to the water, I could hear Cheyenne laughing and yelling with joy, "Oh my God, Mom, it was awesome! You have to do this!" Then, with incredible precision, Eric and Cheyenne shoot right over the boat and land as gently as a swan upon the shallow water of the cove.

I could finally breathe. I was so proud of my gutsy girl. I jumped into the water and hugged her and Eric and thanked him over and over for giving my daughter the thrill of a lifetime.

That's when he said, "Ok, now it's your turn."

I answered, "I beg your pardon. I am sure you are under some gross misapprehension if you think for one moment that you are getting my ass up there! My heart is not strong enough to survive that and Cheyenne would be an orphan. You see, sweetie, I drank, smoked, and did illicit drugs for the better part of my young life. I have reversed some of the toxic effects of all that with a better diet, vitamins, regular trips to the gym and a great deal of kinky, rigorous, and physically strenuous sex over the years, but… I am quite sure this experience would kill me."

"You'll be fine," he says. "It's really not scary at all. Once you are up there, it's so quiet you can hear your heartbeat. You will feel so alive and free. Just do it. You only live once."

I could have ignored him, but then Cheyenne starts with the "Y.O.L.O., Mom, Y.O.L.O.! I did it and you're way tougher than me." She kinda made me feel like a big, fat, pussy. *So*, since I would rather die than have my kid think I didn't have balls, I agreed. Maybe she wanted the life insurance?

Reluctantly, I suited up, prayed hard, waved goodbye to my little buddy as if I would never get to hug her again, and off we went. The "Oh my Gods" started right then and continued full force while I went up and up and up, higher and higher, all while watching the line unravel from the boat. The islands and Cheyenne were getting smaller and smaller. I held onto the bar in front of me with a one-handed death grip and Eric, my hero at my side, with the other. Once we reached altitude, the spool on the boat jams and we jolt for a moment. Eric immediately cuts the line! I screamed and closed my eyes.

He was right… instantly it became quiet. I couldn't hear even the wind, not traffic below on the highway. Not one sound except for me screaming, "Fuck you, Eric, you lying bastard! Jesus Christ, help me! Oh my God, I'm gonna die! Please don't let me die, I will never get to have sex again! Please take me down! Oh my God, I honestly think I'm gonna die. I am not ready to die! Oh God, please let me live. I'll miss my kid. ERIC, you suck! Burn in hell!"

He was wrong about my being able to hear my heartbeat; my screaming was much too loud. But bless Eric's sweet little heart and his infinite patience because he somehow got me to stop screaming and open my eyes. He did not, however, get me to loosen my Kung Fu grip on that kite bar. I really never understood what the term "white knuckling it" meant until that day. I did actually try to look down and could for about one-and-a-half seconds, then I realized that quite possibly, *I was about to die*, and my eyes slammed shut once again. In truth, Eric is an absolute master. He was like a bird himself having done this very adventure a few thousand times. He asked me at one point if I would like to dive a little, to which I replied, "Would you like to keep your balls?" at the top of my lungs.

So, kindly or for fear of his own life, he did not do anything out of the ordinary. He just slowly and ever so smoothly took me back down to Earth. He was truly a kind, gentle, amazing man…

and so damn cute too. When we landed and I stood in the water, I realized it is true: you only do live once as far as we all know, so I was really glad I grew some balls. After giving birth to my daughter, that experience is about at the top of my list of rushes in life.

We all had dinner that night at a great restaurant on the next Key over where you can feed sharks and listen to a steel drum player jam beneath the tiki torches. Best of all, Cheyenne and I got to make great new friends who still keep in touch with us. If you're ever in Miami, Florida, or surfing Facebook, check out Hang-gliding Miami and tell Eric and Chris I sent you.

I took Cheyenne to her first drag show at the 801 Bourbon bar on Duval Street. Holy hell, what a ball! (No pun intended.) Cheyenne was laughing herself silly and even got some pictures taken with the cast. It was too cute. One of the artists came out with an enormous set of balls underneath "her" gown. She would sing this burlesque-style tune, lift up the gown and the balls would swing out. Hysterical!

Last of all on the way back to the mainland, we stopped on Key Largo, and I gave Chey one of the best surprises ever. When planning this trip, I had bought her a special surprise gift that I hoped would help her decide which path to take in her future. I got her a "trainer for a day" gig at a dolphin rescue and rehabilitation center called Dolphins Plus. It was amazing for her because her

dream has always been to work with animals, especially marine mammals. She got to not only swim free with them, but she also got to do training maneuvers, feed them, and get in the lagoon with them and swim free. I got to go in too. We swam with five adult dolphins and a baby! Just us and the dolphins. It was magical. The feeling of climbing down into their world is incredible. They are rather large mammals and, though friendly, still could kick your ass if they wanted to. It was unreal indescribable.

I also arranged for Cheyenne to get in the lagoon and swim with a sea lion named Ono. She got to pet her, hold her, and get pulled through the water while hanging onto her tail flipper, and she even got to play games with her. The joy on Cheyenne's face was so bright it was just like looking into the sun. I swear it was seriously worth every bit of the money I spent. I figured if I got this for her, it might give her the extra encouragement to pursue that in college, *or* it would let her know that even though that is a cool-looking job, it may not be something she wants to do every day. In the end, the choice is hers, but at least I opened the door.

The Stuff Dreams are Made Of

When Cheyenne was little and I was still struggling on my way up, I remember asking her, "So tell me kiddo, when mom gets rich and famous, what kind of car would you like me to get for you? I promise if there is a way, I will get it for you!"

Her reply: "A Lamborghini. A bright green one!"

I'm not joking, that's what she said. I thought *wow, that's my girl!* But I was also thinking ...I better get REAL famous, real fast. This made me pursue my dream even more.

Years later, even though I had become a national name and a great success financially, I was nowhere rich enough to buy her that Lambo. But a promise IS still a promise, especially when it comes to my daughter. So, I found a place in Las Vegas, (Cheyenne's favorite vacation spot) where I could rent a lime green Lamborghini convertible for a day. So, on her twenty-first birthday, I did.

I surprised her with a trip to Vegas, and the car. When she saw it, her eyes were wider than I had ever seen them. Even better... I let her drive! I know her heart pounded as she pulled out onto the desert highway and hit the gas. I will never forget her seeing big, beautiful smile, and the wind blowing through her long blonde hair. We raced through the desert and wound through the canyon. Every time she let off the gas and the car purred, she squealed with delight.

There is no sound like the sound of a Lamborghini. After a couple of hours and endless photos, we headed back to town so Cheyenne could cruise the Vegas Strip and "show off". There was not a person that did not look her way. We heard many hoots and hollers from guys at us and the car.

Finally, we pulled up at Caesars Palace and grabbed a photo out front, tossed the keys to the valet, and went inside for a cocktail like a couple of Rockstars. Of all the things I have ever done for her, that was one of the best.

From the moment my eyes caught hers on the day she was born, nothing and no one has been more important to me, including myself. There were many times in my life that I thought I found my "soul mate," but only once I truly did.

2010 - Rocky Mountain Park

Bags Makes the Big Time

Throughout the years I've had the opportunity to work with some of the biggest names in the business. Some stars I've worked with are really cool. Kid Rock, well, you all know he is the shit. Funny story… his manager got pissed when my agent advertised my name before his on my website when we played together in South Carolina.

I also got a call from the promoter about a month before the show saying there was a problem, and that the town folk were trying to ban the show due to the nasty language. I said, "What? You mean they are trying to keep Kid Rock from playing?" and he said, "No, Bags. They are trying to keep *both* of you from playing!" I was honored to be in Kid's company on that comment.

The show did go on, however, but it was a nightmare. The promoter didn't get his insurance binder in time, and they couldn't open the gates until like three hours before showtime. We had no dressing room, and Kid was pissed. I had to get dressed in a field surrounded by pickup trucks. Seriously, about five guys pulled their pickups into a circle like covered wagons during a war party raid in the old west! I hung out in the center.

I don't need to tell you the fans were a tad bummed that they had to wait outside the fairground's gate forever. But Kid put on an amazing show and all ended well. I, sadly, did not get to even get a picture with him or get to meet him all personal as they had another show in the next town and took off promptly. I will always be bummed about that.

I also had the chance to work with Artemus Pyle again in the Catskills at Mountain Thunder. He is a quiet, rather reserved man, but a sweetheart. At least he was to me and my friends. Hank Williams Jr. is awesome, too.

A different year at The Boogie I got to meet Kenny Wayne Shepard who is really very shy, and Pat Travers, who was unknown to me at the time but is a bit of a legend. It was funny because I was sitting in the lobby of the hotel with a couple of friends, and I said in my *I really don't give two shits what anyone thinks of me tone*, "So, who the hell is this Pat Travers dude anyway? I've never even heard of him." Just then, Pat turns slowly around from the coffee maker where he had been standing the whole time and gives me the sexiest smile ever.

His eyes said, *Ha ha, you silly bitch; you are so busted*, just as my buddy hits me and says, "Uh, Bags… that would be Pat right there." Damn. Pat and I have played together a few times since. He is not only an incredible artist, but also a gentle soul and a great guy.

The Kentucky Headhunters are pretty damn cool, too. I worked with them a bunch and even had them perform at my own bike rally in PA. I have partied on their bus and have a picture of me and Richard Young where you can see my tampon string hanging out of my rebel flag bikini. We're very close.

Bad Company and Confederate Railroad were terrific. The original lead singer, I hear, was really sweet. He supposedly was hung like a bear. Guys with large peckers usually have too little blood to their brains to think of too much besides beaver, really. I am sad I never got to eat him… I mean meat, meet. Whatever.

The guys of Black Oak Arkansas were fun. Jim Dandy is like pushing seventy and can still hold his own up on stage, spandex and all. I really like those guys. They were humble despite the incredible fame they had in the '70s.

Trent Tomlinson is another friend I met during this time who is unbelievably talented. I think he is one of the greatest country songwriters on the planet. He's sexy, too. He had two songs on the Top 10 Country charts and was partying like a rockstar.

I worked with Dr. Hook who was verbally short and really grouchy, which sucked because his song *Sharing the Night Togeth-*

er was my life's happy song. I didn't actually get to *meet* David Allan Coe, though I have worked rallies next to him twice. I heard he is a grouch too. They could have been having a bad night, but when a so-called star that I am on the bill with doesn't see fit to make time for a pre-show hello with me, I tend to think less of them. I always make time for people. Always.

Let's Hear it for the Girls

During this time, there were a few women in my life who helped and encouraged me. I will forever be grateful for these bitches. Skyy was my first actual roadie and has probably written more of my material by accident than anyone else. When I first started having merchandise, she was my sales whore at some of the bigger rallies. I think guys were afraid *not* to buy my stuff for fear she would kick the shit out of them. Skyy is seriously the funniest bitch I know.

She was with me when I played at the Famous Broken Spoke Saloon, and we had a blast. Jay Allen put us up in Rapid City in a decent hotel that happened to be the same place the wrestling midgets were staying. I was beat after the show, so I headed to bed. Skyy said she was going to mosey on down to the bar to see what kind of trouble she could get herself into. I told her to have fun, be careful, and off to sleep I went. Seven o'clock that morning, Skyy came bursting through the door. I jolted out of my sleep and said, "Well, well, where in the hell were you all night?" to which she enthusiastically replied in her deep southern accent, "Honey, I fucked me a midget!"

I do *not* need to tell you what my face looked like. I barely got out, "YOU DID WHAT?" because I was both hysterical, and in shock. Ok, nothing she ever did really shocked me, but I must admit, forming the visual was, well…odd.

She proceeded to give me a play-by-play of the experience: "Honest, Honey, he didn't look so much like an actual midget as a real little man. But I'll tell ya, there was nothing midgetty about his dick! Ooh… girl. This thing was like a freaking beer can! Not a twelve ounce, but a big ole, damn sixteen."

Through my hysteria, I asked, "So, how did that work exactly? I mean, you are not short!"

She said, "Hell, he just laid me down on the bed, put a pillow under my ass, grabbed my ankles, stood up, and just went at it like a howler monkey on crack!"

I almost died.

Wallace

I also have to give a shoutout to my girl, Jeanene Wallace, a.k.a. "Broke Back Barbie." She's done more for me in the past few years than anyone else.

WALLACE
aka
BROKE BACK BARBIE

Beeche Time

I first played at Benny's Bike Rally in Michigan 2008. This event proved to be another amazing opportunity for me. After playing that event, I decided to film my first real DVD the next year. I found an awesome videographer guy to shoot it. The show went off perfectly and it was a great time for all.

A woman named Sandy attended that first rally in Michigan. Afterwards, Sandy went and told all of her friends about the ol' Bag Lady. So, when I was coming back the following year, she made plans to bring her gang. The guys in her group were skeptical. They were all saying things like, "C'mon, man, a comic at a bike rally?" or "I don't like chick comedians" or "No comic can make me laugh," and blah, blah and blah! But she convinced them that this was no ordinary comedy gig, so they came.

They loved the show! She and her friends approached me after the show to offer me a cocktail, and we all started chatting. We hung out together that night and became grand friends...Especially me and Sandy "Beeche". We exchanged emails and numbers and promised to keep in touch. I didn't know it at the time, but gal would become my very best friend in life aside from my daughter.

I found out later about a comment she made to a guy she had brought with her to the show. "One day I am going to work for that chick," Sandy told them. When I got home, I started getting emails from her, so we chatted a bit. The conversation turned into "I would love to work for you," and then she even got a bit pissed when I didn't reply back soon enough. I started thinking, *This chick is a badger!*

She kept after me till finally I said, "Ok! Here's the deal. If you find me the name of that soldier in my DVD I filmed at the Michigan rally, I will hire you." (The soldier's last name was Smith.) I figured she would never be able to find him, so I was safe. She found not only his APO address, but also his shirt size in just three days! So, Smith got a DVD and a care package, and I got a new employee.

Beeche started by canvassing gigs for me out her way in Michigan and actually got me some. So, I invited her to come out to hang in the Rockies for a month, which turned into seven years. We have had some of the best times on the road, and she truly is and has been one of the best road buddies ever. She has been all over the country with me and has never let me down. I know, at least in my world, friends often become family. I had a sister I only met once (at this point), but Beeche has become more of a sister to me than anyone could. In case you didn't already assume this… I require a great deal of patience. To her credit, she has a ton of it. I have had many people help me through the years, but no one does it like the Beeche.

Beeche has an awesome husband, Paul AKA the "Purse Snatcher," who came out a few months after her, and they have lived in the Rockies ever since. "Snatcher" got his name while they were on tour with me in Florida when I played at the Vietnam Vets' compound. I had a dressing trailer on the back of the property and had put my stuff in it along with a few other gals. I was hanging out at the bar after the show and asked Paul to run back to it and grab my purse for me. So, he did. The trouble was… when he came back, he had grabbed the wrong purse. So, here he goes trotting back across the entire compound again with purse in hand, puts it back and grabs another. Once again, he made the trip across the compound and hands me a purse. Wrong purse *again*, so back he went.

Now, mind you everyone is watching this big, tall dude run across the compound with various purses. I can't imagine what they were thinking. To their credit, they just watched. Finally, the third time was the charm! He handed it to me and his wife, Beeche, looked at him and said, "Way to go, Purse Snatcher!" And that, my friends, is how bikers get their nicknames!

Beeche and Snatcher have been the best helpers and friends I have ever had. She truly loves me and my daughter like her family. She never had much family either. She and her "brother" were both adopted by a farmer and his wife. Back then farmhands were needed, and kids were not allowed to be just kids. They had to work from the time they could walk by taking care of the animals and crops. Beeche was close to her adoptive dad but not so to the mom. The son was the mom's favorite and Beeche knew it.

Beeche and I traveled together to many of my shows. I could always be myself around her. Hell, I even pissed in a Stella Artois glass in a traffic jam in downtown Denver while she drove us to a show. I can't pee in front of just anyone. She has also seen me light my farts. She said the flame shot three feet! Yep, we are that close.

The Beeche has been the only person I have met yet who could run my entire life. She helped watch Chey, took care of the house, including doing my laundry like a Chinese laundry lady! She is amazing from backstage, music, and costumes to filming shows, public relations, and running my merchandise table like a pro. It was wonderful to have help like that. I was lucky to meet such a great human. Many artists who tour extensively have agents, managers, assistants, and P.R. people and

Sandy Beeche

merchandise people. Hell, most of them even have people answer their email for them. Me? I did it all by myself for years, until I met the Beeche.

One time, Beeche and I decided to have some fun with folks, and *she* dressed like Bag Lady and went out onstage first. I had always wanted to do comedy there as myself out of costume, so we figured this would be fun. I loved watching "myself" onstage and having the opportunity to see people's reactions when "I" walk out. I often miss that part because I am so pumped for the show. The people fell for it… until she opened her mouth. They knew right away that something was up. To her credit, she kept doing the bit and killing it until I walked out onstage as me. I was all "domina-trixed" out in my kinky garb. She has watched enough of my shows to know how to roll as Baggie. The crowd caught on to our little game and seemed to really enjoy it.

Sadly, I lost my Beeche in July of 2017 to cancer. She was the best friend I ever had, and my heart is broken. I will be forever grateful to her for everything she has done for me and will never be able to repay her for her absolute loyalty, love, and kindness. I love you, Beeche, always. See you on the other side.

"Baggy & Clyde"

Being a comic and something of a celebrity has been wonderful for the most part. It also has its drawbacks. Relationships are really difficult to maintain, and I am not quite sure why. I think part of it is that since my stripper days through today, I am used to being in the spotlight and being looked up to and treated with great kindness, respect and even adoration by those that follow and enjoy what I do. When you make people laugh, you make them feel happy. So, they like being around you, as well as are grateful for the lightheartedness you bring their way.

So, in a relationship I suppose I expect—maybe even demand—that my man treats me with the same respect and adoration, at least more often than not. As with most relationships, in the beginning it is all fun and games. I mean literally. Having grown up in the sex business and now being a comic who has the ability to travel to so many awesome places and be treated like royalty, can give the man who is with me the feeling that life is always going to be a walk in the park. I think guys I have dated think, *Wow, I don't have to work much, if at all, because I'm dating a celebrity.* That SUX, and they are wrong. Very wrong.

One time, I was surfing the web on a biker site I used for promoting my shows and was inviting folks from back home in The Burgh to come see me play in West Virginia. (I was still living in Colorado at the time.) Suddenly, I saw the most handsome face I had seen in years on my screen. He had a kind of Bob Seger look about him, long brown hair, deep blue eyes, and a body by Fisher! Well, I am not one to chase a dude, and in fact, I always play it rather casual and friendly. So, I sent him a note and invited him to bring his girl and come to the show.

The next day I get a note back that said, "Are you the same Bag Lady that did a birthday party for a guy named Rizzo, in South Park, Pittsburgh, in like 1991?" I almost shit. I was in fact that Bag Lady! So, this dude *knows me*? Damn! Well, long story short... I wrote, he wrote, we talked on the phone for a few months. So he made plans to come to see me!

Finally, it was the weekend of the show. We agreed to meet, and since I had a suite with two bedrooms, I offered to give him his own room when he got there. My plane landed in Pittsburgh, and my best friend Skyy and her man picked me up. I was stoked as hell to finally meet him.

On the way down to West Virginia, I called to tell him I'm there, and he said,..."Ah, damn, I don't think I am going to be able to make it. This chick friend of mine is going through some drama with her old man and..." I cut him off and said, "WHAT? You're kidding me, right? Tell me you're joking?" He said no and that he was sorry and before he got out another word, I cut him off and said, "So, you are going to blow me off after all this time waiting to meet, for some damn drama queen that you ain't gonna fix over a weekend? Well… *Fuck you!*" CLICK! I hung up on his ass.

He called back, but I just let it go to voice mail. I was driving through the beautiful, rolling hills of the West Virginia mountains where there was no service. That's why I didn't see the five other times he called till ninety minutes later when I got to the resort. The last call was a voicemail. All I heard was, "I'm on my way." CLICK! (Well, well… men do love a bitch, apparently.) Hold your ground girls and guys. Nobody respects a pushover.

So, he arrived on his bike, soaking wet in the crotch from hitting a thunderstorm on the way. After searching high and low around the huge property, finally found me and my sis, Skyy, in the lounge setting up the show.

I have to say he wasn't much to look at first, sporting a do-rag, Bag Lady-style safety glasses, wet crotch, a pissy look on his face, and saddlebags thrown over his shoulder. I was glad he came, so I hugged him and said, "Hi! So great to meet ya!" There was so much I didn't know at the time.

Looking back, I commend him on beating a terrible anxiety disorder and manning up to make a trip into the unknown to meet a whack job like me. Anxiety or not, he had balls. Big ones.

So, I took him to our suite. The place was gorgeous with bedrooms on either side of a big living room, complete with fireplace and kitchen *and* a big hot tub. I think he was taken aback a bit with it. Clyde was raised in a nice neighborhood, but he was a simple hard-core biker guy, and I am sure he had never hung out in any kind of swanky digs like these. We dropped his stuff and went down to have a beer. I took him backstage with me while I got ready for the show.

I killed it… he laughed his ass off, and all went well. When we get back to the room, and I suggest we jump into our private hot tub together. He was all for it, of course, until I said, "You brought a bathing suit, right?" The look on his face was priceless, and his response was, "You're kidding, right?"

"Why would I be kidding?" I asked, "I don't know what kind of women you run with, but we don't even know anything about each other, really. And I don't do the first date sex thing, ok?" I went on to say, "I just want to soak with you, relax and get to know each other. Is that a problem?" In a way he seemed relieved, so that's what we did. I laid back on his big, strong, chest and we just hung out and talked. It was wonderful, and nothing happened but a kiss or three. Ok, maybe ten.

As a side note, in case you don't already know this one… Men don't generally marry sluts, or at least women they perceive as sluts. And women truly don't want to feel like they are expected to be one. I am all for a woman having strong sexual needs and desires like a man. Hail to you wild gals for satisfying those needs. However, if what you truly *desire* is a soul mate/life mate, knight in shining leather or pressed polyester, you almost never get it when you give it ALL up… all the time. I encourage you to read John Gray's awesome and educational book *Men Are from Mars, Women Are from Venus*. It's so true!

After the hot tub, we hugged goodnight and went to our respective rooms. I did, however, run into his a few times for some more kissing! But that's where the night ended. The next morning, we got up and I wanted to go to breakfast. He just wanted a peanut butter sandwich. Really? I was a little disturbed by the fact that he wouldn't join me for a nice breakfast, especially since whatever we wanted was free.

But rather than argue, I went down to the restaurant alone. I met some wild Vietnam vets who recognized me from the show, so

I sat with them. Finally, Clyde showed up and joined us. I had no way of knowing at that time that he was battling a lifelong eating disorder. But for the moment all was well with the world, and he sure was beautiful. He had a lightning wit and an *I don't give a crap* attitude that—at first—was sexy, so I went with it.

So, we did another show the next night and had a blast. After the weekend, I was heading off to Sault St. Marie, Michigan with Skyy and other friend Will to do a show for the Veterans with a new band called Blackberry Smoke. I kissed Clyde goodbye and off we all went. The

Upper Peninsula of Michigan is simply awesome, magical actually. Kid Rock was right.

Clyde and I kept in touch after the Michigan gig. I went back to Pittsburgh to see him again before I flew home to Colorado. He had a cute little house in the woods, and I stayed there with him for two nights. I had only been with one person since Storm in many years, so when we started kissing… it was on. When I finally saw him naked, all that could come out of my mouth was, "My God, you are beautiful." I am pretty sure he'd never heard that exact sentence before. I doubt many men get called beautiful, but he was exactly that. The tattoos, the perfect amount of fur on the chest and his package were glorious. I mean *it* was visually pretty!

We did the long-distance dating thing for about a year-and-a-half and saw each other about once a month. He would fly to Colorado or I would go home to Pittsburgh and do shows he helped me set up. He was a great promoter. In fact, together we put on one hell of a motorcycle rally in Westmoreland County PA. called "Motorcycles, Metal, and Mayhem" in 2010. For the first year we had around 1,900 people! Not bad.

Prior to this, I suggested he take a year's leave of absence and come to Colorado with me, but he said the Union wouldn't give him a leave of absence (that turned out to be a lie). Clyde made it clear that he wanted to be married before he moved west with me. I wasn't ready to be married, but I threw caution to the wind and proposed to him ON STAGE at the rally. You know what they say about those marry in haste… they repent in leisure.

I remember being in a hotel in Seattle on our way to Alaska about two months before the "big wedding day" and pleading with him to please let us cancel the wedding. He fought me tooth and nail and kept trying to convince me that it was all going to work out between us. I should not have listened to my gut. He had moved in one week before the wedding while I was working in Iowa. I came home to find he had not only taken over my house but dictated authority to all my friends who came to help him unload the truck. I am sure the look on my face when I walked through the door and saw all my shit rearranged was priceless.

The night before the wedding, Beeche and I went to pick up my dress. The Bridal Store happened to be one block from my favorite bar. Coincidence? I think not. So, we were like, *what the hell*? I put the dress and we went out for one last hoorah. We had a blast dancing the night away. Somehow, I got the blue cube caulk on my dress.

The wedding was fun for everyone… except me. Friends flew in from back East and the Midwest, including his parents. Everyone in the wedding party went to the costume shop and rented 1800s old west outfits. We had *Tombstone* cowboys, an Indian, and even a big Mexican bandolier… Hoggie. My friend Hoggie is a badass biker from Pittsburgh who dressed like that just for me. He had lung trouble and could hardly breathe at that altitude, but he hung in there. The girls all wore saloon girl outfits, except for me and Cheyenne who wore gowns. My gown kept me in the bathroom for an hour trying to pin the bitch up with the help of my very patient, very well-meaning friend Chicago dog Diane. Bless her Virgo heart! (If you are ever near Denver, she has an amazing restaurant on West Colfax Ave. called Chicago.) I was frazzled to say the least. On top of which, I didn't want to be doing this in the first place!

I was sober for the event but, well, he was drunk by the time we got to the bridal suite. He was in the hot tub naked before he even began to unlace my dress. *That* did it! I kicked him the hell out of the room and slept very well alone on our wedding night. He ended up drinking all night and slept in the best man's room. In the morning, they were both M.I.A. and hungover. I ended up taking the entire gang, including Clyde's parents and kid, to Estes Park and Rocky Mountain National Park for the day. Hell, they'd come all that way, and they wanted to see some things.

The time we spent together was a mix of amazing and awful. Geminis are like that… one extreme or the other. Dr. Jekyll or Mr. Hyde. One is an angel, and the other is a handful, to say the least.

I saw a bunch of stuff that was broken between us before we ever went through with the wedding, and I knew in my heart it wasn't going to last. He was negative about many things and I didn't like the person I was becoming around him. I just didn't think we were going to make it.

In the course of that first year, Clyde and I flew around the country to rallies. We had fun mostly, but his drinking was a drag. When you are sober and a drunk comes onto you, even one you dig, it is a huge turn-off. Just sayin'. Also, dumb stuff happens when you drink. He liked his beer a bunch, and all is will say is there were issues between us and I couldn't make it work.

Finally, after 18 months I bailed.

I really wish Clyde would have learned how to manage me… and his drinking. Things might have gone better. I grew a bunch of resentments in that relationship and those were some of them. He made me think he was going to come out west to learn how to help run Roadhouse Comedy with me, so I could just tour and be funny instead of doing it all by myself all the time. But that never happened. It was sad really, but in the beginning of a relationship when physical attraction was the main event and time spent together is only fun-filled, wild weekends here and there, it was hard for me to really see his darkness.

Still, Clyde was a good man. He just had some demons to deal with, and I hope he did. He tried to do—and most often did—the best he could for me. I know part of our problem was my being spontaneous and impatient. I also have never been able to stay long where I am not really happy. I wish him all the best things in life. Mostly, I pray he finds true happiness.

My Name in Lights

One of the positives that came out of that relationship is that it provided an opening for me to fulfill one of my childhood dreams… to see my name in lights on the Strip in Las Vegas! Even as a frightened fifteen-year-old crying in between songs in those shithole strip clubs, I knew I was destined to make it to Las Vegas. Up until that point, I had visited Vegas several times, but never had the opportunity to play at any of the venues.

Around this time, I went to Las Vegas with Clyde because he had a job interview out there. While he was at his interview, I wandered into the Four Queens knowing there was a show room there. I asked the guy at the box office who handled the bookings for the Canyon Club showroom, and he gave me the guy's name. I called and left a message and the guy called me back. He was a biker and rock singer named Jay Boleyn. He and his wife managed the restaurant in the hotel. His wife was really sweet, gorgeous girl named Gaylen.

I sent them my website and information they looked at it and called me right away and hired me immediately! This was my big break. Because Vegas doesn't do much to help you promote yourself *unless* you are already a huge star, Beeche, Cheyenne, Skyy, Becky from St. Louis and me worked the street the night of the show like hookers. We handed out fliers and pleaded with people to go to

my show. Friends from all around the country also came to support me. They are party animals. Beeche rented us a limo so I could really feel like the Rockstar I think I am.

We packed out the place! I played the Four Queens two different times and sold out both times. I was told that the bar made more money during my shows than during any other performances the club had that year.

Cheyenne thought it was just awesome and I could see how proud she was of me. She was only eighteen when I first played Vegas, so she was limited to what she could enjoy there. I had taken her there a few times when she was even younger, and she was hooked. Since I had to perform every night, I couldn't be as much fun as usual. Thankfully, my crazy friends took her to see Thunder from Down Under, the male revue, at the Excalibur Hotel. She squealed with delight as the gorgeous, hot, naked men danced about and jumped up on tables shaking all that goodness in her face. Honestly, I was jealous that I couldn't go, but work is work even for a comic. I did redeem myself the last night there and took Chey to see Chippendales. It was a great show but not the same as Thunder.

Seeing my name in lights and my promo video playing over and over on Fremont Street on the Four Queens marquis was absolutely incredible. I remember just standing there looking at it for like an hour almost oblivious to all the people walking by.

I thought—in that moment—that I had arrived.

The Lost and Found

Ever since I was a little girl, playing Vegas was always my biggest dream. I figured for years that if I got there, I would finally be able to call myself a big star. I was amazed, however, how depressed I became after seeing my name in lights. I headlined my own shows in Vegas twice, and though it was truly a thrill, in the end it was under-whelming. On the "shooting for the stars" scale, I should have shot higher. The fantasy of my name on the Las Vegas Strip didn't feel as I thought it would. Not really. I've heard NFL players and coaches talk about this same depressing feeling the day after winner the Super Bowl.

I know my daughter and friends sure thought it was a cool experience, and it was. But what now? For two years I felt I was standing at a dead end. I had no idea which direction to go in or how to get there. When you don't anything in your future, it is nearly impossible to find your way. I was a still playing most of the major motorcycle rallies across the USA and going to Alaska twice a year, but I felt lost.

To add to my confusion, I also went back to drinking in 2007 shortly after the breakup with Storm. I remembered how it happened… I was performing in Kennett, Missouri with their hometown hero, a magnificent country artist named Trent Tomlinson. (Sheryl Crow is also from Kennett.)

After my show, Trent's dad came up and said, "Damn girl, you are funny as hell! Come to the bar and let me buy you a drink."

I replied, "Why, thank you sir, but I don't drink."

He said, "The hell you don't" and put his arm around me and to the bar we went. He ordered us each a shot of Jack Daniels. I'll never forget the way that damn whiskey felt going down. I think I was tired of being lonely and in pain, and I just caved. I hadn't been to a meeting in years and never did "the steps." This was treacherous territory for a newly sober person like me.

And just like that, two years of sobriety went out the window. In the end, that one drink set me back ten years.

At first, I kept my drinking in check. Don't get me wrong…I had a blast. But as with most true alcoholics, it took more and more booze to keep me happy. I found it strange that most of my fans and even my good friends had no idea I had a drinking problem. I was a fun drunk, unless I was annoying my own kid when I would get my wine on and sing Dean Martin songs into the wee hours by the fireplace on snowy nights in Colorado. God bless her for her patience!

But soon I started to look and feel like hell. I gained a ton of weight, looked bloated, had stomach trouble, and acid reflux issues. There were signs and—fortunately—I saw them. I also lost a couple of friends to the drink, or the effects from years of it, and they were my age. I knew I had to give it up again, but how. I could NOT quit on my own. I knew going back into the meetings would be one of the hardest things ever, if not nearly impossible.

As God would have it, a friend from my old AA group called me up one day just to say "hi." Many of them had called to check on me over the ten years I was running and gunning again, which says a lot. On the other end, no one from the bars EVER called to check on me when I quit drinking and went into AA. They just found another drinking buddy.

I told her I needed to stop again, but just couldn't get myself to go back into "the rooms" of AA. Her suggestion: Pray.

Her exact words were "Every night and every morning, stop and ask God to take away the desire for a drink. Just do that out loud and God will help you find your way back." *Ok, I though, that seemed easy enough, why not?* So, I did. Every night and every morning for almost two weeks I prayed that prayer. I still drank—mind you—but I prayed too.

On about the eleventh day, I woke up and… I swear to you, I did not want a drink. Not even a little, and I have not since. The desire completely went away. It was truly amazing. Today I am over four years sober.

About six months into being sober, I thought…*I wonder if God could help me quit these damn cigarettes too!?* So, I prayed on it again. Every night and every morning. "God, please help me to stop craving these nasty cigarettes. Thank you." It only took about seven days this time and POOF! I woke up one morning and simply didn't even think about them. I swear it was seriously amazing to me. No cravings, no grouchiness, nothing.

I did the same thing with eating. I wanted to clean up the way I ate and resist things that were unhealthy. I prayed for help, sincerely from my heart like I did with the other struggles, and He helped me with that too. I became a bit of a gym rat with my awesome daughter. This changed the way I looked at food, and I felt like a new person in about three months.

The good Lord showed me three times in a row that He had my back. I had no choice but to give everything in my life over to Him:

my finances, my relationships, my daughter, everything. I went out for a walk in the woods sat on a log and said, Lord, I give my life and everything in it to you. I trust you. You have blessed my life beyond anything I could ever have hoped for and it is time for me to give back and do your work. Do with me what you will and help me to help others. Please show me what you want from me and I will do it.

I can't explain it, but in my very soul I feel like He hears me every time I speak to Him. I literally feel a warmth come over me when I pray out loud. I had to be patient, but the answers and help always came right in the nick of time.

Family Ties

Decades after "meeting" my sister (not really since our dad wouldn't let see each other), I found Michelle again in 2017. I searched on LinkedIn, the professional networking site, and saw the profile of a woman who matched the small amount of personal information I had been given. Michelle worked as a corporate

Sister Michelle

executive and was living, at the time, in Dallas, TX. She was excited I had reached out to her. We texted back for forth for months before ever even speaking on the phone.

Finally, I was scheduled to perform near Dallas. I texted Michelle and asked her to come to the show. I remember the first time I saw her after all those years. Michelle met me in the dressing room of the Iron Horse Saloon. We hugged and chatted briefly, and then she stayed for the show and we had dinner together afterwards. It is hard to explain that feeling. She and I clicked like old friends! She is opposite of me in that she went the corporate route and has the upper crust lifestyle in a Texas suburb. But inside…we're the same: wild, funny, and hardworking with huge hearts. Michelle is one of the most generous people I know. On top of it all, she's gorgeous.

About a year later I found out that our father had died. I remember waking up that morning thinking about my dad. I hadn't seen him for decades, so I rarely even thought of him. Hours later I received a call from Michelle saying Dad had died. For reasons I will never understand, my father failed to make any effort to get to know me or my daughter. Losing him wasn't sad for me, as it was for Michelle, but I still mourned the loss of the relationship I would never be able to have with my father.

About a year or so after meeting Michelle, my mom died. She had a stroke ten years prior, so I'm grateful I had her for that long. In the last few years of her life, Mom and I were the closest we had ever been. Shortly after her health problems started, she admitted that she had failed as a mother. She knew it all along, but it wasn't until after her stroke that she finally owned it. She used to call me on the phone and announce herself as "This is your conditional-loving mother." *What mother says that, even in jest?*

But, when faced with frailty of her own humanity, she asked for my forgiveness. And—by the grace of God—she got it. I learned so much from my mom…the good, the bad, and the ugly.

Mom left me her house after she died. At first, I was disappointed to have to go back to Pittsburgh. I never wanted to leave Colorado again if I could help it. And living in her house brings back horrible memories of the abuse and craziness from years earlier. I never could have predicted, though, how grateful I would be to have a place to live when the lockdowns started and every entertainer on the planet was instantly unemployed for the next year. But God knew.

Even though I lost my sense of freedom and identity when I left Denver, some of the benefits of coming back to Pittsburgh were unexpected. Shortly after moving into my mom's house, I re-connected with Linda after years of living out-of-state. She had kept tabs on me all of those years! So, when I returned to the 'Burg she connected Cheyenne and me with some of her Christian friends. One of Linda's closest friends, Connie Geier, has a granddaughter who is around Chey's age… Valerie. Those two clicked immediately! They even look like sisters. Val and her husband are officers and work with Cheyenne's boyfriend for our local police department.

I met the grandmother and granddaughter several times but didn't meet the daughter, Amy (Val's mom), until months later. Val knew what a crazy conservative I am, and she told me her mom was, too. We both knew before meeting each other that we would get along famously, but I had no idea that Amy—who had just published her second book and recently started a small publishing company—would be the exact person I needed to help me finish MY book. I handed over to her a 138,000-word mess of hay mixed with cow dung which I had written over the past six years, and less than three months later we were sending this book to print.

Sue and Amy

Once again, God had used Linda in my life in ways I could never imagine. She even invited me to speak to a group of friends at her house and give my testimony. Although I stand up in front of crowds of 20,000 on a regular basis, speaking to a small group of women about what Jesus is doing in my life was intimidating. I never had a lot of women friends, as I always felt more comfortable with men, but these ladies love and accept me for who I am.

Last Days and Final Thoughts

I am famous—or should I say infamous—all over the world, thanks to our troops. I even had a four-page write up in VIBES, the only Harley magazine in Japan! (Thank you, Mino Uemura, from Tokyo!) Even with all my success, I still had days where

things looked really hopeless. The thing is, now I see that they never were. God always saw to it something always came through. I have often wondered why I have been so blessed in my life.

Like many of you, I've felt a deep sense a loss since the beginning of 2020. We know, without question, evil exists on this earth now more than ever. At least they

Lois, Suzanne, Linda - March 2021

no longer try to hide their wickedness from us. Dark forces are trying to brainwash and even destroy our children. Please, please, turn off the mainstream news and seek out books and web sites where you can learn the truth about all the shit going on.

Educate yourself, I'm begging you.

In closing, I want to say thank you. I tried to talk about EVERY SINGLE ONE OF YOU in this book but, thanks to my editor, I had to rein it in. Even if I missed you, please know I didn't forget our times. Friends and lovers all!

I also did not realize how many amazing men I have had the incredible pleasure to share time with. I am grateful for every one of them. They all taught me something and made me feel beautiful during our time together. I pray I did the same for them.

Recently, God brought me Michael, a wonderful man that doesn't drink, smoke, or drug. He is kind, funny, handsome as hell, and a biker! My daughter and my five dogs are all healthy and happy, and even though I had to leave Colorado for the time being, I kept my company there and will return to the west soon. For now, I am at peace. I am in a position to do for others, and I think that is truly why we are all here.

To me, life is about sharing experiences. The memories made help pull you through when times get rough—and eventually they will. My journey has been about laughter, kindness, and loving others along the road. Sometimes, even when we don't know why, change happens for a reason. In the moment, we can't always see it, but if you truly trust God with all your heart, and try to let go of judgement and resentments, you will see why things happened as they did and be able to find joy in your life.

Michael

Thank you for sharing this journey with me. I hope I inspired a few of you to write your own story! (When you do, I know the perfect person who can help you make it happen.)

It is hard to put an entire well-lived life into three hundred pages. I suppose that is why many people write more than one book. For now, I want to leave it here. Maybe someone will turn it, or some part of it, into a movie. Hell, maybe I will! It's not like I haven't had to reinvent myself many times over the years. I never regret taking chances.

There is no way to describe the feeling of having people love what you do. There is no drink or drug that ever gave me the high I get when I'm on that stage in front of all of you. Whether I was performing in front of a group of one hundred or 10,000, you have given me some of my greatest joys in life. I love making you all laugh, and I thank YOU for always making me feel loved in return.

"Big Poppa"

Now that we've reached the end, I'll be starting my next book. Stay tuned.

Until we meet again, may God bless every single one of you. Continue to fight the good fight and find the courage to chase your dreams.

Respectfully,

Suzanne

Suzanne "Bag Lady Sue" Austin

Bag Lady Sue...

Ride on, my friends!
Perry, Amy, Michael, Suzanne

...thanks you all!

Wayne THUMPER Betts

Special thanks to the following photographers.
Pictures used with permission:

Rob of USBiker Parties -
www.usapikerparties.com

Jeannette of Spirit Capture Photography -
www.spiritcapturephotography.com

About the Author

At the age of fifteen, Suzanne found herself on the streets with nowhere to go. Although she had some loving, caring adults in her life during the formative years—her aunt, uncle and grandmother—everyone who looked out for her and her brother had died by the time she turned twelve. After suffering abuse from her mom's boyfriends on multiple occasions, the courts took her from her home.

After running away from county shelters, Suzanne was determined to take care of herself. One night, she saw an ad in the evening paper looking for dancers. They were great money for that time, and she thought, well, I can dance. From childhood, her dream was to see her name in lights on the Vegas strip, so she figured this was

her shot. Suzanne would spend many years dancing in bawdy burlesque clubs, and experiencing things most kids never do.

In her late twenties Sue enrolled in a comedy competition through a radio station in her hometown of Pittsburgh PA. She had no idea at the time how this would change the course of her life. Through combining her stripper act and love for comedy, she created the character of "Bag Lady Sue." The Bag Lady has been entertaining audiences—especially at biker rallies and veteran's charities—all across the United States for the past thirty years. In addition, she has performed for our troops on and off military bases, and her videos have been shared all around the world.